Vol. XIV No. 2

Bible Expositor and Illuminator
Large-Print Edition

SPRING QUARTER March, April, May 2023

	Looking Ahead	2
	Editorials	3

Jesus Pleases His Father

UNIT I: By His Works

Mar.	5—Jesus' Baptism—Mark 1:4-13	4
Mar.	12—Overcoming Temptation with the Word—Matt. 4:1-14*a*	18
Mar.	19—Doing the Father's Work—John 5:19-29	32

UNIT II: By His Sacrifice

Mar.	26—Submitting to the Father's Will—Matt. 26:36-50	46
Apr.	2—Crucified for Sinners—Matt. 27:38-54	60
Apr.	9—Risen from the Dead! (Easter)—John 20:1-10, 19-20	74
Apr.	16—Proofs of the Resurrection—Luke 24:36-53	88

UNIT III: By His Teachings

Apr.	23—The Bread of Life—John 6:22-35	102
Apr.	30—The Light of the World—John 8:12-20; 12:44-46	116
May	7—The Good Shepherd—John 10:7-18	130
May	14—The Resurrection and the Life—John 11:17-27	144
May	21—The True Vine—John 15:1-17	158
May	28—Jesus Prays for Believers—John 17:6-21	172
	Topics for Next Quarter	188
	Paragraphs on Places and People	189
	Daily Bible Readings	190
	Review	191

Editor in Chief: Kenneth Sponsler

Edited and published quarterly by
**THE INCORPORATED TRUSTEES OF THE
GOSPEL WORKER SOCIETY
UNION GOSPEL PRESS DIVISION**
Rev. W. B. Musselman, Founder

Price: $9.39 per quarter*
shipping and handling extra

ISBN 978-1-64495-315-0

This material is part of the "Christian Life Series," copyright © 2023 by Union Gospel Press. All rights reserved. No portion of this publication may be reproduced in any form or by any means without written permission from Union Gospel Press, except as permitted by United States copyright law. Edited and published quarterly by The Incorporated Trustees of the Gospel Worker Society, Union Gospel Press Division. Mailing address: P.O. Box 301055, Cleveland, Ohio 44130-0915. Phone: 216-749-2100. www.uniongospelpress.com

LOOKING AHEAD

This quarter is titled "Jesus Pleases His Father," and it gives us a fascinating glimpse into the manifold ways Jesus did that perfectly during His life and ministry on earth. Going through these lessons should challenge us to follow Him in pleasing the Father as well.

Our first unit begins with a lesson that takes us to Jesus' baptism in the Jordan River. It was there that the Father unambiguously announced His full approval of all that Jesus said, did, and thought: "Thou art my beloved Son, in whom I am well pleased" (Mark 1:11).

Lesson 2 shows us how Jesus successfully met this challenge we all face: being tempted by Satan. In His use of God's Word to repel the tempter, He left us the best example we could hope for. Lesson 3 underscores how Jesus always followed His Father's example in all things (John 5:19).

Our second unit focuses specifically on the great sacrifice Jesus made on our behalf—His ultimate reason for coming. Lesson 4 shows us that this sacrifice was the hardest thing that any human has ever had to bear. Jesus quailed before it but resolved to see it through. Lesson 5, covering the crucifixion itself, brings us to the ultimate in love ever displayed for unworthy sinners.

Lesson 6, by contrast, brings us to Easter and Jesus' triumphant resurrection. The resurrection was the Father's ultimate stamp of approval on Jesus' life and sacrifice (cf. Rom. 1:4). Lesson 7 shows us Jesus' care for His disciples in remaining with them long enough to see that they were prepared for the mission ahead of them.

Our final unit turns our attention to Jesus' teachings. We often do not consider how greatly Jesus pleased His Father by accurately presenting the truth to His hearers. In lessons 8 through 12, we focus on Jesus' proclamation of Himself as the Bread of Life, the Light of the World, the Good Shepherd, the Resurrection and the Life, and the True Vine. We could spend years on these truths and never plumb their depths.

In our final lesson, we are allowed into the hallowed chamber of Jesus' prayer life—specifically His prayer to the Father on our behalf. There we learn how much we are on His heart and how greatly He desires us to be one with Him, with the Father, and with one another.

—*Kenneth Sponsler.*

PLEASE NOTE: Fundamental, sound doctrine is the objective of The Incorporated Trustees of the Gospel Worker Society, Union Gospel Press Division. The writers are prayerfully selected for their Bible knowledge and yieldedness to the Spirit of Truth, each writing in his own style as enlightened by the Holy Spirit. At best we know in part only. "They received the word with all readiness of mind, and searched the scriptures daily, whether those things were so" (Acts 17:11).

EDITORIALS

Pleasing the Father, Displeasing Men

KENNETH SPONSLER

The testimony of God the Father regarding Jesus is strikingly unambiguous: "This is my beloved Son, in whom I am well pleased" (Matt. 3:17). "Behold my servant, whom I have chosen; my beloved, in whom my soul is well pleased" (12:18). "This is my beloved Son, in whom I am well pleased; hear ye him" (17:5). God never made such unqualified statements about anyone else, for no one before or after Jesus ever lived a life that was fully pleasing to the Father, without blemish or lapses. He alone fulfilled God's standard of holy perfection.

It may seem puzzling, then, that Jesus decidedly did not please all people. We might think that One who embodied perfect holiness and perfect love would attract everyone to His side, winning them over by His sheer goodness of heart and life. But over and over again we see in the Gospels that this was not so: "And they [the people in Nazareth] were offended in him" (Matt. 13:57). "And the Pharisees went forth, and straightway took counsel with the Herodians against him, how they might destroy him" (Mark 3:6). "Then the Jews took up stones again to stone him" (John 10:31).

In going to the cross to bear our sins, Jesus fulfilled God's loving plan to secure our salvation. We have perhaps concentrated on that truth so much that we sometimes forget the human side of the equation: Jesus was crucified because He aroused the anger, fear, and hatred of many people—chiefly the religious authorities of the day, but also of the crowds at large. The chief priests engineered the trial of Jesus before Pilate, but the mob joined them in the cry for His execution (Matt. 27:20, 23). Jesus had no illusions about their attitude toward Him: "If the world hate you, ye know that it hated me before" (John 15:18).

This picture, of course, must be kept in proper balance: Jesus did indeed attract great crowds and was immensely popular, especially early in His ministry. The disciples were the first to drop everything for Him. "And straightway they forsook their nets, and followed him" (Mark 1:18). But they were not alone. The disciples came to Him while He was praying in an isolated locale to report, "All men seek for thee" (vs. 37). The crowds coming to hear Him teach were so great that He once had to borrow a boat to have room to speak to them (4:1-2).

This great following, motivated to a substantial degree by Jesus' miracles of healing and provision (John 6:26), largely evaporated when He uttered truths too uncomfortable for many to hear (vss. 60, 66). And this fact leads us into the main reason why Jesus aroused opposition: He did not come to give people what they wanted but what they needed—a restored relationship with God that first required acknowledgment of their sin and their brokenness before Him.

Jesus told His own brothers, "The world cannot hate you; but me it hateth, because I testify of it, that the works thereof are evil" (John 7:7). His mission, although including innumerable acts of mercy and blessing, was first

(Editorials continued on page 186)

LESSON 1   MARCH 5, 2023

Scripture Lesson Text

MARK 1:4 John did baptize in the wilderness, and preach the baptism of repentance for the remission of sins.

5 And there went out unto him all the land of Judaea, and they of Jerusalem, and were all baptized of him in the river of Jordan, confessing their sins.

6 And John was clothed with camel's hair, and with a girdle of a skin about his loins; and he did eat locusts and wild honey;

7 And preached, saying, There cometh one mightier than I after me, the latchet of whose shoes I am not worthy to stoop down and unloose.

8 I indeed have baptized you with water: but he shall baptize you with the Holy Ghost.

9 And it came to pass in those days, that Jesus came from Nazareth of Galilee, and was baptized of John in Jordan.

10 And straightway coming up out of the water, he saw the heavens opened, and the Spirit like a dove descending upon him:

11 And there came a voice from heaven, *saying,* Thou art my beloved Son, in whom I am well pleased.

12 And immediately the Spirit driveth him into the wilderness.

13 And he was there in the wilderness forty days, tempted of Satan; and was with the wild beasts; and the angels ministered unto him.

NOTES

Jesus' Baptism

Lesson Text: Mark 1:4-13

Related Scriptures: Matthew 3:1-17; Luke 3:15-22;
Matthew 17:1-7; Mark 9:2-8; Luke 9:28-36

TIME: A.D. 26   PLACES: wilderness of Judea; Jordan River

GOLDEN TEXT—"There came a voice from heaven, saying, Thou art my beloved Son, in whom I am well pleased" (Mark 1:11).

Introduction

The pivotal verse of the book of Mark is 10:45, which says, "For even the Son of man came not to be ministered unto, but to minister, and to give his life a ransom for many." Everything presented before this verse shows Jesus ministering to the people around Him, and everything presented after it shows Him moving toward and then giving His life as a ransom for sinners.

Each Gospel seems to purposely attempt to reach a specific group of people. When Matthew presented Jesus as the Messiah-King, he appealed to Jewish people. When Luke presented Him as the perfect Man, he appealed to Greek people. When John presented Him as the Son of God, he appealed to everyone. Mark presented Jesus as the the Servant-Redeemer.

It is possible that Mark was the earliest of the Gospels, and there is evidence from church fathers that the author received much of his information from Peter. Mark is the John Mark mentioned in Acts 12:12, 25 and 13:5, 13. He was a cousin of Barnabas (Col. 4:10) and might have been the young man mentioned in Mark 14:51-52.

LESSON OUTLINE

I. THE PREPARER—Mark 1:4-8

II. THE PREPARED—Mark 1:9-13

Exposition: Verse by Verse

THE PREPARER

MARK 1:4 **John did baptize in the wilderness, and preach the baptism of repentance for the remission of sins.**

5 **And there went out unto him all the land of Judaea, and they of Jerusalem, and were all baptized of him in the river of Jordan, confessing their sins.**

6 **And John was clothed with camel's hair, and with a girdle of a skin about his loins; and he did eat locusts and wild honey;**

7 And preached, saying, There cometh one mightier than I after me, the latchet of whose shoes I am not worthy to stoop down and unloose.

8 I indeed have baptized you with water: but he shall baptize you with the Holy Ghost.

John's ministry (Mark 1:4-5). The three Synoptic Gospel authors (Matthew, Mark, and Luke) all introduce the forerunner of Christ, that is, John the Baptizer, before describing the beginning of Christ's ministry. John was the son of the priest Zacharias (Luke 1:5-25, 57-63), so he could have been involved in a ministry in the temple in Jerusalem. Instead of ministering in such dignified surroundings, however, he did his work in the wilderness. {Since his ministry centered around baptizing people, he is called John the Baptist in all three Synoptic Gospels (Matt. 3:1; Mark 6:14; Luke 7:28).

John ministered as a herald, or announcer, for the arrival of the Messiah.}Q1 Important Roman officials were always preceded by a herald, so when one arrived in town, everyone knew someone significant was coming. This is another reason Mark did not include an account of Jesus' birth; he was specifically trying to reach the Roman people, and they would comprehend the importance of John's work relative to the Messiah. Their attention would then be drawn toward the One he was announcing, and that was exactly what Mark wanted.

John's "baptism of repentance" (1:4) should not be confused with Christian baptism. Today, following their conversion, believers are baptized in a ceremony that pictures the death, burial, and resurrection of Christ, all of which are past. John's baptism was preparatory for the coming of the Messiah. Baptism was known to the Jews, for it was required of Gentiles entering into Judaism. John's baptism, however, was for the Jews, God's covenant people, and it required repentance in anticipation of the arrival of the Messiah.

{Those who were baptized by John gave testimony to the fact that they had repented of their sins and as a result were forgiven.}Q2 Forgiveness was not a result of the baptism but of their repentance.

As John ministered, many came from all over Judea to hear him and respond to his message. (In Jesus' day Judea was one of five provinces of Israel, and Jerusalem was the capital city.) The Greek text indicates that people were heading out to the wilderness in great throngs, eager to be baptized and prepared for the Messiah.

{The concept of repentance is important for us. It means "to think differently" or "to reverse a pattern of thought." Implied in the term is the concept that a deliberate change of thought has occurred and led to a change of direction in one's life. First Thessalonians 1:9 illustrates this well: "For they themselves shew of us what manner of entering in we had unto you, and how ye turned to God from idols to serve the living and true God." A person who has truly repented of sin will experience a changed life.}Q3

John's lifestyle (Mark 1:6). {John appeared on the stage of history as the last of the Old Testament line of prophets. According to Jesus' statements in Luke 7:24-28, he was the fulfillment of Malachi 3:1. Matthew quoted a longer statement in which Jesus indicated that John was actually the fulfillment of the Elijah prophecy in Malachi 4:5, but it required faith to accept this (Matt. 11:14). When the angel appeared to Zacharias announcing John's birth, he said John would minister in the spirit and power of Elijah (Luke 1:17). All these statements pointed to John's ministry as the forerunner of the Messiah.}Q4

John's attire would have reminded the Jewish people of Elijah, the premier Old Testament prophet. Second Kings 1 describes the time when King Ahaziah sent men to ask a false god a question. They were met instead by Elijah with a warning message (vss. 2-4). When they reported back to the king, he asked what kind of man had met them. They said, "He was an hairy man, and girt with a girdle of leather about his loins" (vs. 8). The king knew immediately that it was Elijah. We know, therefore, that John's attire was very similar to Elijah's.

John's attire and diet were characteristic of someone who spent his time residing in a wilderness area. Locusts were a permitted food in the Mosaic law (Lev. 11:22), considered to be among the clean foods allowed. It is significant to note that while John expected people to accept and respond to his message, his meager attire and diet marked him out as very different. It was his choice to live frugally and apply himself wholeheartedly to the ministry God had given him.

John's message (Mark 1:7-8). The Greek word translated "preached" in verse 7 means "to herald" or "to proclaim." John had been sent specifically to announce the arrival of the Messiah, and what we find here is a brief synopsis of his message. God never intended for John to be the most prominent figure relative to His plan of salvation. That was meant for Jesus, and John's ministry was to introduce Him. John perfectly understood his role, as seen in his statement in John 3:30: "He must increase, but I must decrease."

{In Mark's text John revealed his genuinely humble attitude in the statement "There cometh one mightier than I after me, the latchet of whose shoes I am not worthy to stoop down and unloose" (1:7). The task of removing the sandals of a guest was relegated to the lowest servant in a household, for it was one of the most menial tasks a servant ever had to perform. This was John's way of indicating how superior he knew the Messiah was to him.}^Q5 He did not want people to idolize him but rather to look for the One coming after him.

{This One would baptize them with the Holy Spirit instead of water.}^Q6 In the course of Israel's history, several identifying signs had been given to them. In Abraham's day the sign of circumcision was given to indicate the covenant relationship God had established with His chosen ones. In Moses' day the sign of Sabbath observance was given in the law, indicating that God had a special relationship with this nation He had just brought out of Egypt. In John's day the sign of a right relationship with God was water baptism.

When the Messiah Himself arrived, however, a new sign was going to be baptism with the Holy Spirit. He would be given as a gift to all who became God's children through salvation. "The One who would give the Spirit as an identifying sign of relationship would be the true Messiah—not the one who gave the external preparatory sign. Messiah's baptism would not be external but internal" (Pentecost, *The Words and Works of Jesus Christ*, Zondervan).

THE PREPARED

9 And it came to pass in those days, that Jesus came from Nazareth of Galilee, and was baptized of John in Jordan.

10 And straightway coming up out of the water, he saw the heavens opened, and the Spirit like a dove descending upon him:

11 And there came a voice from heaven, saying, Thou art my beloved Son, in whom I am well pleased.

12 And immediately the Spirit driveth him into the wilderness.

13 And he was there in the wilderness forty days, tempted of Satan; and was with the wild beasts; and the angels ministered unto him.

Jesus' baptism (Mark 1:9). Jesus was now "about thirty years of age" (Luke 3:23). Although His baptism was immediately followed by Satan's temptation in the wilderness, this was the beginning of His public ministry. Matthew gives us a bit of information not found in either Mark or Luke, namely, that John initially objected to baptizing Jesus: "But John forbad him, saying, I have need to be baptized of thee, and comest thou to me?" (3:14). Jesus insisted, telling him it was "to fulfil all righteousness" (vs. 15).

Since John's baptism was done as an external evidence of a person's repentance of sin, and since Jesus had never sinned, there was no need for Jesus to be baptized in the same way as other people. His baptism, therefore, had to fulfill other purposes rather than giving evidence of repentance. It was also not the same as today's Christian baptism, for there was not yet a death, burial, and resurrection with which to be identified. Jesus' baptism, therefore, was different from all others.

Jesus had been living in Nazareth in Galilee. From there He went to John. Galilee was the northernmost province of Israel, and Nazareth was the hometown in which Jesus lived as a child. It was there that He presumably worked in Joseph's carpenter shop, waiting for the right time to enter His public ministry. The summary given in *The Bible Knowledge Commentary* (Walvoord and Zuck, eds., Victor) offers reasons for Jesus' baptism:

"Mark did not state why Jesus submitted to John's baptism; however, three reasons may be suggested: (1) It was an act of obedience, showing that Jesus was in full agreement with God's overall plan and the role of John's baptism in it (cf. Matt. 3:15). (2) It was an act of self-identification with the nation of Israel whose heritage and sinful predicament He shared (cf. Isa. 53:12). (3) It was an act of self-dedication to His messianic mission, signifying His official acceptance and entrance into it."

Jesus' approval (Mark 1:10-11). {The word "straightway" means "directly" or "at once" and could be translated "immediately." This word occurs forty-two times in Mark, furthering the concept of Jesus as a Servant eager to do His Father's will.}Q7 John baptized Jesus in the Jordan River, {and as they were coming up out of the water, there was an immediate display of God's approval of His Son. The heavens opened and the Holy Spirit descended upon Jesus while the voice of God the Father lovingly addressed His Son, who pleased Him greatly.}Q8

Someone was once heard to say that he would recognize Jesus when he arrived in heaven because He would be the one with a dove sitting on His shoulder! It is important to realize that the description given here is not of an actual dove but rather of the descent of the Spirit in a form similar to that of a dove. Luke 3:22 says the "Holy Ghost descended in a bodily shape like a dove upon him." There was a definite form visible, but the word "like" indicates only a similarity, not the exact same thing.

What is most important about this scene is the fact that at that moment, Jesus was anointed by the Holy Spirit to fulfill all the functions of His messianic office. Peter, when preaching in Cornelius's house, explained that Jesus' ministry began after His baptism by John. He explained that "God anointed Jesus of Nazareth with the Holy Ghost and with power" so that He "went about doing good, and healing all that were oppressed of the devil" (Acts 10:38).

The voice from heaven expressed God's complete approval of Jesus and the ministry on which He was embarking. Scripture gives ample evidence of the love that flows between the Father and the Son. Isaiah 42:1-4 is a classic passage—not only as an expression of God's delight in His Son (called "my servant" here), but also as a prophecy of the time when the Holy Spirit would come upon Him. The rest of that passage describes the very effective type of ministry Jesus would have among people during His time on earth.

Jesus' temptation (Mark 1:12-13). While all three Synoptic Gospels say that Jesus went into the wilderness to be tempted after His baptism, only Mark indicates that it was immediate and forceful. The word "driveth" indicates He was thrust under a strong, constraining impulse from the Spirit. This is much more forceful than in Matthew and Luke's accounts, which describe Him as being led or brought by the Spirit (Matt. 4:1; Luke 4:1). {What is significant about this is the fact that He was not driven there by Satan but rather by the Holy Spirit of God.

The impression this gives us is that Jesus took the offensive in the battle with temptation and evil.}Q9 This was a case of God the Father putting His Son to the test and proving Him to be free of sin and eminently qualified to fulfill His messianic role. Of course, it was also a case of Satan doing his best to entice Him away from that role in order to ruin the plan of redemption.

{The fact that Jesus could truly be tempted proves His humanity. He was not exempt from Satan's attacks and can therefore fully identify with us when we face them. Hebrews 2:18 assures us, "For in that he himself hath suffered being tempted, he is able to succour (help) them that are tempted." While it was impossible for sinful people to live according to all the demands of the law, Jesus fulfilled that law by coming in the flesh and being victorious over temptation.}Q10

For forty days Jesus was in the wilderness being tempted by Satan. It seems, therefore, that there were many more temptations than the three recorded in the Gospels. Mark 1:13 says that there were wild animals in the area (but no human companionship) and that the angels of God ministered to Jesus. A spiritual battle greater than we could ever imagine occurred there. Thank God that Jesus understands what we go through when we too are tempted.

—*Keith E. Eggert.*

QUESTIONS

1. What was John's primary ministry, and what activity was that ministry centered around?
2. What were people indicating when they were baptized by John?
3. What is repentance, and what results when a person repents?
4. Why was the comparison of John with Elijah important?
5. How did John convey his recognition of the Messiah's greatness?
6. What made Jesus' baptism different from all other baptisms?
7. What does the term "straightway" indicate in the Gospel of Mark?
8. What occurred that confirmed to Jesus that He was pleasing God?
9. Why is it important to note that Jesus was led, or driven, by the Spirit into the wilderness to be tempted?
10. Why are the results of Jesus' temptation important to us?

—*Keith E. Eggert.*

Preparing to Teach the Lesson

It has often been said that leaders are born, not made. But some leaders are in the making for long periods of time. They are groomed for leadership and are made aware of that from a very early age. Prince William of England is one good example of this. Our lesson explores Jesus' preparation for leadership.

TODAY'S AIM

Facts: to show how the Father prepared Jesus for leadership.

Principle: to show that when God wants us in leadership, He calls us specifically for that task.

Application: to encourage students to be sensitive to God's calling for leadership in their lives.

INTRODUCING THE LESSON

At some time or other in our lives, we probably have had the experience of knowing and observing great leaders at work. They fascinate us, and deep down we want to be like them. Have we ever wondered, though, how long it took them to become the leaders they are? To some, leadership comes easily. Others may require lengthy training for the task that lies ahead of them.

Jesus knew from the very beginning about the calling upon His life. It was a calling to die, but it also was a calling to lead others to Him, for in Him alone is eternal life. In our lesson this week we explore how the Father prepared Jesus for a unique leadership role.

DEVELOPING THE LESSON

1. The forerunner of the Messiah (Mark 1:4-6). God chose a very unlikely forerunner to announce the arrival of the Messiah. The prophet Isaiah had already talked about him many centuries before. He was the unrefined and bold John the Baptist. John was probably a cousin of Jesus. His parents were Zacharias and Elisabeth, and he was just a few months older than Jesus.

John lived and preached in the wilderness. He told people to turn from their sins in repentance and turn to the living God. This would lead to their receiving the forgiveness of God. John raised the curiosity of the people with his unique message and his boldness. In fact, people came from all over Judea to see him and hear him preach in the wilderness.

John also was known as the baptizer. When people repented of their sins, he baptized them publicly as an outward sign of their decision to follow in the ways of God. This was done in the waters of the Jordan River.

John dressed in a strange manner. He wore clothing made from camel hair that was secured with a crude leather belt. He ate locusts and wild honey. All this probably was a part of the reason people flocked to see and to hear him. He was certainly an unusual sight, even in the wilderness, but there was no denying the power of his message.

2. The message about the Messiah (Mark 1:7-8). John's message was simple and forceful. It compelled people to pay attention to him, for it was about the Messiah, who was coming after him. The Jews certainly knew about this Messiah. He was the One whose coming was prophesied in their holy Scriptures.

John acknowledged that the Person who was coming after him was far greater than he was. In fact, He was so great that John was not even worthy to untie His sandals. In the ancient Eastern world, a slave took care of the footwear of his master and his master's guests. John said that he was not even worthy to perform the lowly task of taking care of the Messiah's sandals.

John then proclaimed something that was very intriguing. He said that he baptized with water but that the One who was coming would baptize people with the Holy Spirit. The coming of this Messiah would change things. He would be like no other. He would be the fulfillment of their hopes and dreams.

God was about to break into their lives in a unique way, and their hopes would be fulfilled. The people did not fully understand the implications of this, but it reminded them of the words of the prophets. It certainly caused them to think.

3. The Messiah declared (Mark 1:9-11). The time for the public manifestation of the Messiah had come. Jesus came down from Nazareth with the specific purpose of being baptized by John in the Jordan. It must be remembered that Nazareth was the little village where Jesus was raised. It seems that nothing significant had ever happened in Nazareth (cf. John 1:46). The baptisms John performed were public events. It appears that crowds stood by the Jordan River and watched as John baptized the people.

Something special happened when Jesus was baptized. As the onlookers watched, the heavens parted and the Holy Spirit descended upon Jesus in the form of a dove. Ask the class members why they think the Holy Spirit is often portrayed as a dove. In the Bible, the dove often symbolizes purity and innocence.

The voice of God the Father then came from heaven, declaring that Jesus was His beloved Son and that He was fully pleased with Him. Everyone present heard that affirmation. It was a public announcement from God that the promised Messiah had come and that the Father's stamp of approval was on Him. Clearly the Messiah had arrived and was to be listened to.

4. The Messiah tested (Mark 1:12-13). Satan does not waste any time in working against the plans of God. Hardly had the Messiah been announced than the Holy Spirit led Him into the wilderness, where Satan waited to tempt Him.

Trials and testing will come to all of God's servants. Jesus was in the wilderness for forty days being tempted by Satan.

ILLUSTRATING THE LESSON

Jesus was proclaimed, manifested, and then tested. God's leaders often follow a similar path.

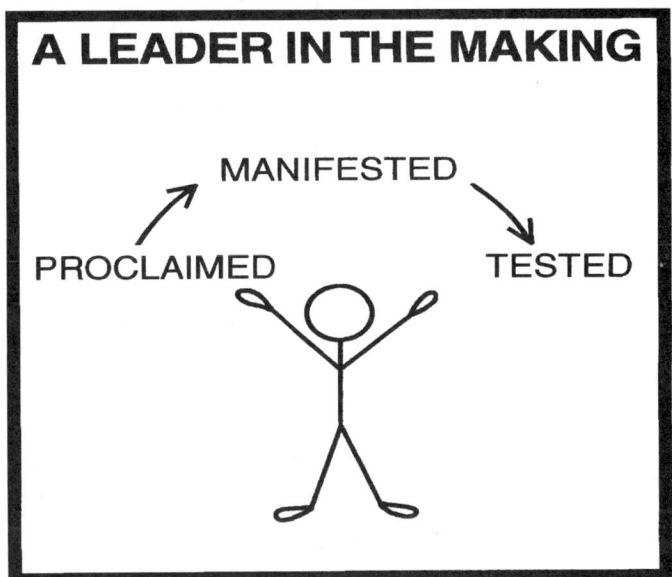

CONCLUDING THE LESSON

Our lesson this week has shown us that God has His unique ways of preparing His servants for leadership. God has a meticulous plan for all of His children. Let us be sensitive to God's plan for our lives.

ANTICIPATING THE NEXT LESSON

In our lesson next week we will focus on the temptation of Christ. What successful tactic did He use against Satan's deceptions?

—A. Koshy Muthalaly.

PRACTICAL POINTS

1. Religious rites mean nothing apart from the confession of sins that brings divine forgiveness (Mark 1:4-5).
2. God's work demands faithfulness, not conformity to society's standards (vs. 6).
3. There is no place for self-promotion in serving the Lord; He must be preeminent (vss. 7-8).
4. The presence and power of the Lord are essential to serving Him successfully (vss. 9-11).
5. The Holy Spirit never leads us into difficult places and then abandons us (vs. 12).
6. With God's help we can endure any temptation (vs. 13).

—Jarl K. Waggoner.

RESEARCH AND DISCUSSION

1. In what ways did John the Baptist's ministry differ from Jesus' (Mark 1:4-5, 8; cf. Matt. 3:1-12; 4:17)?
2. How might John's unusual appearance have helped or hindered his ministry (Mark 1:6)? Why are we so quick to judge others on the basis of appearance?
3. How would you characterize the ministry of John the Baptist? Why was it so important?
4. What similarities are there between Jesus' baptism and the believer's water baptism (Mark 1:10-11) How are they different (cf. Matt. 28:19)?
5. Why is it important to us in a practical sense that Jesus was "tempted of Satan" (Mark 1:13)?

—Jarl K. Waggoner.

ILLUSTRATED HIGH POINTS

One . . . after me (Mark 1:7)

John and his ministry had already been prepared, even from the time of conception in his mother's womb. Zacharias and Elisabeth were serving God in Judea. The Lord God chose that godly couple and devised and directed the whole process of John's preparation for leadership. John carried on his ministry very faithfully; however, when Jesus arrived on the scene in Palestine as the specially anointed envoy from heaven, the major responsibility of teaching the kingdom and calling people to repent passed to Him.

It is likely that in your church there is an associate or assistant minister. Though that person has a somewhat less prominent position, he is nonetheless required to be prepared in the best possible way for his important activities.

We should not avoid confronting essential issues with the teachings of Scripture. A church could be guilty of doing less than what is required.

Jesus . . . was baptized (vs. 9)

The Christian ministry demands proper preparation for the Lord's service. Jesus submitted Himself to baptism by John, and God the Father showed His full approval. Later, Jesus endured the wilderness temptation experience as part of His preparation.

If your church is in the process of choosing a spiritual leader, the responsibility of the church authorities is to make sure that leader is well prepared. The process will not mirror the Lord's unique experiences, but the special spiritual preparations to fit the specific needs of your church are essential.

If you have a leader who appears to need additional preparation, pray for him and work with him.

—P. Fredrick Fogle.

Golden Text Illuminated

"There came a voice from heaven, saying, Thou art my beloved Son, in whom I am well pleased" (Mark 1:11).

The baptism of Jesus was a turning point in His life. Behind Him were thirty years of formative growth, the adult portion of which was spent as a tradesman in Nazareth. The arrival of John the Baptist on the scene signaled that it was time for Jesus to lay aside His trade and begin His ministry, which was the reason for His coming.

As Christians, we ought to give ourselves to God for whatever purpose He might have for us. Some do this at the time of their salvation or at baptism, and as a result some even change professions as they sense God's leading. Not every new Christian will be so redirected by the Lord, but we all should be willing to go where God leads us.

Jesus' baptism by John demonstrated His identification with sinners, though He Himself was sinless. It was the righteous thing to do, for it was God's will for Him (Matt. 3:15); likewise, baptism is God's will for all believers. It is our way of publicly identifying with the death, burial, and resurrection of our Lord (cf. Matt. 28:19; Rom. 6:3-6). In some sense, it is our initiation into the plan and purpose for which we were saved.

Jesus' baptism also was the opportune time for the Father to send the Spirit to Him to empower Him as needed in the days ahead. The first ministry of the Spirit in Jesus' life was to send Him to the desert to be tested and then to enable Him in various ways and at numerous times for the rest of His earthly ministry (Luke 4:14).

Jesus was prepared for leadership by the Spirit's enabling, and by His obedient life He pleased His heavenly Father immensely. So much was the Father pleased at the baptism of our Lord that He spoke in an audible voice from heaven to announce that fact.

Such a phenomenon as God speaking aloud to someone today certainly is within His ability and prerogative, but one must not look for or expect God to do so. Occasionally, people who have committed criminal acts will claim that God told them to do what they did. Many of them are no doubt sincere in their belief that they heard the voice of God, but their actions prove otherwise. Satan and his demons are actively seeking ways to get Christians to do evil things, and surely what some think is God is nothing other than an evil spirit.

God is pleased with us when we have chosen to identify with His Son by baptism. We should accept His pleasure by faith, however, rather than look for some sign from heaven.

The other matter here that applies to Christians today is the presence of the Holy Spirit and the empowerment He brings. As the Spirit led Jesus through testing and enabled Him to perform the many wonders that authenticated Him and His message, so the Spirit seeks to lead each of us as well. We will be tested—perhaps many times in our lifetime—but He is our way of escape if we will accept it (I Cor. 10:13).

We also can do much more for God if we rely on the Spirit rather than on our own strength. The sad truth is that many refuse to attempt great things for God or to serve in some capacity because they look no further than their own abilities. Let us commit ourselves to trusting God to supply what we lack in serving Him.

—Darrell W. McKay.

Heart of the Lesson

What is leadership? Are leaders made or born? God calls leaders, and then He prepares them for their task. He does not expect them to be ready right away. Instead, one step at a time, God works through leaders to train them to be positive, Christlike influences on others.

Our text talks of two important people who were called by God for unique ministries as leaders.

1. John the Baptist (Mark 1:4-8). John was an unusual character. He lived in the desert, ate locusts and honey, and wore a rough robe made from camel hair.

John had a dynamic, urgent message that certainly did not tickle people's ears. He told people to repent, or turn from their sin, because the kingdom of heaven was coming soon. He told people to watch for the Messiah.

The Jewish people longed for the Messiah to come. Could it be that God was sending the Messiah at last?

Surprisingly, people walked perhaps twenty miles from Jerusalem to hear the message John preached in the wilderness. Crowds responded to his fervent call for repentance and baptism in the Jordan River.

Repentance means more than feeling sorry for one's sin. Anyone can feel bad about falling short. John was calling for true repentance—completely changing direction in life. Before repenting, a person is content to walk in darkness. When he repents, he acknowledges his sin. He renounces his life of bondage to sin. He puts his faith in God and turns to a new, abundant life of righteousness.

John prophesied much about the coming Messiah. He said he was not even worthy to unloose the Messiah's sandals. He knew he himself was not the light; rather, he was the one to humbly point the way to the Light of life (cf. John 1:8).

John performed baptisms with water. He told the people that the Messiah would baptize them with the Holy Spirit. The Messiah would purge the people of their sins and purify them.

2. Jesus of Nazareth (Mark 1:9-13). When He was about thirty years old, Jesus came to see John out in the wilderness. Mark simply says that Jesus "was baptized of John in Jordan." Matthew tells us that when Jesus came to be baptized, John resisted baptizing Him, declaring that it was more appropriate that he be baptized by Jesus (3:13-14).

Certainly, because Jesus is God, He did not need to repent, but it seems that He wanted to be baptized in order to publicly identify with the people. Through baptism He was identifying with sinners He had come to save.

When Jesus came up out of the water, God the Father's voice told everyone present that Jesus was His Son, whom He loved and with whom He was pleased. Then the Holy Spirit, in the form of a dove, descended and landed on Jesus. In this way, the whole Trinity was represented that day.

This event marked the beginning of Jesus' public ministry. The Spirit led Him from the public baptism to the lonely wilderness, where Satan tempted Him to turn away from holiness and to sin. In this place Jesus "was in all points tempted like as we are, yet without sin" (Heb. 4:15). When the temptation ended, God the Father sent angels to minister to Him.

God the Father prepared Jesus, His divine Son, for leadership on earth. How much more do we as humans need to be prepared so that we too can be the leaders God wants us to be?

—*Judy Carlsen.*

World Missions

This week's lesson, "Jesus' Baptism," highlights the beginning of Jesus' earthly ministry. The Holy Spirit's role in these events reminds us that He is always at work calling out disciples for leadership roles. In addition, the Spirit is always pioneering new Christian ministries. There are few churches, Christian schools, or missions that remain unchanged for two hundred years.

The modern missionary movement had its beginning with Spirit-led men like William Carey. Missions historians call this beginning period, starting about 1800, the period of "classical missions." Most of the early mission societies were denominational. Over time, most were integrated into the churches that controlled them. Many became ecumenical in viewpoint (Fiedler, *The Story of Faith Missions*, Regnum).

Faith missions date from the founding of Hudson Taylor's China Inland Mission (now OMF) in 1865. Taylor originally had no intention of launching a new mission, but after several years in China as a missionary, he had become frustrated over the lassitude of classical missions. Finally, he decided it was time to open a faith missionary endeavor.

The hallmark of faith missions is the emphasis on evangelism in preference to doctrinal issues. The faith principle was embodied in the position on remuneration for workers. Taylor's principle number four holds, "Missionaries receive no salary, but expect that God will supply their every need through the hands of his children."

The missionaries that you know may serve under denominational boards or faith mission societies. In general, Taylor's principle of faith support is still followed by many societies today. After approval for service, the candidate will approach the home church and other churches and individuals who know the missionary about taking on a portion of the financial need. When the whole sum is raised, the candidate can proceed to the field. Most faith missions assess some of the missionary's support for administrative and other expenses.

The winning of souls and the planting of new churches is the full and ultimate goal of all missionary activity. The Holy Spirit sovereignly calls His laborers into the harvest. He also makes the places of service plain to the societies and the missionaries.

One of the evidences that missions are a divine undertaking is that workers rarely wind up in places with great climates and with people who are eager to hear the gospel. Many missionaries labor on in unwholesome climates and disease-ridden areas among hostile peoples. One society lost its first nine missionaries in Africa to disease, travel hazards, and tribal violence. The society did not give up. Today there are hundreds of churches where those missionaries fell in their faithful service to God.

There is no higher calling in all the world than to take the gospel to people who really do not want it. Missionaries can be sure that the Holy Spirit will guide them to the place of His choosing. Faithfully presented, the gospel will achieve the Lord's particular purposes. Whether the field remains difficult and unresponsive or a great spiritual harvest ensues through the work of the Spirit on hearts He has prepared, faithfulness is what God looks for.

—Lyle P. Murphy.

The Jewish Aspect

Mark clearly identified the ministry of John the Baptist as the direct fulfillment of the prophecies of Isaiah 40:3 and Malachi 3:1 and 4:4-6 (Mark 1:2-3). John's responsibility was to introduce the Messiah to Israel.

There are many Old Testament prophecies about the Messiah's coming, but Isaiah 40 introduces the portion of Isaiah that reveals the Messiah as the Suffering Servant of Israel.

John's own words in Mark 1:7-8 show that he was completely aware of his role as the prophet who would present the Messiah. His ministry, as successful as it was in attracting large and steady crowds, did not promote himself but focused the attention of the people on Jesus.

Central to John's message was the call to repentance. This call was similar to Elijah's prophetic ministry as revealed in Malachi 3:5-6. In addition, John's way of life and his appearance also were reminiscent of Elijah (cf. II Kgs. 1:8).

There were many false expectations of what the Messiah would be like. It was necessary for John to begin in advance to focus the attention of the people on the spiritual nature of His mission.

In the Old Testament, God dealt with Israel as a whole, yet it was still necessary for each individual to respond in faith to God's actions and instructions. Such was the case with John's ministry as well.

Jesus would present Himself as Israel's King, and a major focus would be on individuals' personal holiness and their relationship with God.

The rite of baptism was not new to the Jews. Gentile converts to Judaism were required to be immersed in water for purification and conversion. John's baptism, however, served a different purpose. He insisted on repentance prior to water baptism. His baptism was more than a mere ritual. It was an outward demonstration of a contrite heart. The Messiah's mission would be one of salvation, but only those whose hearts were receptive would benefit.

John minimized his own role by announcing that the Messiah would perform a greater baptism, one involving the Holy Spirit. The implication was that spiritual preparation was necessary in order to receive this greater baptism.

When the moment arrived for John to reveal the Messiah, God provided him with evidence of the Messiah's identity. The Holy Spirit in the form of a dove descended upon Jesus as He submitted to John's baptism.

The dove was a symbol to the nation of Israel. Jesus was the ideal representative of Israel. It was a dove that brought hope to those on the ark after God's judgment from the Flood. Jesus would be God's pardon from judgment. The dove was a symbol of the Holy Spirit.

At His baptism, Jesus was anointed by the Holy Spirit. The word "Messiah" means "anointed." Jesus began His ministry with this anointing.

The descent of the Spirit was accompanied by the voice of the Father declaring His pleasure with His Son. The words uttered by the Father are reminiscent of Isaiah 42:1, a passage clearly referring to the Messiah.

It is clear that Jesus' coming was in fulfillment of God's promises to Israel. Even though many did not properly perceive His purpose, He came as the Messiah.

—Carter Corbrey.

Guiding the Superintendent

Believers experience life in a society that places a premium on instant gratification. Accompanying this demand for immediate fulfillment is a partner in crime called stress. Facing the demands of this terrible twosome poses several dangers for the child of God.

First, yielding to the temptation of on-the-spot contentment opposes the biblical principle of waiting patiently for the Lord's guidance (cf. Pss. 25:5; 119:81-83). Second, the accompanying partner, stress, robs the believer of the personal peace that God desires to give His people (cf. Phil. 4:4-9).

Finally, embracing the principle of instant gratification leads to weakness of character. The desert experiences of Moses and Jesus are necessary ingredients of a mature, strong character. Periods of preparation are mandatory in order to demonstrate spiritual leadership that furthers the kingdom of God. Mark reminds us of this principle in this week's lesson text.

DEVOTIONAL OUTLINE

1. John's wilderness ministry (Mark 1:4-8). John the Baptist conducted a powerful and popular ministry of baptism and preaching. His appearance and diet were ruggedly simple, and his message was powerfully clear. He was sent to prepare the way for someone whose ministry would prove to be more powerful and prominent.

Although John attracted a great deal of attention, he never intended that the attention remain on him. He made it clear that he was simply there to point to One who was coming, One who would so far eclipse his ministry that no contrast seemed too extreme. Indeed, as John pointed out, whereas he was busy baptizing people with water, the Coming One would baptize people with the Holy Spirit.

2. Jesus' baptism (Mark 1:9-11). While John the Baptist was conducting his ministry of baptism and preaching, Jesus Christ "came from Nazareth of Galilee, and was baptized of John in Jordan."

As Jesus stood in the Jordan River, several supernatural events occurred. First, "the heavens opened" (vs. 10). Second, the Spirit of God in the form of a dove descended on Jesus. Finally, the heavenly voice of God the Father affirmed the unique spiritual relationship of Father and Son and declared the Father's unqualified approval. Jesus pleased the Father in all He did, including the humble way He began His ministry here.

3. Jesus' wilderness experience (Mark 1:12-13). Immediately following Jesus' baptism and affirmation by the Father, the Holy Spirit directed Jesus into the Judean wilderness for a period of forty days. During this time, He experienced both Satan's temptations and angelic ministrations.

CHILDREN'S CORNER

It is never too early to begin preparing young lives for future spiritual leadership. A powerful component of this preparation is the assurance that God the Father does not hesitate to voice His approval (cf. Mark 1:11).

Help the children know that God delights in His Son, Jesus Christ, and also in those who believe in Him and desire to do His will. Because Jesus pleased His Father, He can and will help children who trust Him to please the Father in all they do.

—*Thomas R. Chmura.*

LESSON 2   MARCH 12, 2023

Scripture Lesson Text

MATT. 4:1 Then was Jesus led up of the Spirit into the wilderness to be tempted of the devil.

2 And when he had fasted forty days and forty nights, he was afterward an hungred.

3 And when the tempter came to him, he said, If thou be the Son of God, command that these stones be made bread.

4 But he answered and said, It is written, Man shall not live by bread alone, but by every word that proceedeth out of the mouth of God.

5 Then the devil taketh him up into the holy city, and setteth him on a pinnacle of the temple,

6 And saith unto him, If thou be the Son of God, cast thyself down: for it is written, He shall give his angels charge concerning thee: and in *their* hands they shall bear thee up, lest at any time thou dash thy foot against a stone.

7 Jesus said unto him, It is written again, Thou shalt not tempt the Lord thy God.

8 Again, the devil taketh him up into an exceeding high mountain, and sheweth him all the kingdoms of the world, and the glory of them;

9 And saith unto him, All these things will I give thee, if thou wilt fall down and worship me.

10 Then saith Jesus unto him, Get thee hence, Satan: for it is written, Thou shalt worship the Lord thy God, and him only shalt thou serve.

11 Then the devil leaveth him, and, behold, angels came and ministered unto him.

12 Now when Jesus had heard that John was cast into prison, he departed into Galilee;

13 And leaving Nazareth, he came and dwelt in Capernaum, which is upon the sea coast, in the borders of Zabulon and Nephthalim:

14 That it might be fulfilled which was spoken by Esaias the prophet.

NOTES

Overcoming Temptation with the Word

Lesson Text: Matthew 4:1-14*a*

Related Scriptures: Luke 4:1-13; I Corinthians 10:9-13; I John 2:12-14

TIME: A.D. 26　　　　　　　　　　　　　　　　PLACE: wilderness of Judea

GOLDEN TEXT—"But he answered and said, It is written, Man shall not live by bread alone, but by every word that proceedeth out of the mouth of God" (Matthew 4:4).

Introduction

Every day that we live, we are tempted to sin. From all directions sin attacks us.

When Jesus lived on earth, He also had to face temptations. Even before He began His public ministry, Jesus was tempted by Satan. As Satan tried to undermine God's program of salvation, he tempted Jesus to use His divine power independently of God's will. He also tried to get Jesus to reveal Himself by performing an impressive feat rather than by following the Father's plan. Furthermore, he sought to get Jesus to grasp for authority without going to the cross.

This incident was not the only episode of temptation that Jesus faced. Throughout His three-year earthly ministry, Jesus had to resist the attacks of Satan in many forms. He had to put the will of God ahead of His own comfort.

As Jesus resisted each of these temptations, He kept His focus on doing what He had come to earth to do.

LESSON OUTLINE

I. **PREPARATION FOR TEMPTATION**—Matt. 4:1-2
II. **PROCESS OF TEMPTATION**—Matt. 4:3-10
III. **PROTECTION AFTER TEMPTATION**—Matt. 4:11-14*a*

Exposition: Verse by Verse

PREPARATION FOR TEMPTATION

MATT. 4:1 Then was Jesus led up of the Spirit into the wilderness to be tempted of the devil.
2 And when he had fasted forty days and forty nights, he was afterward an hungred.

Alone in the wilderness (Matt. 4:1). Many Christians have learned by experience that spiritual high points are often followed by times of testing. In fact, we may be most vulnerable to spiritual failure just after we have experienced a time of spiritual victory.

In Matthew's record of the life of Jesus, the high point of Jesus' baptism was followed by a time of severe testing by the devil. The Bible teaches that the devil is an evil, angelic being who accuses and slanders God's people. The devil's desire is to defeat God in any way that he can. To further his sinister plan, the devil endeavors to lead people into disobedience and sin against God. He has been doing this since the time of Adam and Eve, and he is doing it in the lives of people today. He even tried to accomplish his scheme in the life of Jesus.

{Even though the devil was the agent of the temptation of Jesus, he was not the one who controlled the situation; rather, Jesus was led by the Spirit of God to the place of testing. This is an important fact to note, for it explains how temptation fits into God's plan.}^Q1

According to James 1:13, God does not tempt any person to sin. Instead, He uses even the malicious motives of the devil to further His own good purposes. What the devil intends to destroy Christians, God can turn around to develop them in their spiritual strength. As I Corinthians 10:13 promises, God never allows His people to experience a temptation that they cannot escape through His help.

The temptation of Jesus occurred in the wilderness. This barren, desolate land was significant in at least two ways. First, it was a place in which there was little comfort or companionship. Jesus had to endure the devil's attack without physical support or the help of other people. Second, it paralleled the experience of the nation of Israel, who had been tempted in the wilderness. Would Jesus succeed in an environment like that in which Israel had succumbed?

Hungry after fasting (Matt. 4:2). {The devil waited as Jesus fasted for forty days until He was very hungry. The lack of nutrition made Jesus vulnerable to temptation, especially if the temptation involved something to eat.}^Q2 What Jesus felt was genuine physical need. This, however, was God's will for Him, because the Spirit of God had led Him there.

Hunger is a basic and powerful physical drive. Jesus had to decide whether to remain hungry in obedience to God's direction or to seek to satisfy His hunger by disobeying God's direction. The devil would seek to exploit Jesus' extreme hunger in his attempt to undermine His obedience to the Father.

PROCESS OF TEMPTATION

3 And when the tempter came to him, he said, If thou be the Son of God, command that these stones be made bread.

4 But he answered and said, It is written, Man shall not live by bread alone, but by every word that proceedeth out of the mouth of God.

5 Then the devil taketh him up into the holy city, and setteth him on a pinnacle of the temple,

6 And saith unto him, If thou be the Son of God, cast thyself down: for it is written, He shall give his angels charge concerning thee: and in their hands they shall bear thee up, lest at any time thou dash thy foot against a stone.

7 Jesus said unto him, It is written again, Thou shalt not tempt the Lord thy God.

8 Again, the devil taketh him up into an exceeding high mountain, and sheweth him all the kingdoms of the world, and the glory of them;

9 And saith unto him, All these things will I give thee, if thou wilt fall down and worship me.

10 Then saith Jesus unto him, Get

thee hence, Satan: for it is written, Thou shalt worship the Lord thy God, and him only shalt thou serve.

Independent use of power (Matt. 4:3-4). The devil is masterful in preparing temptations that appear innocent on the surface but have disastrous consequences. At His baptism, Jesus heard God the Father call Him His beloved Son. The devil picked up that title as he spoke to Jesus. In essence he said, "If You really are the Son of God, use Your power to satisfy Your hunger."

The devil did not doubt that Jesus is the Son of God. {Instead, he tried to use Jesus' hunger to drive a wedge between the Son and the Father.}Q3 All around Jesus were stones, perhaps resembling loaves of bread in their shape and size. The Son of God could easily transform them into bread merely by speaking a word. Jesus in fact did use this kind of divine power later in His ministry when He fed the multitudes.

The present situation, however, was different. {Jesus was hungering in the desert because the Spirit of God had directed Him to fast. To use His divine power to satisfy His hunger at this time would have been something of a spiritual declaration of independence. Jesus would not be living under the authority of the Father but following His own way. In reality, the devil was attempting to get Jesus to act just as Adam and Eve had, by putting personal desire ahead of God's direction.}Q3

{Jesus responded to the devil's suggestion by quoting the Word of God.}Q4 He cited Deuteronomy 8:3, which told of Israel's experience in the wilderness many centuries before. In that passage, God said that He had led Israel into the wilderness in order to determine whether they would keep His commandments (vs. 2). God wanted Israel to know that obedience to His word is the most important value in life, even more important than satisfying physical hunger.

Applying this biblical truth to His own experience, Jesus chose to obey God rather than use His divine power to satisfy His hunger. He passed the first test by keeping obedience to God as the first priority in His life. Jesus did not let physical need blind Him spiritually. He knew what God had directed Him to do, and He remained faithful to God's word despite the personal discomfort He felt.

Impressive display of power (Matt. 4:5-7). The first test was in the privacy of the wilderness, but the second test occurred in the public setting of Jerusalem. The devil led Jesus to the roof of the temple. The point on the southeast corner of the temple area was some 450 feet above the valley below. In fact, the Jewish historian Josephus said that it was so high that to look down from it made people dizzy.

At that highly visible place, the devil challenged Jesus to prove that He really was the Son of God by jumping off. To make the temptation particularly powerful, Satan used Scripture to make his point. Quoting from Psalm 91:11-12, he said that God had promised to send His angels to bear Jesus up.

{The devil cleverly misapplied God's Word as he sought to tempt Jesus to sin. The passage in Psalm 91 was never intended to encourage God's people to be careless or to presume upon God's gracious protection. Instead, it promised that God would deliver His people who fell into difficulties as they followed His will.}Q5

What Satan urged Jesus to do was quite different. He wanted Jesus to use miraculous, impressive means to prove He was the Son of God. Throughout His ministry Jesus was pressured to perform miracles. Miracles in themselves, however, did not guarantee a response of faith. The devil had no interest in being convinced that Jesus was indeed the Son of God. Instead, he wanted Jesus to stoop to human means of attracting a following rather than keep to the plan laid out by God the Father.

Once again Jesus countered Satan's temptation by an appeal to Scripture. Satan had taken Psalm 91:11-12 out of context. Jesus, however, used Deuteronomy 6:16 in a way that agreed with its original context. In the Deuteronomy passage, God said, "Ye shall not tempt the Lord your God, as ye tempted him in Massah."

The incident at Massah, recorded in Exodus 17:1-7, was a time when the people of Israel demanded a miracle of the Lord. That insistence, God said, was putting Him to the test. In the same way, Satan tempted Jesus to compel God the Father to perform a miracle in order to impress people rather than to humbly follow the plan the Father had already given.

Illegitimate offer of power (Matt. 4:8-10). The first two tests were subtle attempts to get Jesus to work outside the plan of God. The final test was a much more blatant temptation. The devil took Jesus into a very high mountain. There, like Moses viewing the land of Canaan from Mount Nebo, Jesus could see all the kingdoms of the earth before Him.

Jesus knew that the earth rightfully belonged to Him and that He would eventually reign as King over it all. Nevertheless, before He could rule over the earth, Jesus had to redeem the earth from its sin. He had come to earth as a man so that He could be God's Substitute for sinful humans on the cross.

Before Jesus could wear the crown, He had to endure the cross. As Jesus' prayer in the Garden of Gethsemane showed, this was a painful experience for Him to bear. Because of His love, Jesus was willing to die on the cross, but He asked the Father if there were some other means that could accomplish the same effect.

Satan made Jesus a tempting offer. He said that he would give all of the earth to Jesus if only He would fall down and worship him. In other words, {Satan was saying that Jesus could be King without having to go to the cross.}^Q6 What a tragedy it would have been had Jesus accepted this proposal! By grabbing the crown for Himself, Jesus would have forfeited salvation for humans. Besides, Satan was a usurper. Only God could give authority over the earth, and He would one day give it to Jesus (Phil. 2:9-11; Rev. 5).

Jesus rejected this temptation outright. He ordered Satan to leave. Once again He quoted the Bible, which commands that only the Lord is to be worshiped and served (cf. Deut. 6:13). Instead of thinking that the end would justify the means, as we frequently are tempted to do, {Jesus fixed His focus on worshipping the Lord and obeying His Word.}^Q7 No one else is to share the worship that belongs exclusively to God. No projected benefit can ever justify disobeying what God has said. Jesus resolutely loved God and lived by His Word.

PROTECTION AFTER TEMPTATION

11 Then the devil leaveth him, and, behold, angels came and ministered unto him.

12 Now when Jesus had heard that John was cast into prison, he departed into Galilee;

13 And leaving Nazareth, he came and dwelt in Capernaum, which is upon the sea coast, in the borders of Zabulon and Nephthalim:

14a That it might be fulfilled which was spoken by Esaias the prophet.

Served by angels (Matt. 4:11). Jesus had passed the tests successfully. Rather than yield to temptation, He had stood in obedience to the Word and will of God. Although He would face temptations again in His life, for the present the devil left Him. {To help Jesus in His weakened, famished condition, angels came and ministered to Him. It is likely they provided food to nourish Him physically and fellowship to encourage Him emotionally.}Q8

Secluded in Galilee (Matt. 4:12). The ministry of John the Baptist was centered in Judea. That part of the country was the heart of Jewish life; so it was where people would expect prophets to minister. Jesus, however, did not fit the typical pattern. His ministry was to have a different geographical focus.

As Matthew 14:3-5 relates, John's forthright preaching brought upon him the wrath of Herod, the Roman-endorsed ruler of the provinces of Galilee and Perea. John spoke against Herod's unlawful marriage to Herodias, his sister-in-law. Herod arrested him and wanted to put him to death, but he feared the Jewish multitudes who regarded John as a prophet.

{With John unable to continue his public ministry, it seems the Jewish religious leaders headquartered in Jerusalem turned their attention to Jesus (cf. John 4:1-3). Sensing it was not the time to engage this opposition, Jesus left Judea and traveled north to the province of Galilee.}Q9 There He would begin His great Galilean ministry of teaching, preaching, and healing (Matt. 4:23).

Settled in Capernaum (Matt. 4:13-14a). Although Jesus had lived for many years in Nazareth, He did not choose to make His hometown His base of operations. Along the Sea of Galilee lay Capernaum, a bustling town centered around the fishing industry. Capernaum became the headquarters for Jesus' Galilean ministry.

{In the time of Jesus, Galilee was a vibrant commercial area. Several major roads crossed the region; so it saw a continual flow of people from throughout the Mediterranean world. Although Galileans were often ridiculed by the people of Judea, in reality they were much more involved in international life than were the inhabitants of Jerusalem. Galilee was thus an ideal location for Jesus to proclaim the good news.}Q10

Seven hundred years earlier, the Prophet Isaiah had foretold that the northern tribes of Zebulun and Naphtali would see a great light (Isa. 9:1-2). The region of Israel that had suffered most from foreign invaders in the Old Testament would be the first to hear the Messiah. This prophecy was fulfilled in the early ministry of Jesus.

—Daniel J. Estes.

QUESTIONS

1. What does the fact that the Spirit of God led Jesus into the wilderness tell us?
2. How did Jesus' physical condition make Him especially vulnerable to temptation?
3. Why did the devil encourage Jesus to use His power to turn stones into bread?
4. How did Jesus counter the devil's temptations?
5. How did the devil misuse Scripture in tempting Jesus?
6. What shortcut did the devil propose to Jesus for getting what rightfully belonged to Him?
7. Why was Jesus successful in overcoming Satan's attacks?
8. How did the angels help Jesus after His tests?
9. Why did Jesus leave Judea and go to Galilee?
10. Why was Galilee a strategic center for Jesus' early ministry?

—Daniel J. Estes.

Preparing to Teach the Lesson

Jesus was fully God. At the same time, He was fully man. As a genuine human being, Jesus was as capable of being tempted as we are, but as God He could not sin. Hebrews 4:15 tells us that He was "in all points tempted like as we are, yet without sin." This week's lesson deals with Jesus' temptation in the wilderness.

TODAY'S AIM

Facts: to examine Matthew's account of the temptation of Jesus.

Principle: to teach that the Word of God is our best defense against temptation.

Application: to encourage students to overcome temptation as Jesus did.

INTRODUCING THE LESSON

New products usually undergo rigorous testing before being introduced to the market. A product that cannot endure severe testing in the laboratory cannot be expected to do well in real-life situations. A visitor to a testing laboratory might think that good items are being needlessly abused. In reality, the abuse of the product is not meant to destroy it but to prove its worthiness. Who would trust his life to a car or plane that had not been thoroughly tested?

Jesus had been baptized by John. His public ministry lay before Him. Before that ministry began, He was to be tested. His testing would take the form of a personal temptation from Satan himself.

DEVELOPING THE LESSON

1. The setting for temptation (Matt. 4:1-2). Note that the Spirit led Jesus into the wilderness to be tempted. A somewhat similar situation is recorded in Job 1:6-19. In both cases it was Satan who did the testing within the parameters of God's sovereignty.

Satan came to tempt Jesus after Jesus had fasted for forty days and nights. Jesus, as a genuine human being, would have been physically weak by this time. Discuss this strategy of the enemy. He often attacks us in times of weakness. Jesus was not spiritually weakened by physical deprivation, however.

The wilderness site of Jesus' temptation has been traditionally identified as a mountain southwest of Jericho. Locate this area on a map.

2. The appeal to the flesh (Matt. 4:3-4). Ask class members to try to imagine going without food for forty days and nights. Ask them to share examples of people who have been lost or shipwrecked without food. Try to imagine what self-discipline would be required not to create food if you had the power to do so.

What would have been wrong with Jesus' turning stones into bread? Jesus turned five loaves and two fish into food to feed more than five thousand people (Matt. 14:19-21). There was nothing wrong with that. One writer noted, however, that "the Father's will was for Him to be hungry in the desert with no food. To submit to Satan's suggestion and satisfy His hunger would have been contrary to God's will" (Walvoord and Zuck, eds., *The Bible Knowledge Commentary,* Victor).

God has given us physical appetites for good reason. All of these appetites must be satisfied within the framework of God's will. Certain things that are right in one context could be wrong in another. Discuss this concept with your students. Ask them for examples. Explain what absolutes are. God's Word reveals that some things are never right, regardless of the social context.

Notice that Jesus quoted Scripture as He resisted Satan's temptation. Read Deuteronomy 8:3. The best antidote against temptation is to have our minds thoroughly saturated with the Word of God.

3. The appeal to pride (Matt. 4:5-7). Satan twisted Scripture back to Jesus. Read Psalm 91:11-12 and compare it to the quotation in Matthew 4:6. Anyone can twist the Scripture to make a point. We need to be careful not to do this ourselves.

Why would it have been wrong for Jesus to cast Himself off the temple? Such a feat certainly would have attracted attention! It was not the Father's will for Jesus to misuse His power for such frivolous and self-seeking displays. John identified "the pride of life" (I John 2:16) as worldliness. Ask students to suggest examples of pride-of-life temptations that confront people today.

Jesus responded to this temptation by quoting Deuteronomy 6:16. It would be presumptuous to expect God to rescue Him after doing something known to be against His will. Read James 4:3. God does not make His power available in order to satisfy selfish desires.

4. The appeal to ambition (Matt. 4:8-11). Satan's final tactic was to offer Jesus all the kingdoms of earth if He would fall down and worship the evil one. Jesus did not deny that those kingdoms were under Satan's control. Refer to II Corinthians 4:4 (cf. John 12:31). Fictitious stories have been written about people selling their soul to the devil for temporal favors. Your class may be able to cite examples from literature.

Jesus did not have to worship Satan in order to have all the kingdoms of the world. They all will be His anyway. Read Revelation 19:16, where Jesus is designated "KING OF KINGS, AND LORD OF LORDS."

Jesus quoted Deuteronomy 6:13 and 10:20 in response to the last temptation. God alone is worthy of worship! Jesus had successfully endured all that the enemy had thrown at Him. Angels then came to minister to Him.

5. Aftermath of temptation (Matt. 4:12-14a). Locate the geographical references given in these verses. John's ministry was concluding. Jesus' public ministry was just now beginning.

ILLUSTRATING THE LESSON

Three arrows coming at Jesus illustrate the three temptations Jesus resisted with the Word of God.

CONCLUDING THE LESSON

Jesus was tested comprehensively but was victorious over every temptation that was presented to Him. Temptation is real for all of us. In fact, we are tempted in the same basic areas as Jesus was. We can be thankful for the example of victory that Jesus set. Jesus' experience demonstrates how important it is to learn the Scriptures.

ANTICIPATING THE NEXT LESSON

Encourage students to read John 5:19-29 and ponder the interaction between the Father and the Son.

—*Bruce A. Tanner.*

PRACTICAL POINTS

1. God does not abandon us in times of temptation (Matt. 4:1; cf. I Cor. 10:13).
2. It is always a sin to pursue legitimate ends through illegitimate means (Matt. 4:2-3).
3. Our desire for God's Word should exceed even our desire for physical sustenance (vs. 4).
4. God's promises are not given to us so that we can test Him or show off our faith (vss. 5-7).
5. Let us be ever vigilant, for even the most godly people can be tempted by the worst sins (vss. 8-9).
6. God's Word, as it is known, understood, and consistently applied, is our best defense against Satan's temptations (vss. 10-11).
7. We must remember that the circumstances we encounter in life are God's way of fulfilling His plan for us (vss. 12-14).

—Jarl K. Waggoner.

RESEARCH AND DISCUSSION

1. How can we explain Matthew 4:1 in light of Jesus' teaching that we should pray that God not lead us into temptation (6:13)?
2. What does 4:2-9 tell us about the tactics Satan uses against believers?
3. Why was it necessary for Jesus to be tempted? How do we benefit from His temptation and His response to it (cf. Heb. 4:15)?
4. What are some ways that Christians can "tempt the Lord" (Matt. 4:7)?

—Jarl K. Waggoner.

ILLUSTRATED HIGH POINTS

Fall down and worship (Matt. 4:9)

People from several churches got together for a trip to Israel. One of the pastors who had been to Israel numerous times before explained the various sites they visited. Each evening, the people would get together to discuss the day's adventures.

One evening they were discussing what they had seen thus far on their daily trips. One of the older men asked to make a comment.

He said, "This trip has proved to me that people are the same today as they were in biblical times. Even though God revealed Himself in many wonderful ways to the people, they turned from Him to seek and worship other gods."

He went on to explain that even when Jesus lived before man's very eyes and performed miracles, many still hated and rejected Him. The hatred and rejection continue today.

John was cast into prison (vs. 12)

A pastor was speaking on how Christians had suffered for the Lord down through the years. He said, "Walking in close fellowship with the Lord and serving Him faithfully does not guarantee that you will not suffer persecution in this life."

He then went on to tell of several Christians who had suffered and died for their faith. He told about how even teenage Christians were killed. He spoke of Andrew, a young African who witnessed boldly for the Lord. He did not receive his tribal scars or make blood sacrifices, which the young people were commanded to do.

Andrew made it known that he was going to obey God and not man. For this disobedience to tribal practices, he was severely beaten and then buried alive.

—V. Ben Kendrick.

Golden Text Illuminated

"But he answered and said, It is written, Man shall not live by bread alone, but by every word that proceedeth out of the mouth of God" (Matthew 4:4).

John the Baptist had just baptized Jesus, albeit reluctantly, since he realized that this was the prophesied Messiah, God's beloved Son. John knew he was unworthy to even unlace His sandals, never mind baptize Him (John 1:27)! Almost ironically, the voice of the Lord had suddenly proclaimed this very truth from heaven, accompanied by a vision of the Holy Spirit coming to rest on Jesus as the Anointed One.

Now Jesus was compelled by that same Holy Spirit into the desert to fast and to endure temptations from Satan. This series of temptations was intended to prepare and confirm Jesus for the commencement of His earthly ministry. Early Christian ascetics, such as Anthony and Simon Stylites, followed Jesus' example (albeit it with questionable practices and theology) by enduring similar extended periods of fasting and temptation in the desert.

Unsurprisingly, Satan chose food as Jesus' first temptation. He must have reckoned this as foremost among Jesus' vulnerabilities at that time, and so he made it his first attempt to distract Jesus from God's priorities.

Satan's tactics have not changed since his temptation of Christ. He still tempts us wherever we are most vulnerable at any given time in an effort to distract us from God's priorities for our lives. But in contrast to Jesus, we often fall for his tricks. We must be ever vigilant in relying on the Holy Spirit, as Jesus did. Nevertheless, we always have this promise from the apostle James: "Resist the devil, and he will flee from you" (4:7).

In resisting this particular temptation, Jesus quoted Deuteronomy 8:3. In doing so, He met Satan's earthly priorities with God's spiritual, heavenly ones. Earthly food is necessary for a human's earthly life, but every word that comes from the mouth of the Lord is of even greater necessity for our spiritual and eternal life.

Therefore, Jesus contended, God's Word is what is most essential, not physical food. Thus, He declined to use the power God had bestowed on Him for such a mundane purpose. God has already filled the earth with a bounty of earthly food, but Jesus' mission from the Father was to fill it with the spiritual food of God's Word!

Christian, do you hunger for God's Word in your life? Many of us may need to admit that we often seem content to spiritually starve ourselves rather than regularly avail ourselves of the bounty of God's nourishing Word all around us, especially if we have the privilege of living in the United States.

If you are a newly converted or young Christian, one of the essential signs that your faith is genuine is a pronounced hunger for God's Word, the Bible. Should you find such a hunger lacking, you should seriously examine your commitment to Christ to make sure it is authentic.

Although more mature believers tend to acquire a greater familiarity with the Scriptures so that they carry the Word within them everywhere they go, such familiarity should not be allowed to give rise to neglect or apathy. Immerse yourself in God's vital Word daily!

—*John Lody.*

Heart of the Lesson

What is the longest distance you have ever run—a quarter mile, a half mile, perhaps even a mile or more? Some competitive running events reach lengths of one hundred miles.

Two things are certain about extreme lengths in distance running. First, no one can compete without extensive preparation. Second, the pressure to drop out of the race far exceeds anything the average runner has ever experienced.

1. The preparation (Matt. 4:1-2). When is a person ready to do something—after college, after an apprenticeship, after five years on the job? Businesspeople often speak of a learning curve, meaning the time it takes a person to become proficient at something.

Strange as it may seem to us, Jesus was on a learning curve. It consisted, among other things, of learning obedience through suffering (Heb. 5:8). As Jesus was about to make the transition from being a private figure to being in the public eye, the Father had another lesson in store for His Son.

Instead of taking His Son from the wilderness directly to Jerusalem, the Father led Him to an even more isolated wilderness setting (Matt. 4:1-2). There, some finishing touches would be applied.

2. The provocation (Matt. 4:3-10). You should take two main thoughts from Jesus' temptation.

First, the temptation was real. Jesus could have done any or all of the things Satan suggested, and the things Satan offered to give in exchange were His by right. Would people really have protested, for example, if Jesus had reclaimed "the kingdoms of the world" (Matt. 4:8) at the hands of Satan instead of going to the cross?

If someone wants to influence the outcome of a sporting event, he tries to corrupt the star—someone who can change things but still make it look good. Players on the bench are not important. Satan's temptation was skillfully targeted. The same propositions, presented to us, would have been less fatal to God's plan.

Second, extreme conditions provide a stern test of character. Believers who are near death have been known to struggle as their flesh asserts itself in spite of a life of Christian service.

Jesus must have been near death after the forty-day fast. Notice, though, that the Scriptures provided an answer at each point of temptation and that His dependence on them surfaced at a time of deep need. Like a distance runner, He was conditioned for an extreme endurance test. We do not know when these tests will occur, but we are responsible for being prepared.

3. The provision (Matt. 4:11). The race—or that phase of it, at least—was over for Jesus. The special ministry of angels verified the intensity of the ordeal.

We may learn from the angels' ministry that God provides extraordinary grace for those who are required to endure extraordinary things for Him.

4. The prophecy (Matt. 4:12-14*a*). As you study Matthew, notice the presence of prophecy. John's ministry was prophesied (3:3), and Jesus' choice of where to live fulfilled yet another of Isaiah's prophecies (4:14).

Jesus knew that faithfulness to God's calling cost John, His relative, freedom and would eventually result in his death. Fortified by His wilderness experience, Jesus embarked on the same path.

—Ken Schafer.

World Missions

Jesus' temptations not only serve as a major prelude to His ministry; they also reveal Jesus' approach to ministry. Jesus' goal was to focus on God and God's truth. This is evident in Matthew 4:10 when Jesus said, "Get thee hence, Satan: for it is written, Thou shalt worship the Lord thy God, and him only shalt thou serve." Jesus was quoting Deuteronomy 6:13.

People were created by God to worship Him, yet a great many people throughout the world worship other gods. They have, as Paul has written, "changed the glory of the uncorruptible God into an image made like corruptible man, and to birds, and fourfooted beasts, and creeping things" (Rom. 1:23).

Jesus, however, came to redirect our worship to the one true and living God. As a result of Jesus' ministry, a great many Koreans have turned from Buddha to worship and serve the one true and living God. I once met one such Korean woman while I was teaching a three week course at Asian Theological Seminary (ATS). She shared with me her testimony, which I now share with you.

"When I married my husband," said Grace, "neither his family nor my family were Christian. They were all Buddhists. My husband neglected me since he was busy doing business outside. I had to take care of my mother-in-law, who was very sick.

"Seeking the peace of her heart," Grace recalled, "one day my mother-in-law wanted to attend the worship service at Paul David Yong Cho's Full Gospel Church."

In looking back on that special day in her life many years ago, Grace remembered, "The Holy Spirit struck my whole self. Crying and weeping, I became a child of my eternal Lord and Saviour." Although it was her mother-in-law who was seeking peace, Grace was the one who found it. She turned from Buddha—a false and lifeless idol—to worship the one true and living God.

"Life," Grace said, "became meaningful to me. For the sake of my Lord I could endure any persecution of the rest of the family, especially of my husband." Grace shared how for many years she found comfort in I Peter 3:1, which says, "Ye wives, be in subjection to your own husbands; that, if any obey not the word, they also may without the word be won by the conversation of the wives."

Perhaps you can imagine how difficult this was for Grace, or maybe you share a similar experience. To her credit, she continually obeyed Scripture and continually prayed for her family's conversion. "At last," she told me, "God worked wonders in my life. My husband is now a believer, as well as his family." Grace's obedience to Scripture was rewarded, her prayers were answered, and her God was glorified.

Grace told me back then that she serves her Lord and Saviour. Her mission, like that of Jesus, was to pursue God's call. Her goal was not to draw attention to herself but to focus on God and His truth. She was serving as a missionary to young people in Manila while she attends ATS. Upon graduation, she said, "If God is willing, I hope to go to Myanmar (Burma) as a missionary."

Although her husband's family were Christians, Grace told me that her immediate family were not believers yet; so she asked me, "Please pray for their conversion and my ministry."

Please join with me today in praying for Grace, her ministry, and the salvation of her family.

—Herbert W. Bateman, IV.

The Jewish Aspect

Jesus is presented to us in Scripture as Prophet, Priest, and King. It is the theory of some Bible scholars that Satan's temptation of the Lord was a test of each of these offices. Satan's goal was to seize the worship due only to God. If Jesus could be tempted in any area of His ministry to men, Satan would secure a tremendous advantage (Lange, *Lange's Commentary on the Holy Scriptures,* Zondervan).

Theoretically, all Israel was eagerly awaiting the Messiah. In fact, however, only a few were, and they were largely from among the common people. What kind of Messiah did Israel expect?

One sect of the Jews, the Essenes, shunned public life and lived in their own community in the rocky cliffs near Qumran above the Dead Sea. The origin of the Essenes is not known. The first mention of them dates from the second century before Christ.

The Essenes led a spartan lifestyle and were an exclusive group. Their doctrines were secret. They looked for a Messiah and considered "that they were the righteous remnant, sole heirs to God's covenant" (Packer, Tenney, White, eds. *Illustrated Encyclopedia of Bible Facts,* Nelson).

The Pharisees were the ritualists of Israel. They were never satisfied with a Messiah of whom it was said, "This man receiveth sinners, and eateth with them" (Luke 15:2). It seems likely they would have applauded a messianic demonstration in which angelic hosts spared the Messiah's life (Matt. 4:6).

The Sadducees were the antisupernaturalist/humanists of Israel. A righteous messianic kingdom with genuine spiritual values would have held no attraction for them; so Satan's purpose to have Jesus lose His kingdom and avoid the cross would have been appealing to these leaders who denied an afterlife.

The majority of Israel was not ready for the Messiah of Old Testament prophecy. They ignored and rejected the prophecies of Messiah's lowly birth, suffering, dying, and rising again, which Jesus fulfilled to the letter.

Jesus in His early ministry was in His hometown of Nazareth. Although those living there heard of Jesus' great miracles, they would not believe He was the Messiah (cf. Luke 4:16-30). Jesus therefore would testify, "A prophet hath no honour in his own country" (John 4:44).

Not much has changed in Jewish concepts of the Messiah. Most do not believe in a personal Messiah. Some Jews speak of a messianic age in which war, violence, poverty, and racism are abolished through genuine brotherhood and good works. They do not realize that those things are secured for Israel and for all mankind through Christ's redemption (Eph. 1:7) and the new covenant (Jer. 31:31-33).

The fact that young Jews are turning to faith in the Messiah, Jesus, may be an exciting indication of the near closing of this age (cf. Rom. 11:25-26). In the last half century, greater numbers of Jews have been saved than in any period since the days of Jesus and the apostles.

Israel today is a state with problems of sin and apathy, similar to problems it had in Jesus' day. The religious elite in Israel are no more enlightened biblically than were the Essenes, Pharisees, and Sadducees. There are, however, a growing number of believing Hebrew Christians in the Holy Land.

—Lyle P. Murphy.

Guiding the Superintendent

Immediately after Jesus' identity was publicly made known at His baptism, Satan desired to test the Son of God. This description of Jesus' temptation has great meaning for us because it shows that He resisted temptation just as He expects us to do.

DEVOTIONAL OUTLINE

1. Test of selfish satisfaction (Matt. 4:1-4). This time of satanic testing was not unforeseen by the Father. In fact, God's Spirit led Jesus into the barren wilderness specifically so that He would be tested.

The fact that Jesus fasted for forty days before these temptations came shows that He prepared Himself for the testing that He knew would come. It also highlights one of Satan's tactics in waiting until one is physically drained to launch his most severe attacks.

Satan's first assault was directly related to Jesus' physical hunger and exhaustion. He suggested that if Jesus was truly divine, He could turn the desert stones into bread, which He desperately needed. Jesus' response, however, was that satisfying physical needs was not as important as obeying His heavenly Father.

2. Test of selfish pride (Matt. 4:5-7). Next the devil took Jesus to the highest point of the temple, possibly where priests blew trumpets to alert the city to important events. Satan urged the Lord to throw Himself from that height and prove Psalm 91:11-12, which states that God's angels protect those who trust in God.

Jesus refused to oblige Satan on the grounds that He would be unnecessarily testing the goodness of His Father. He quoted Deuteronomy 6:16, which says one should not tempt the Lord. God should be trusted for who He is, not because He does everything one asks Him to do.

3. Test of selfish advancement (Matt. 4:8-11). Satan then took Jesus to the top of a high mountain and showed Him the grandeur of the great nations of the world. He offered to give them to Jesus if He would simply bow down and worship him. Jesus again countered the devil's temptation with Scripture, quoting Deuteronomy 6:13 and 10:20. These verses declare that no one is fit to be worshiped except God Himself.

4. Rejection of selfish recognition (Matt. 4:12-14a). Jesus chose to make His ministry headquarters in Capernaum in Galilee. Mainly because of their frequent contact with Gentiles, Galilean Jews were viewed with contempt by the people of Judea (cf. John 1:46; 7:52). Although Jesus could have established Himself as a religious expert in Jerusalem, the Jewish center of worship, He was willing to be despised along with the Galilean Jews.

CHILDREN'S CORNER

Jesus was obedient to His Father and obeyed His word perfectly. Children should follow His example.

A lot of temptations are out there in today's world, even for children. But Jesus showed that they do not need to give in to them. Just as with others, children are prone to selfishness and other wrongs, but they can depend on Jesus in facing Satan's temptations. It is not too early for them to start memorizing Scripture to use in defeating his evil lures.

—Todd Williams.

Scripture Lesson Text

JOHN 5:19 Then answered Jesus and said unto them, Verily, verily, I say unto you, The Son can do nothing of himself, but what he seeth the Father do: for what things soever he doeth, these also doeth the Son likewise.

20 For the Father loveth the Son, and sheweth him all things that himself doeth: and he will shew him greater works than these, that ye may marvel.

21 For as the Father raiseth up the dead, and quickeneth *them;* even so the Son quickeneth whom he will.

22 For the Father judgeth no man, but hath committed all judgment unto the Son:

23 That all *men* should honour the Son, even as they honour the Father. He that honoureth not the Son honoureth not the Father which hath sent him.

24 Verily, verily, I say unto you, He that heareth my word, and believeth on him that sent me, hath everlasting life, and shall not come into condemnation; but is passed from death unto life.

25 Verily, verily, I say unto you, The hour is coming, and now is, when the dead shall hear the voice of the Son of God: and they that hear shall live.

26 For as the Father hath life in himself; so hath he given to the Son to have life in himself;

27 And hath given him authority to execute judgment also, because he is the Son of man.

28 Marvel not at this: for the hour is coming, in the which all that are in the graves shall hear his voice,

29 And shall come forth; they that have done good, unto the resurrection of life; and they that have done evil, unto the resurrection of damnation.

Doing the Father's Work

Lesson Text: John 5:19-29

Related Scriptures: Luke 2:41-52;
John 5:1-17; 8:25-30; 10:31-39; Philippians 2:5-11

TIME: A.D. 28   PLACE: Jerusalem

GOLDEN TEXT—"Verily, verily, I say unto you, He that heareth my word, and believeth on him that sent me, hath everlasting life, and shall not come into condemnation; but is passed from death unto life" (John 5:24).

Introduction

Those who have carefully studied the chronology of Jesus' life tell us that John 5 recounts events near the beginning of His second year of public ministry. By that time, He was quite well known in both the northern and the southern areas of Israel. Most of His second year was spent in Galilee.

In John 5 we find Jesus making a visit to Jerusalem to attend a Jewish religious feast. He faced antagonism there, where He was not as popular as He was in Galilee. It began after He miraculously healed the man beside the pool of Bethesda (vs. 5). Once the man told the Jewish leaders who had healed him, they determined to kill Jesus, primarily because He had done this work on the Sabbath (vs. 16). When they confronted Jesus, He told them that He was simply carrying on the work that His Father had been doing (vs. 17). That inflamed them even more. Now, along with working on the Sabbath, He had made Himself equal to God.

LESSON OUTLINE

I. THE FATHER AND THE SON—John 5:19-23

II. PEOPLE AND THE SON—John 5:24-29

Exposition: Verse by Verse

THE FATHER AND THE SON

JOHN 5:19 Then answered Jesus and said unto them, Verily, verily, I say unto you, The Son can do nothing of himself, but what he seeth the Father do: for what things soever he doeth, these also doeth the Son likewise.

20 For the Father loveth the Son, and sheweth him all things that himself doeth: and he will shew him greater works than these, that ye may marvel.

21 For as the Father raiseth up the dead, and quickeneth them; even so the Son quickeneth whom he will.

22 For the Father judgeth no man, but hath committed all judgment unto the Son:

23 That all men should honour the Son, even as they honour the Father. He that honoureth not the Son honoureth not the Father which hath sent him.

Their relationship (John 5:19-20). {When Jesus said He was working just as His Father was working, He not only claimed equality with God, He also claimed to have the authority of God. Since the Jewish leaders considered His statement to be blasphemy, they believed He should be put to death.}Q1 Jesus amplified His claim in verse 19 when He further based His authority on His relationship with God by saying He did everything the same way His Father did. He was, in fact, so unified with His Father that He could do nothing on His own.

Kenneth Gangel observed, "The equality factor explodes in dimensions the Jews must have found mind-boggling. Jesus, equal in nature with God; His goals, identical with God's goals; His will, only subordinate so that people through Him could see the Father" (Anders, ed., *Holman New Testament Commentary,* Broadman & Holman). In the world of Jesus' day, the Romans ruled. To them, the Jews' religious activity meant little. To the Jews, the highest authority of all was their religion. Jesus was challenging them at the heart of their beliefs.

A similarity exists in the Muslim religion today. What is making it so difficult to establish democracy in Muslim countries is the fact that in their minds religion and politics cannot be separated. Religious authorities are to be the political leaders, governing the people and directing national interests. {In the minds of the Jews in Jesus' day, the highest authority rested in their religious leaders. When Jesus explained His Sabbath actions on the basis of a higher authority than theirs, they reacted instantly and negatively.}Q2

Furthermore, Jesus claimed that God loved Him (His Son) and revealed to Him everything He was doing. This claim of unity meant that Jesus was doing only what God wanted done. In addition to that, Jesus said that other, even greater, things were going to be done by Jesus as God directed Him in the future. This probably means that the healing of the infirm man was nothing compared to what was yet coming. For example, Jesus would later raise people from death (chap. 11).

Their ability to give life (John 5:21). The Jews believed God had the power to give life. He did so first at Creation but also at other times. For example, the prophet Elijah raised a widow's son to life after the boy had died (I Kgs. 17). During the drought he had announced to King Ahab, Elijah was cared for by a widow at Zarephath (vs. 9). One day her son died. The prophet took him to the upper room where he was staying. After Elijah stretched himself over the boy's body and cried out to God three times, God restored the boy's life.

Sometime later God did the same thing through Elijah's successor, Elisha (II Kgs. 4). Elisha regularly stopped at a home near Shunem where the woman was a believer in God. She persuaded her husband to build a small upper room where Elisha could stay whenever he passed through their territory. When her son also died unexpectedly, she quickly traveled to get Elisha. As had Elijah, Elisha stretched himself over the boy's body repeatedly and prayed until finally the boy sneezed seven times as his life returned.

Perhaps the most interesting resurrection is the following: "And Elisha died, and they buried him. And the bands of the Moabites invaded the land at the coming in of the year. And it came to pass, as they were burying a man, that, behold, they spied a band of men; and they cast the man into the sepulchre of Elisha: and when the man was let down, and touched the bones of Elisha, he revived, and stood up on his feet" (II Kgs. 13:20-21).

{Since the Jews were acquainted with the Old Testament Scriptures, they had no problem hearing that God can give life.}Q3 Even Isaiah had written, "Thy dead men shall live, together with my dead body shall they arise. Awake and sing, ye that dwell in dust: for thy dew is as the dew of herbs, and the earth shall cast out the dead" (Isa. 26:19). They did have a big problem, however, when they heard Jesus say that He could also give life to whomever He chose. Once again, He claimed equality with God.

{What is especially precious to us is the fact that Jesus gives spiritual as well as physical life. It is through Him that we can have eternal life and be assured of heaven.}Q4

Their handling of judgment (John 5:22-23). {Jesus also claimed that the Father had conferred upon Him the authority to judge all things. He went so far as to say that the Father does not judge anyone but instead has committed all judgment to the Son.}Q5 This too is something greater than the healing of the man by the pool, and it also emphasizes the equality of Father and Son. {Jesus stated that there is a reason the Father has committed all judgment to Him: that all should honor Him as they do the Father.}Q6

Psalm 9:7-8 shows that God is the Judge: "But the Lord shall endure for ever: he hath prepared his throne for judgment. And he shall judge the world in righteousness, he shall minister judgment to the people in uprightness."

Jeremiah described a different situation when he wrote, "Behold, the days come, saith the Lord, that I will raise unto David a righteous Branch, and a King shall reign and prosper, and shall execute judgment and justice in the earth. In his days Judah shall be saved, and Israel shall dwell safely: and this is his name whereby he shall be called, THE LORD OUR RIGHTEOUSNESS" (Jer. 23:5-6).

An important transfer of authority is described in Daniel: "I saw in the night visions, and, behold, one like the Son of man came with the clouds of heaven, and came to the Ancient of days, and they brought him near before him. And there was given him dominion, and glory, and a kingdom, that all people, nations, and languages, should serve him: his dominion is an everlasting dominion, which shall not pass away, and his kingdom that which shall not be destroyed" (7:13-14).

So important is it that people recognize Jesus' equality with His Father and His authority to judge that Jesus said anyone who does not honor the Son does not honor the Father either. The apostle Paul wrote in Philippians 2:9-11 that one day every knee will bow and acknowledge the supremacy of Jesus Christ. But that follows this life. How much better to acknowledge Him now!

PEOPLE AND THE SON

24 Verily, verily, I say unto you, He that heareth my word, and believeth on him that sent me, hath everlasting life, and shall not come into condemnation; but is passed from death unto life.

25 Verily, verily, I say unto you, The hour is coming, and now is, when the dead shall hear the voice of the Son of God: and they that hear shall live.

26 For as the Father hath life in himself; so hath he given to the Son to have life in himself;

27 And hath given him authority to execute judgment also, because he is the Son of man.

28 Marvel not at this: for the hour

is coming, in the which all that are in the graves shall hear his voice,

29 And shall come forth; they that have done good, unto the resurrection of life; and they that have done evil, unto the resurrection of damnation.

Importance of belief (John 5:24-25). {The Greek words that begin this paragraph are *amēn, amēn,* which has been translated, "verily, verily." It is intended to emphasize the certainty of the next statement. One might say, "I can tell you this with complete assurance of its truth." We are meant to pay special attention to what Jesus said next.}Q7 When we read His statement, we realize that the entire gospel is given here, much as it is in John 3:16.

{The truth Jesus stated is that anyone who hears His words and believes in the God who sent Him will be guaranteed eternal life, which will result in escape from judgment.}Q8 Usually the wording of salvation truth emphasizes believing in Christ rather than in the Father. Since Jesus had been referring to His unity with the Father, it is understandable that He would say belief in the Father will result in eternal life. They are so completely unified that to genuinely believe in one is to believe in the other.

The phrase "is passed from death unto life" (5:24) becomes even more important when we understand that in the Greek text, the perfect tense is used here. In this verse, that indicates a completed action took place sometime in the past and has continuing results. {When we believed in Jesus Christ as our personal Saviour, we passed from death into life, and we remain there.}Q9

Paul wrote, "Wherefore, as by one man sin entered into the world, and death by sin; and so death passed upon all men, for that all have sinned" (Rom. 5:12). Before salvation we are spiritually dead. Paul also wrote that "the wages of sin is death; but the gift of God is eternal life through Jesus Christ our Lord" (6:23). When we believe in Jesus Christ, we become spiritually alive. At that moment of belief, we leave the realm of death and enter the realm of life. This spiritual life is also called everlasting (or eternal) life.

Once again Jesus stressed the certainty of His next remark: there would be a time—in fact, it had already begun—when the spiritually dead would hear His voice and live. This is the meaning we get from the little phrase "and now is" (John 5:25). The context is Jesus' ability to give life, not the future resurrection that will lead to judgment. It is true that in the future the physically dead will hear His voice and come alive again. In the present, however, the spiritually dead can hear and receive eternal life.

Authority for judgment (John 5:26-27). As humans, we do not have life in ourselves; we receive life from our heavenly Father. He is not dependent on any other source of life. He is life, and He is the source and Creator of all life. There is no life except what comes from God. Jesus said the Father had given Him the same capacity. He has life in Himself and is not dependent upon any other source for life. This explains the previous verses. He can give life because, like His Father, He is the source of life.

John's reason for recording this conversation of Jesus was probably his concern that his readers understand not only that Jesus possesses life in Himself but also that He has the power to give life to others. John 1:4 states, "In him was life; and the life was the light of men." It is the spiritual life that we receive from Jesus that gives us spiritual light, that is, understanding of God and His ways. Apart from Jesus, we could never receive such insight and we would be eternally lost and separated from God.

Not only was authority over life given to Jesus by His Father; so too was the authority to render judgment. God did this because Jesus is the Son of Man, a title that comes directly from the prophecy of Daniel 7:13-14. There He is called the Son of Man and described as receiving an everlasting dominion over all of creation. The title emphasizes His human nature and is the one Jesus used most often in referring to Himself. It is especially meaningful to know that the judgments rendered will come from One who shared our human life.

Power for resurrection (John 5:28-29). {Here Jesus spoke of a future event, as opposed to what He seemed to refer to as something present in the phrase "and now is" in verse 25. There is a physical resurrection coming that will involve every person who has ever lived.}^{Q10} This refutes any teaching that death ends everything and that there is nothing beyond this life. There are, in fact, two resurrections mentioned in Jesus' words: a resurrection of life and a resurrection of damnation. Not everyone goes to heaven.

{One resurrection leads to heaven, while the other proceeds to a place of condemnation. The word translated "damnation" is the Greek word *krisis,* which refers to a tribunal at which justice according to divine law will be rendered. The first resurrection involves believers, that is, those who have a right relationship with God through His Son, Jesus. The second involves unbelievers, that is, those who have not received Jesus Christ as Saviour. It will be a just judgment, for God is just (cf. Gen. 18:25).}^{Q10}

In this text there is no distinction of time regarding the resurrections, but further study of the Scriptures leads many to believe they do not happen at the same time. Here Jesus referred only to the universality of resurrection. Everyone is going to face God at one time or another. Those who "have done good" (John 5:29) are those who have believed in Jesus and trusted Him for salvation. This is the only real "good" anyone can do, because goodness and good works do not earn heaven. Those who "have done evil" are those without Christ.

Perhaps no other passage in the Bible relays so effectively the seriousness of the decision we make regarding who Jesus is and what He came to do. Jesus came to earth for the purpose of dying in payment for our sins. "As many as received him, to them gave he power to become the sons of God, even to them that believe on his name" (1:12). It is a serious matter to not believe.

—*Keith E. Eggert.*

QUESTIONS

1. Why did the Jews become upset when Jesus said He was working in the same way as His Father?
2. Why did the Jews disagree with the idea that Jesus had authority from God higher than theirs?
3. Why did the Jews have no problem hearing that God gives life?
4. What makes it especially meaningful to us to know that Jesus gives life?
5. What did Jesus claim regarding His authority to judge?
6. Why did He say that it is important to recognize His equality with God?
7. What is the significance of Jesus' words "verily, verily" (John 5:24)?
8. What certain truth did Jesus state about believing in Him?
9. What takes place when people believe in Jesus Christ?
10. What did Jesus say about resurrection? Who is going to be there, and what are the destinations?

—*Keith E. Eggert.*

Preparing to Teach the Lesson

The deity of Jesus Christ is the foundational doctrine of our Christian faith. The Apostle John's purpose was to reveal Jesus Christ as the Son of God. This week's lesson reinforces the deity of Jesus by revealing aspects of His unique relationship with the Father.

TODAY'S AIM

Facts: to teach the unity of the Father and the Son, specifically on issues of life and judgment.

Principle: to affirm the unity and equality of God the Father and God the Son.

Application: to help Christians appreciate the unique unity of the Father and the Son.

INTRODUCING THE LESSON

Those who build know the value of a solid foundation. Before a building is erected, great pains are taken to establish the footing upon which that building will stand. Sunday school children echo Jesus' words when they sing, "The wise man built his house upon a rock."

Our house of faith must also be built on a firm foundation. That foundation is the fact that Jesus is indeed God. Any doctrinal structure that falls short of that basic truth is flawed from the start.

In this week's lesson we see how Jesus revealed truth that clearly established His unique, divine relationship with God the Father.

DEVELOPING THE LESSON

1. Father and Son in agreement (John 5:19-20). "Some have mistakenly said that Jesus was here disclaiming equality with the Father. On the contrary, the whole context argues the opposite" (Scofield, ed., *The New Scofield Reference Bible,* Oxford). The Son does not act independently from or contrary to the Father. Note that continuous love characterizes the Father-Son relationship. Remind the class that Father, Son, and Holy Spirit are not three Gods but one God existing in three Persons.

2. The Father trusts His Son (John 5:21-22). The giving of life is the prerogative of God alone. Therefore, if the Father and the Son both give life, both the Father and the Son are God. Read Luke 12:5 and Hebrews 9:27. Life and death are expressions of God's sovereign will.

Discuss the concept of divine judgment. God has created us all, and we will all give account to Him. The Son has been given authority to judge. Refer to Romans 14:10 and Revelation 20:11-15.

3. Father and Son in equal honor (John 5:23). Consider the people to whom Jesus was speaking. Challenge class members to listen to Jesus' statements through the ears of His Jewish listeners. Why would Jesus' statement about the Father and the Son deserving equal honor be so offensive to them? If such a claim were not true, it would be the epitome of blasphemy.

4. Eternal life (John 5:24). The Father has sent the Son. However, it is not enough just to believe in the existence of God. Read James 2:19. Jesus' Jewish opponents certainly believed in God, but they needed something beyond that. Note that Jesus linked hearing His word with believing in God. Refer to John 14:6. Discuss "heareth my word" (5:24). What does that statement mean? Certainly the

Jews were hearing His words. What did He expect?

Note the promise of everlasting life to those who believe in the Father through the Son (cf. John 3:16; cf. 1:12; Rom. 8:1).

5. Life in the Father and in the Son (John 5:25-29). Explain "the hour is coming, and now is." Jesus was not speaking of a literal sixty-minute hour, but of the time of "his coming onto the stage of history" (MacDonald, *The Believer's Commentary,* Nelson). "Jesus' life-giving power can call a person out of the grave (11:43), everyone from their tombs (5:28-29), or anyone in spiritual death (vs. 24) to eternal life" (Walvoord and Zuck, eds., *The Bible Knowledge Commentary,* Victor).

Read John 5:26, and refer back to verse 21. Father and Son are coequal in matters of life. Read verse 26, and refer back to verse 22. The Father has committed judgment to the Son. In Scripture, repetition is often for emphasis. It is important that we be aware of this wonderful, mystical relationship of Father and Son within the Godhead.

Physical death is not the end for anyone. All who have died will be brought back to life at the appropriate time. Refer to I Thessalonians 4:13-18, which refers to Christians. Refer to Revelation 20:11-15, which foretells the resurrection of the unsaved. Some will be raised to eternal fellowship with and glorification of the Lord. Others will sadly be doomed to a state of eternal punishment and separation from God.

Read John 5:29. At first glance, this verse appears to present works as the criterion for a person's eternal destiny. This is not the case. Scripture interprets Scripture. Refer to Ephesians 2:8-9 and Titus 3:5.

Those who have done good are those who obey Him (John 14:15), abide in Him (15:5-7), and walk in the light (8:12; I John 1:7). In the words of Edwin Blum, "They are saved by the Lamb of God who, as their substitutionary Sacrifice, takes away the penalty of their sin. Salvation is by faith in Christ" (Walvoord and Zuck).

ILLUSTRATING THE LESSON

The judge in the illustration highlights that God, all three Persons, judges humanity.

CONCLUDING THE LESSON

The Jews of Jesus' day had no understanding of the Trinity, and they could not grasp who Jesus was. The claim of Christianity is that Jesus, God the Son, is coequal with God the Father. In this week's lesson text, Jesus revealed His relationship to God the Father. He shares the Father's unique characteristics, making Him coequal to and in perfect agreement with the Father. The Father has committed the judgment of all to the Son, before whom we all shall give account.

ANTICIPATING THE NEXT LESSON

Next week we see that Jesus' emotional anguish was very evident in Gethsemane. Read Matthew 26:36-50.

—*Bruce A. Tanner.*

PRACTICAL POINTS

1. Just as Jesus was dependent on the Father, so we must recognize our dependence on Christ (John 5:19; cf. 15:5).
2. Our love for someone will be evident in our desire to share with that person (5:20).
3. The wonderful things Jesus did should prompt us to honor Him as God (vss. 21-23).
4. Because we cannot believe what we never hear, we must earnestly study the words of Christ (vs. 24).
5. Life—natural, spiritual, and eternal—is a precious gift from God (vss. 25-26).
6. The judgment after death is as certain as death itself (John 5:27-29; cf. Heb. 9:27).

—Ralph Woodworth.

RESEARCH AND DISCUSSION

1. Since Jesus is the Son of God, why could He not do anything without the Father (John 5:19)?
2. What are some of the greater things the Son would do that would cause the people to marvel (vs. 20)?
3. If the Son could not do anything without the Father, why was He given the responsibility of judging (vs. 22)?
4. What are some things we can do to honor the Son (vs. 23)?
5. If everlasting life comes from hearing and believing, can those who have no opportunity to hear be saved (vss. 24-25)?

—Ralph Woodworth.

ILLUSTRATED HIGH POINTS

He that heareth (John 5:24)

In the fall of 2003, a string of southern California wildfires claimed twenty-four lives. When complaints were made that not enough warning was given by authorities, one fire official said, "We begged people to leave the area, but they didn't take us seriously. Some wanted to stay and fight the fire in their backyards with garden hoses. . . .Some looked like they were packing for a trip. The ones who listened to us and left the area immediately, lived. The ones who didn't, died."

Like the people who ignored the fire wardens, there are many today who are ignoring the Judge of the world and His warnings.

Authority to execute judgment (vs. 27)

How often people criticize God and take issue with Him when He allows tragedies to happen. "How could a good God allow such things?" they ask.

Consider this: Suppose you went to a court house to watch a trial but were told that because of overcrowding, you had to watch the trial on television.

For the next few hours, you can see only what the camera shows you. You do not hear all the testimony. You do not hear all the questions put to the witnesses. You do not see all the evidence. You are not privy to the conversations between the lawyers and the judge.

When the jury comes in with a verdict, how well are you able to discern whether justice has been done?

How, then, can men judge God? The Lord sees the motives of every heart. He knows what sins have been committed. Besides being all-knowing, He is all-merciful. Who can match Him as the righteous Judge of all?

—Ted Simonson.

Golden Text Illuminated

"Verily, verily, I say unto you, He that heareth my word, and believeth on him that sent me, hath everlasting life, and shall not come into condemnation; but is passed from death unto life" (John 5:24).

To not honor the One to whom all authority and ultimate judgment have been given is not at all a wise thing to do. Yet it happens all the time today, seemingly with increasing intensity and hatred. Christians are told to be tolerant, yet sincere believers in Christ are treated with intolerance by a world that acts much the same as the religious leaders of Jesus' day.

What made matters worse for the hostile crowd that shadowed Jesus and sought to kill Him was the fact they had incontrovertible evidence before them of His divinity but still could not bring themselves to believe in Him. To not believe in Jesus, then or now, is to lose out on the very thing mankind so desperately wants and needs—life that never ends and the absence of judgment. Jesus told those so vehemently against Him that the one they hated with great passion was the very one they should listen to and honor by believing in Him. Let us look at how He expressed Himself.

Our golden text begins with a double *amēn* (in the original), which is translated "Verily, verily." meaning "Truly, truly." Every word Jesus spoke is important, and the same can be said for the entire Bible. But when Jesus says, "Verily, verily," the reader/hearer should pay special attention.

What Jesus wants any and all to know is that it is extremely urgent to hear what He has to say. To hear means not only to hear with the ear but also to do with the will. It is to be obedient to the words one hears.

A motivating factor to get people to want to listen to Jesus is contained in the truth that Jesus was highly honored by the Father when He gave Him the gifts of authority and ultimate judgment.

Jesus has the authority to give everlasting life to whomever He wills. The way to receive the gift from Christ is certainly not by criticizing Him, let alone by seeking His death. Yet that is how the crowd of religious leaders felt in that day, and those seeking to remove God from the public square, schools, and areas where someone might be offended are no different today. To seek to eradicate God is just like trying to kill Him.

The way to receive the gift of life from Jesus is the way of faith. One must hear His word and believe in the One who sent Him—in other words, to believe Jesus was sent from God as the One the Scriptures promised would come.

To hear His word and believe (obey) is to receive everlasting life. The life Jesus gives is not doled out at death or on Judgment Day. It comes at the time of belief. That is clear by the statement that there is no condemnation in the future for the believer (cf. Rom. 8:1). Jesus stated that the believer has already passed over from death to life. That is the present case for believers, but it has future implications. The believer will not come into judgment on the last day, either.

It is a blessing to be among those who have heard the Word of God and, with sorrowful repentance for sin, embraced Him. For the believer, that was his judgment day and the day when everlasting life was imparted. Because of this, we should honor Christ with our worship.

—Darrell W. McKay.

Heart of the Lesson

The pious Jews of the New Testament persecuted Jesus. They wanted to kill Him because He healed a man on the Sabbath Day. Jesus' good deed and His statement about being equal to God greatly angered the Jews.

The Jewish leaders did not believe Jesus. They were not willing to accept Him. Rather than believe Jesus is the Son of God, the Jews preferred to believe He was of Satan. Since they really did not know God, they did not realize Jesus spoke the truth. Jesus only did what His Father told Him to do.

It is very important for us to believe in Jesus Christ and obey Him. Jesus, the only begotten Son of the Father, was sent to do His Father's will. Jesus always speaks the truth. His word is the final authority. We must hear Him! We must trust in Jesus if we want to be saved.

1. Jesus' authority in power and works (John 5:19-21). The Jewish leaders repeatedly tried to find fault with Jesus. Jesus told them that His power and authority came from His Father. He determined to not work on His own. Jesus is obedient to His Father. He only does the works of His Father, who sent Him.

The Father made it possible for Jesus to turn water into wine (2:2-9), heal the nobleman's son (4:50), and heal the man who was an invalid at the Pool of Bethesda (5:9). Jesus informed the Jewish leaders that He would be shown greater works by His Father, and they would marvel at them (vs. 20).

Jesus and His Father are one. Blessed are they who believe and receive God's Son. Jesus was in perfect harmony with His Father when He healed the man on the Sabbath Day. What state would the world be in if our heavenly Father refused to help us because of the Sabbath Day? Although the Jewish leaders' responses to Jesus were unfavorable, He did not allow them to hinder Him from doing the will of His Father.

2. Jesus' authority in judgment and honor (John 5:22-23). Jesus is the righteous Judge who will one day judge the world. Just judgment requires the judge to know all facts and the intent of the heart of the person who is being judged. Jesus is omniscient (all-knowing). He knows the motives of everyone's heart. He is just, fair and impartial. Jesus will fairly judge everyone.

Honor, glory, and praise belong to Jesus, our Lord and Saviour.

3. Jesus' authority in giving eternal life (John 5:24-27). Jesus made it possible for us to have eternal life. We are promised eternal life if we believe in Him. Jesus is the Saviour of the world. He died in our place. "The wages of sin is death" (Rom. 6:23), but the punishment we deserved for our sins was accepted by Jesus Christ. Life is in Jesus, and He gives life abundantly. He gave His life for us.

4. Jesus' authority over death and resurrection (John 5:28-29). Jesus has power over life, death, and resurrection. One day, at the time appointed by the Father, Jesus will resurrect everyone from the grave. We must have the righteousness of Christ by faith in order to be resurrected to eternal life. Those who do not have faith in Christ Jesus will be resurrected to eternal damnation.

We should never doubt Jesus' power and authority. He has dominion over all creation. The fact that He was resurrected from the dead assures us that we too will be resurrected.

—Arletta Merritts.

World Missions

Christianity is unique in that the Bible, not man, is the authority. The missionary is not the authority. He carries the authority. He translates it and teaches it, but he is on an equal plane with the people to whom he ministers. They all gather around the Book to study what it reveals.

The missionary has the advantage of background and education; so at first the new believers must learn the rudiments of the faith. This is eventually overcome, and the churches, the schools, and everything else come under the control of the nationals. They are equal in capacity and intelligence with the missionary.

I met a native of India once who had pastored a church in Pennsylvania. He related to me how his native village had been evangelized by a missionary sent out from the church he eventually pastored. It had come full circle, clear around the world. The gospel is like that. It is a great equalizer.

Islam has its imams and ayatollahs. The Hindus have their gurus, priests, and holy men. These are the authorities. The Buddhists have their saffron-robed priests. It is similar for other religions. But for Christians the Book is the final authority. Every church can study it and follow it with assurance of its authority. Salvation is by faith in Christ alone, not by membership in a church or by decree of a church leader.

Some religious leaders try to dictate the lives of their followers. They feel that their personal foibles should determine religious teaching. The true believer in Christ, however, turns to the pages of Scripture.

Of course, leadership does indeed make decisions on doctrinal matters. There is a doctrinal statement of faith that everyone follows. If you disagree, you can leave and find a society that you agree with or strike out independently. Even though the Bible is the sole authority for true Christians, there are differences of interpretation. We can cooperate with those of like precious faith even though we do not agree on every minor point.

Missionaries are sometimes pressured by governments to form groups with a centralized structure to make it easier for government officers to control them. There is something about churches that are independent of government control that frightens authoritarian governments. They imagine that Christians are fomenting rebellion. This suspicion occurs in Communist and Muslim countries and under dictators. Such impositions are artificial and unwieldy.

The downside to independence is that sometimes a strong personality breaks off from the main church body because he wants to start his own church that he can control. He violates the basic principle that the Bible is the authority. He sets himself up as dictator of his group and rules the people with an iron hand, taking money, oppressing them, and sometimes exercising life-and-death control. This is not unique to overseas situations. It happens here.

No matter how this may occur, it only makes us appreciate all the more the authority of the Bible. We need to teach that principle here and on the mission field. It takes constant vigilance to uphold it and to warn people against any false teachers.

The ideal result of missionary work is a growing, vital, independent, evangelizing church that plants more of the same. The missionary is then in the role of a trusted friend and adviser.

—Philip J. Lesko.

The Jewish Aspect

Three times daily, Orthodox and other religious Jews pray, "You are eternally mighty, my Lord, the Resuscitator of the dead are You," and, "Blessed are you, HaShem [Lord], Who resuscitates the dead" (Scherman, ed., *The Complete Artscroll Machzor: Rosh HaShanah,* Mesorah). In Orthodox Judaism this belief is so strong that the Mishnah says in Sanhedrin 10:1 that anyone who denies the resurrection of the dead has no share in the world to come.

Sadly, on this issue where we who believe in Jesus would most like to find agreement with our Jewish friends, only a relatively small religious community believes in the resurrection. In our time far more Jews believe in reincarnation or even in no afterlife at all. Reincarnation is different from bodily resurrection. Bodily resurrection means that God will raise us from the dead with new bodies and the same soul. By contrast, reincarnation says that people come back as different people (or even different beings, including animals) with the same souls from generation to generation.

A mystical Jewish book called the Zohar claims that reincarnation is God's way of dealing with people whose lives are not righteous. Souls that return to God laden with sin are sent back to new bodies to get an opportunity to redeem themselves from hell (Birnbaum, *A Book of Jewish Concepts,* Hebrew Publishing). Through the influence of ancient Egyptian and Indian mysticism, this concept of reincarnation has come to be tolerated in Judaism, even in religious circles.

In modern times, many in the Jewish community have become enamored of Eastern religions, such as Buddhism. The influence of Eastern religions has only heightened the belief among many Jewish people in ideas such as reincarnation, as opposed to the teachings of the Jewish Bible and prayer book concerning bodily resurrection.

In Jesus' time few believed in reincarnation, and the doctrine of resurrection was widely accepted. Jesus taught about the resurrection in a very Jewish way.

For example, Jesus said, "The hour is coming, in the which all that are in the graves shall hear his voice" (John 5:28). To a modern reader, it might seem strange for Jesus to refer to people being resurrected by hearing the voice of the Son of man. The Jewish audience, however, would have been familiar with Ezekiel's prophecy: "Prophesy upon these bones, and say unto them, O ye dry bones, hear the word of the Lord" (Ezek. 37:4). God promised to resurrect Israel, and it would be His voice calling them to new life.

Jesus spoke of two destinies for the resurrected. This too was familiar to a Jewish audience. Daniel said, "Many of them that sleep in the dust of the earth shall awake, some to everlasting life, and some to shame and everlasting contempt" (Dan. 12:2).

Jesus spoke the biblical truth of the resurrection in a way that struck a chord with His Jewish hearers. The shocking part was Jesus' claim that His would be the voice calling the dead to life.

As we noted, many of our Jewish friends today do not believe in the ancient doctrine of the resurrection. A vital part of our message to our Jewish friends should be that of Daniel 12:2 and Ezekiel 37. We could also point a Jewish person to the passages already cited in the Mishnah or the Jewish prayer book. Your Jewish friends may appreciate your familiarity with their religious books.

—Derek Leman.

Guiding the Superintendent

Did Jesus ever claim to be God? Some have said that the claims of deity for Jesus Christ found in the Bible are merely pious thoughts expressed by His followers in the years following His ministry. In other words, they say Jesus never claimed such status for Himself while He was on earth.

So far in our lessons this quarter we have focused on the fact that Jesus Christ is indeed the God-Man. Our lesson this week will continue this theme by looking at the authority that Jesus claimed to have. In summary, our text will show that by claiming to be the judge of all mankind, Jesus was claiming a prerogative that belongs only to God.

Jesus had just healed a person on the Sabbath Day (John 5). By doing this He claimed to be doing God's work. This week's passage picks up His discussion where He gave five proofs of His deity.

DEVOTIONAL OUTLINE

1. I am doing God's work (John 5:19-20). By claiming to do God's work, Jesus was claiming that what He did was inspired by God. He even promised that God the Father would lead Him to do even greater works.

2. I am the giver of life (John 5:21). One prerogative of being God is giving life. Jesus claimed to have this ability. In the context, Jesus had just given a crippled person his health. Later, Jesus proved He could give physical life (11:40-44); thus, His claims to provide eternal life were credible (cf. vss. 25-26).

3. I am the final judge (John 5:22-23). Only God has the right to be the final judge of mankind. Jesus and the Father are so united that to reject the Son's authority is to reject the Father also.

4. I determine man's destiny (John 5:24). To trust in Jesus is to receive eternal life and escape eternal judgment. One should not pass over this statement too quickly. Here in a short sentence is the entire good news of the gospel. Jesus will give eternal life and remove any threat of judgment for those who believe in Him.

5. I will then raise the dead (John 5:25-29). The absolute authority of Jesus Christ is the focus of these verses. He declared that by His divine authority He would one day judge all mankind.

It is quite clear from what Jesus said here that there is definitely life after death. Death is never the end; it is a new beginning.

It is also clear from Jesus' words that everyone will be judged after death for deeds done in this life. Jesus also indicated that all humanity can be divided into two groups: those who believe in Him and those who do not. There will come a time when He will call before Him all who are in their graves and judge them.

It is quite obvious that by these five claims Jesus established the fact of His divine authority.

CHILDREN'S CORNER

Many times it is in childhood when one begins to realize just exactly who Jesus Christ is. By focusing on any of Jesus' five claims, help your students understand that He is God.

One of Jesus' great claims in our text is that He is the giver of eternal life. Your youngsters need to see the seriousness of this fact. Every person who has ever lived will one day stand before their judge, Jesus Christ. Encourage your students to be prepared for such a meeting.

—Martin R. Dahlquist.

LESSON 4 — MARCH 26, 2023

SCRIPTURE LESSON TEXT

MATT. 26:36 Then cometh Jesus with them unto a place called Gethsemane, and saith unto the disciples, Sit ye here, while I go and pray yonder.

37 And he took with him Peter and the two sons of Zebedee, and began to be sorrowful and very heavy.

38 Then saith he unto them, My soul is exceeding sorrowful, even unto death: tarry ye here, and watch with me.

39 And he went a little further, and fell on his face, and prayed, saying, O my Father, if it be possible, let this cup pass from me: nevertheless not as I will, but as thou *wilt*.

40 And he cometh unto the disciples, and findeth them asleep, and saith unto Peter, What, could ye not watch with me one hour?

41 Watch and pray, that ye enter not into temptation: the spirit indeed *is* willing, but the flesh *is* weak.

42 He went away again the second time, and prayed, saying, O my Father, if this cup may not pass away from me, except I drink it, thy will be done.

43 And he came and found them asleep again: for their eyes were heavy.

44 And he left them, and went away again, and prayed the third time, saying the same words.

45 Then cometh he to his disciples, and saith unto them, Sleep on now, and take *your* rest: behold, the hour is at hand, and the Son of man is betrayed into the hands of sinners.

46 Rise, let us be going: behold, he is at hand that doth betray me.

47 And while he yet spake, lo, Judas, one of the twelve, came, and with him a great multitude with swords and staves, from the chief priests and elders of the people.

48 Now he that betrayed him gave them a sign, saying, Whomsoever I shall kiss, that same is he: hold him fast.

49 And forthwith he came to Jesus, and said, Hail, master; and kissed him.

50 And Jesus said unto him, Friend, wherefore art thou come? Then came they, and laid hands on Jesus, and took him.

NOTES

Submitting to the Father's Will

Lesson Text: Matthew 26:36-50

Related Scriptures: Psalm 88:1-18; Mark 14:32-42; John 12:20-26; Hebrews 5:7-9

TIME: A.D. 30   PLACE: Mount of Olives

GOLDEN TEXT—"And he went a little further, and fell on his face, and prayed, saying, O my Father, if it be possible, let this cup pass from me: nevertheless not as I will, but as thou wilt" (Matthew 26:39).

Introduction

Following the Passover meal and the institution of the Lord's Supper, Jesus and His disciples, minus Judas Iscariot, went out to Mount Olivet to spend the night. They moved into the Garden of Gethsemane on the western slope.

This week's text records that Jesus offered up three prayers, but it actually involved the same prayer offered three times. He was in dire agony while doing this, "and his sweat was as it were great drops of blood falling down to the ground" (Luke 22:44).

Some believe that this indicated Jesus' human nature and the natural aversion to His coming suffering and death. But His agony was also caused by the prospect of suffering the wrath of His heavenly Father as He bore the sins of the world.

All eleven disciples who had come with Him failed to stay awake, and the twelfth disciple came to have Him arrested.

LESSON OUTLINE

I. FIRST PRAYER—Matt. 26:36-41

II. SECOND PRAYER—Matt. 26:42-43

III. THIRD PRAYER—Matt. 26:44-46

IV. BETRAYAL—Matt. 26:47-50

Exposition: Verse by Verse

FIRST PRAYER

MATT. 26:36 Then cometh Jesus with them unto a place called Gethsemane, and saith unto the disciples, Sit ye here, while I go and pray yonder.

37 And he took with him Peter and the two sons of Zebedee, and began to be sorrowful and very heavy.

38 Then saith he unto them, My soul is exceeding sorrowful, even unto death: tarry ye here, and watch with me.

39 And he went a little farther, and fell on his face, and prayed, saying, O my Father, if it be possible, let this cup pass from me: nevertheless not as I will, but as thou wilt.

40 And he cometh unto the disciples, and findeth them asleep, and saith unto Peter, What, could ye not watch with me one hour?

41 Watch and pray, that ye enter not into temptation: the spirit indeed is willing, but the flesh is weak.

Rest (Matt. 26:36). Judas was familiar with the Garden of Gethsemane and knew that Jesus and His disciples were likely to make their way there that night.

{Jesus instructed the disciples to sit in a certain location while He withdrew to another spot for a session of prayer.}^Q1 They probably thought that He expected them to serve as watchmen and warn Him if anyone hostile appeared. This would be one form of rest from the exertions of the day.

Request (Matt. 26:37-38). After giving His instructions to His disciples, Jesus took His inner circle of Peter, James, and John with Him to another location. A mood of heavy sorrow enveloped Jesus. {He told these three men that His soul was exceedingly sorrowful, even to the point of threatening death.}^Q2

It would appear that Jesus wanted Peter, James, and John to be with Him and lend their support to Him as His time of suffering approached. This certainly was a reasonable request of His three closest disciples.

Resignation (Matt. 26:39). Jesus went about a stone's throw away from the three disciples (Luke 22:41). There He knelt down and, according to Matthew's account, fell on His face to pray. Addressing God as His Father, Jesus asked that, if possible, the cup He was about to drink might be taken away from Him. However, He was prepared to do God's will. He was submissive, surrendered, and acquiescent as an obedient Son.

In considering what the cup represented, we are faced with at least two possibilities. One is that Jesus wanted to avoid enduring the shame and agony of a mock trial, cruel torture, and excruciating crucifixion. His human nature would naturally be repelled by the thought of these prospects; however, He *knew* that He had come to the earth "to minister, and to give his life a ransom for many" (Matt. 20:28; cf. Mark 10:45). He *knew* that He was "the Lamb slain from the foundation of the world" (Rev. 13:8). There was no way to avoid this.

{Perhaps a more likely reason for Jesus' agony in the garden is that He was contemplating the awful prospect of enduring the wrath of His heavenly Father as He bore the sins of mankind.}^Q3 The cup is sometimes used in the Old Testament as a figure of God's wrath (cf. Ps. 75:8; Isa. 51:19, 22), and man's sin has brought God's eternal wrath upon him (John 3:36; Rom. 1:18; 2:5). When Christ took upon Himself man's sin, He experienced the divine punishment that human sin deserved (II Cor. 5:21; I Pet. 2:24). This took place on the cross, and it is what elicited Jesus' cry, "My God, my God, why hast thou forsaken me?" (Matt. 27:46).

Many people have endured great suffering, but only Jesus Christ has known the anguish of assuming the guilt of mankind and experiencing the divine punishment it deserves.

Rebuke (Matt. 26:40-41). After His first prayer, Jesus returned to Peter, James, and John. He found the three men sleeping. Waking Peter, Jesus expressed disappointment that he could not stay awake to watch for even one hour. By this time the two sons of Zebedee also may have been awake to hear the rebuke and to share in it.

{Although Jesus did not mention it to Peter, James, and John, He had been visited by an angel after His first prayer and strengthened by him (Luke 22:43).}Q4

Jesus had been helped by a heavenly being even as He had been deprived of the help requested from His earthly companions.

{Jesus now urged His disciples to watch and pray so that they would not fall into temptation and suffer the consequences of it.}Q5 He wanted them to be prepared for what was coming so that they would not yield to temptation. It was one thing to have a willing spirit, but it was another thing to restrain the weakness of their flesh. Paul later considered this topic when he dealt with the continual struggle of the Spirit with the flesh (Rom. 7:15—8:13). The only way to be victorious is to live by the power of the Holy Spirit.

SECOND PRAYER

42 He went away again the second time, and prayed, saying, O my Father, if this cup may not pass away from me, except I drink it, thy will be done.

43 And he came and found them asleep again: for their eyes were heavy.

Repetition (Matt. 26:42). No response to Jesus by the three disciples is recorded. We assume that they felt chastened, but as subsequent verses show, they were apparently so exhausted that they could not stay awake to profit from what He said.

Jesus moved back to His place of prayer and repeated the request He had made about the cup passing from Him; at least, that is what seems to be implied. His emphasis now, however, was on resignation to do His Father's will if He had to drink from that cup.

Repose (Matt. 26:43). Jesus returned to the place where Peter, James, and John were located. He found them in repose, their eyes weighted down and heavy with sleep. This time it seems He gave them no rebuke. He understood the limitations of their human frames and was not willing to scold them again.

THIRD PRAYER

44 And he left them, and went away again, and prayed the third time, saying the same words.

45 Then cometh he to his disciples, and saith unto them, Sleep on now, and take your rest: behold, the hour is at hand, and the Son of man is betrayed into the hands of sinners.

46 Rise, let us be going: behold, he is at hand that doth betray me.

Repetition (Matt. 26:44). Jesus moved back to His place of prayer and repeated the request He had made before, saying the same words. His willingness to do His Father's will remained constant.

{If the divine Son of God felt it was appropriate to repeat the same prayer three times, there may be a lesson in this for us. God expects all of His children to be persistent in making their requests known to Him.}Q6 The important thing is that they be ready to accept His answers of "yes," "no," or "wait." It is God's will that is vital, not our own will (I John 5:14-15).

Resignation (Matt. 26:45-46). Jesus' resignation to His Father was next transposed to resignation to the situation with His disciples. He returned to Peter, James, and John and again found them sleeping, as were the other eight disciples at their location. Jesus told them to sleep on now and take their rest. The die had been cast. The Son of man was being betrayed into the hands of sinners. The betrayer had joined hands with the chief priests, the elders, and the scribes in a plot to find Jesus and take Him to trial before the Sanhedrin. An attempt would then be made to persuade the Roman authorities to authorize His execution.

The time of sleep for the disciples had now ended, for the officers led by Judas Iscariot were arriving. Jesus commanded His disciples to rise up and get ready to go, for he who was to betray Him was at hand.

{Thus we see a threefold resignation on Jesus' part. First, He was resigned to God's will. Second, He was resigned to His disciples' exhaustion. Third, He was resigned to His betrayal and arrest.}Q7 Once we have resigned ourselves to God's will, we are ready to resign ourselves to whatever else is necessary in order to carry it out.

BETRAYAL

47 And while he yet spake, lo, Judas, one of the twelve, came, and with him a great multitude with swords and staves, from the chief priests and elders of the people.

48 Now he that betrayed him gave them a sign, saying, Whomsoever I shall kiss, that same is he: hold him fast.

49 And forthwith he came to Jesus, and said, Hail, master; and kissed him.

50 And Jesus said unto him, Friend, wherefore art thou come? Then came they, and laid hands on Jesus, and took him.

Plan (Matt. 26:47-48). {If it appears that Jesus was aware of the approach of Judas and the multitude of people accompanying him, that is exactly right. Before the sounds of their approach could be heard by the disciples, Jesus knew they were coming.}Q8 He knew what was in the minds and hearts of men (John 2:25).

Jesus knew the intentions of the approaching multitude. Led by the deceitful Judas Iscariot, who knew the place (John 18:2), this mob came armed with swords and staves, or clubs. Included in this crowd was "a band of men and officers from the chief priests and Pharisees," who were equipped with "lanterns and torches and weapons" (vs. 3). There were "chief priests, and captains of the temple, and the elders" (Luke 22:52).

{Judas Iscariot had given the multitude a sign, saying that the one he kissed in greeting would be Jesus. They were to grab Him and hold Him fast.}Q9 This was the plan, and it was put into motion. It might be noted here that affectionate gestures such as this between men were common to the culture and customs of that time. In fact, men in the Middle East still have a habit of greeting one another with a kiss and even walking together hand in hand without any sexual overtones.

Perfidy (Matt. 26:49-50). We can find more details of this incident in John 18:2-13. "Jesus therefore, knowing all things that should come upon him, went forth, and said unto them, Whom seek ye? They answered him, Jesus of Nazareth. Jesus saith unto them, I am he. . . . As soon then as he had said unto them, I am he, they went backward, and fell to the ground."

Jesus again asked them for whom they sought. They told Him it was Jesus of Nazareth, and He repeated His statement that He was that person. Then He requested that His disciples be allowed to go free. He asked this so that none of the men whom God had given Him would be lost (vss. 7-9).

In spite of the fact that Jesus had identified Himself twice to the arresting mob, Judas came up to Him to hail, or greet, Him as Master and to kiss Him. Jesus said, "Judas, betrayest thou the Son of man with a kiss?" (Luke 22:48).

Then Jesus called him His friend and asked him why he had come. He knew the answer, but He wanted Judas to put it in his own words. No answer by Judas is recorded.

Betrayals by enemies or criminal con artists are despicable, but they are to be expected. Betrayal or deceit practiced by a close friend, however, is much worse. This was particularly true in the case of Judas's betrayal of Jesus, because He was the divine Son of God. Ever since this horrendous incident took place, "Judas" has become a common byword for anyone who deceives or betrays someone else, especially someone close to him.

The case of Judas Iscariot underscores the fact that appearances often shield inner feelings. Despite the fact that Judas Iscariot was numbered among the twelve disciples, his subsequent actions proved he was not truly one of them.

Peter's action in cutting off the right ear of Malchus, the high priest's servant, was rebuked by Jesus. He told him to put his sword back into his sheath, remarking that those who take up the sword will perish by the sword. Jesus could have prayed to His Father and had twelve legions of angels come to rescue Him from the arresting mob, but then the Scriptures regarding His atoning death would not have been fulfilled (Matt. 26:51-54).

The incident regarding Peter's rash act with his sword is mentioned here because it ties in directly with the cup Jesus was destined to drink as recorded in our lesson text. "Then said Jesus unto Peter, Put up thy sword into the sheath: the cup which my Father hath given me, shall I not drink it?" (John 18:11).

If Jesus had not allowed the betrayal to take place and had not suffered and died to atone for our sins, the whole redemptive plan of God would have been aborted. If Jesus had not been willing to drink that cup, we would be hopelessly and eternally lost.

The evil deed was done. The captain and officers of the Jews took hold of Jesus and bound Him (John 18:12). They led Him away to the high priest's house, with Peter following afar off (Luke 22:54).

{One of the saddest reports in the Bible is this: "Then all the disciples forsook him, and fled" (Matt. 26:56; cf. Mark 14:50).}^{Q10} They would go into hiding until after Christ's resurrection and His appearance to them. They soon thereafter would be empowered by the Holy Spirit to go out and begin changing the world. If the Spirit can make that kind of transformation in them, He can do the same for us.

—*Gordon Talbot.*

QUESTIONS

1. What did Jesus tell His disciples to do in the Garden of Gethsemane?
2. How sorrowful did Jesus say that He was?
3. What likely was the cup that Jesus was reluctant to drink?
4. How did Jesus receive strength after His first prayer?
5. Why did Jesus tell His sleepy disciples to watch and pray?
6. What does Jesus' example in repeating His prayer teach us?
7. What three types of resignation did Jesus display in Gethsemane?
8. When did Jesus know that Judas and the mob were coming?
9. How did Judas plan to betray Jesus to the multitude?
10. In what way did all the disciples let Jesus down?

—*Gordon Talbot.*

Preparing to Teach the Lesson

With this lesson we transition from examining some of Jesus' major works to considering His sacrifice. A crucial element in this was His steadfast acceptance of God's will even though it meant enduring great suffering.

TODAY'S AIM

Facts: to examine Matthew's account of Jesus' prayer in the garden and His betrayal and arrest.

Principle: to teach that fervent prayer is a necessary part of Christlikeness.

Application: to encourage Christians to follow Jesus' example, specifically in prayer.

INTRODUCING THE LESSON

My friend Jeff is the pastor of a healthy, growing church in Illinois. The church's facilities have been expanded several times to accommodate the mushrooming congregation. Lives have been changed dramatically as people have found the Lord through the ministry of that church.

I recently learned that Pastor Jeff spends several hours each day in prayer. Although he has many demands on his time, Jeff has determined to discipline himself to truly seek the Lord each day. He has found that this time with God has proved to be extremely valuable to his own spiritual life and to the ministry of his church.

Jesus, even though He was the Son of God, was a man of prayer. His prayer in the garden just prior to His arrest is a prime example of His intensity in prayer.

DEVELOPING THE LESSON

1. Jesus' first prayer (Matt. 26:36-41). Supply your students with background information on Gethsemane. Gethsemane was an olive grove located on the Mount of Olives. Why might Jesus have chosen this place to pray? The olive grove probably would have been quiet and free of distractions. Refer to Luke 6:12, which tells of an earlier time when Jesus went to a mountain to pray all night. Can we draw lessons from Jesus' example?

Jesus left most of the disciples at one location and then proceeded a little farther with Peter, James, and John. He then left them and went on even farther by Himself. Discuss why Jesus went off by Himself to agonize in prayer. Read Jesus' own teaching on prayer in Matthew 6:6. What are the advantages of being by oneself in serious times of prayer? The presence of others can sometimes inhibit a person's prayer.

Note Jesus' emotional state (Matt. 26:37-38). Discuss His probable reasons for being so sorrowful. Such honest portrayals of Jesus' emotions remind us of His true humanity. Read Hebrews 4:15 and Isaiah 53:3. One lesson we can learn from such a portrayal of Jesus' emotions is this: If Jesus could experience the full range of human emotions, we should appreciate the fact that even Christians sometimes have negative feelings.

Jesus prayed, "Let this cup pass from me" (Matt. 26:39). Discuss how this demonstrates Christ's humanity. This plea from Jesus teaches us that we can and should be honest in expressing our requests to God. Read John 12:27, in which another example of Jesus' inner struggle is recorded.

Jesus also prayed, "Nevertheless not as I will, but as thou wilt" (Matt. 26:39). Note that God's will had a prominent place in Jesus' prayers (cf. 6:10). For some people the object of prayer seems to be to persuade God to acquiesce to their will. Christlike prayer means submitting ourselves to His will. Read I John 5:14. Discuss the importance of submission to God's will in prayer.

What had Jesus expected from Peter, James, and John? Those three men made up Jesus' inner circle. They were the closest to Him. How did they disappoint Him? Discuss the importance of standing by our friends in prayer during their times of need. What reason did Jesus give for prayer (Matt. 26:41)? How does this warning apply to us?

2. Jesus' second prayer (Matt. 26:42-43). After admonishing the sleeping disciples, Jesus went back to pray again. Jesus' persistence in prayer should teach us persistence also. Note again Jesus' resignation to the Father's will. Emphasize that submission to God's will is the highest form of prayer.

3. Jesus' third prayer (Matt. 26:44-46). Jesus' perseverance is further demonstrated in His third prayer. His disciples' lack of support did not dissuade Him. Sometimes we too need to persevere without others' help.

Jesus was fully aware of the coming betrayal. He had prepared Himself for this terrible crisis through prayer.

4. Jesus' betrayal and arrest (Matt. 26:47-50). Identify the "great multitude" that came to arrest Jesus. Read John 18:3. The Jewish leadership had enlisted Roman help to arrest Jesus. This was a joint operation of temple police and Roman legionnaires. Perhaps such a force was sent out to confront Jesus and the Eleven because there was fear of a popular uprising in Jesus' defense.

The sign that would identify Jesus was a kiss. A kiss on the cheek was normally a friendly salutation. The worst kind of guile, however, was behind Judas's kiss. Satan was clearly at work in this evil deception. We can only guess the tone of Judas's voice when he said, "Hail, master" (Matt. 26:49). Note the graciousness of Jesus as He addressed the betrayer Judas as "friend" (vs. 50).

ILLUSTRATING THE LESSON

The bulk of this week's lesson text deals with Jesus' prayers in the garden. His practice of praying serves as a perfect example for us.

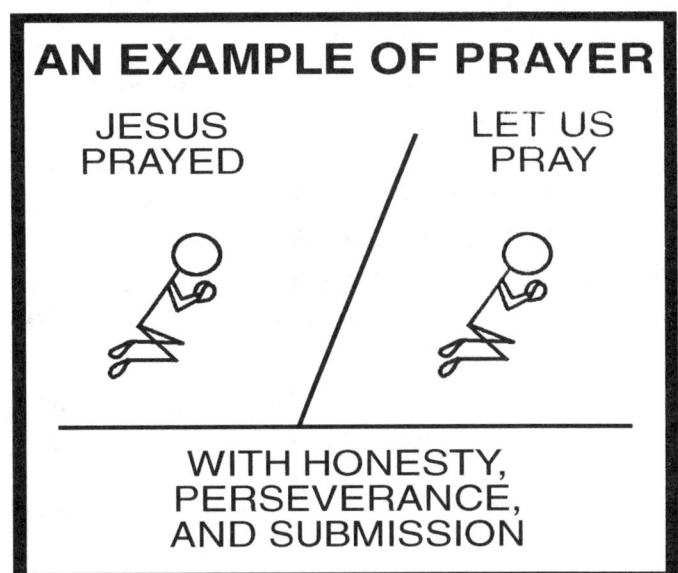

CONCLUDING THE LESSON

Jesus was drawing nearer and nearer to the Cross. As that terrible event loomed ahead of Him, He paused in the quiet Garden of Gethsemane to pray to the Father. Jesus in prayer serves as an example to us all. His honesty, persistence, and ultimate submission to the Father's will beckon us to imitate Him. Through Jesus' prayer we see that praying can be a very intense, soul-searching endeavor. Encourage your students to follow Jesus' example in prayer.

ANTICIPATING THE NEXT LESSON

Next week's lesson takes us to the scene of Jesus' crucifixion. We will see the extreme malice of Jesus' enemies as well as the deep emotional anguish of our Saviour as He hung on the cross.

—*Bruce A. Tanner.*

PRACTICAL POINTS

1. Experiencing emotional turmoil can prepare us to minister to others (Matt. 26:36-38; cf. Heb. 4:15-16).
2. Submissive obedience is a mark of Christlikeness (Matt. 26:39).
3. The discipline of prayer is demanding, but it is necessary for overcoming temptation (vss. 40-41).
4. Do not hesitate to repeat heartfelt prayers (vss. 42-44).
5. A time of spiritual rest is necessary to prepare Christ's followers for a time of spiritual battle (vss. 45-46).
6. Spiritual betrayal is no coincidence; it always involves a definite plan of action (vss. 47-48).
7. Not everyone who calls Jesus "Master" will enter His kingdom (6:49-50; cf. 7:21-23).

—Thomas R. Chmura.

RESEARCH AND DISCUSSION

1. How important is it to have a spiritual accountability partner, and what level of intimacy should you strive for (Matt. 26:36-38)?
2. What does verse 39 reveal concerning the perfect humanity of Jesus Christ?
3. What type of spiritual exercise and discipline will combat the dangers of spiritual lethargy (Matt. 26:40-41; cf. Eph. 5:14-17)?
4. What does Christ's response to His disciples' repeated weakness teach you about His compassionate grace (Matt. 26:42-45)?
5. What is at the heart of spiritual hypocrisy (vss. 48-49)?

—Thomas R. Chmura.

ILLUSTRATED HIGH POINTS

I go and pray yonder (Matt. 26:36)

Jesus prayed, and God answered. The answer was that there was no way for Christ to escape what lay ahead. It was a part of the divine plan from before the foundation of the world.

We have often heard it said that God answers every prayer. Sometimes He says no. At times the answer is wait, and then there are times when He grants our request. The key, of course, is to pray according to His will and be willing to accept whatever answer He gives.

Jesus knew what His Father's will was. He also knew what it would cost Him to fulfill that will. How grateful we should be that He did not shy away from giving His life to pay the penalty for our sins!

Findeth them asleep (vs. 40)

A former minister attended the church where I grew up. He was known for his tendency to fall asleep during church services. Perhaps the only reason he did not sleep during the Sunday school class was that he was occupied, being the teacher of the adults.

This man slept not only during the sermon but in the other parts of the service as well. In fact, on occasion, when he was invited to share in a service, he would fall asleep while sitting on the platform with the minister. His excuse was that he pretty much knew what the pastor was going to say.

It is true that Jesus' disciples had been awake a full day, but they were also fishermen who were accustomed to working through the night (cf. Luke 5:5). May we be ever alert to take advantage of the worship and preaching of the Word. Our alertness will encourage the pastor and be a special blessing to those around us.

—David A. Hamburg.

Golden Text Illuminated

"And he went a little further, and fell on his face, and prayed, saying, O my Father, if it be possible, let this cup pass from me: nevertheless not as I will, but as thou wilt" (Matthew 26:39).

Our lesson text for this week takes us from Jesus' prayers in Gethsemane to His actual arrest by the mob of armed men led by Judas Iscariot.

Our golden text records the first of Jesus' three prayers in the garden, all of which are of similar content; He asked the Father to let the cup of His impending torture and crucifixion pass from Him if possible, followed by His affirmation of willingness to do His Father's will, no matter what.

While Jesus was agonizing in prayer to God the Father over His upcoming ordeal of pain and death for their sins and the sins of the world, His disciples had fallen asleep! Like so many of us, they tended to let their prayer vigils become nap time. Their spiritual dullness and anxiety allowed them to lose focus when Jesus desired their prayers the most.

Jesus' resolve to do His Father's will is a shining example for us. Jesus was as frail and human as any of us, yet He relied upon the power of God through the Holy Spirit to overcome His human weakness and give Himself as an offering for our redemption.

We have the same spiritual resources available to us today that Jesus relied on that fateful night in Gethsemane. But the question remains, will we trust our heavenly Father's will for us as He did?

Submitting to the Father's will for our lives is probably the hardest thing we will ever have to do. Even as Christians with the Holy Spirit dwelling inside us, our fallen human nature craves autonomy. We stubbornly desire to maintain a firm grasp on the tiller of our own destiny, no matter how many times we have experienced the Father's faithfulness in directing our course.

Ask yourself: Did anyone ever have more reason for insisting on self-determination than the divine Son of God? Has anyone ever had greater justification for claiming the right to take control of His own destiny than Jesus did?

Yet Jesus forsook His own welfare for the sake of those He loved. He chose to keep His own will in perfect sync with the will of His heavenly Father so that He could redeem us from our lost sinful condition to become adopted sons and daughters in God's family.

Love is the heart of the matter—love for His heavenly Father and love for us. That is what Jesus meant when He said, "Greater love hath no man than this, that a man lay down his life for his friends" (John 15:13).

The apostle John wrote, "Hereby perceive we the love of God, because he laid down his life for us: and we ought to lay down our lives for the brethren" (I John 3:16). God's love is the love of submission, obedience, and especially the love of self-sacrifice for others.

To truly follow Jesus' example in Gethsemane, we must love God and others enough to trust His will under the most extreme and demanding situations. Such love and trust takes even the best of us a lifetime to cultivate. Start now!

—*John Lody.*

Heart of the Lesson

Is prayer an important part of your daily life? When do you pray? The Bible has scores of verses about prayer and its importance to those people throughout the Old and New Testaments who followed God.

In this week's text we see how Jesus faced the most difficult hours of His life on earth. Although He is God, He is also completely human. Jesus knew what was about to happen to Him, so He turned to His Father in prayer—as He always did while here on earth. In fact, He had prayed all night before He chose His disciples (Luke 6:12-13).

1. Prayer seeks (Matt. 26:36-39). Jesus asked His closest friends to pray with Him as He sought the will of His Father. He sorrowed as He looked ahead to the ordeal to come. Could it possibly be God's will for Him to somehow bypass the pain and torment? The human part of our Lord sought to somehow avoid it all. Knowing that torture and death were indeed God's plan for Him, Jesus prayed for God's will to be done.

It is through prayer that we too can learn God's will for our daily lives. Certainly God speaks through His Word, but He also speaks personally to us in our minds as we communicate with Him in a spirit of humble submission. He can speak to our minds—saying yes, no, or wait.

2. Prayer guards (Matt. 26:40-43). Jesus' disciples let Him down; they fell asleep. They loved the Lord and wanted to help Him by praying, but their flesh was weak. After all, it was late and they had just had a big supper.

Sadly, Satan knows our weaknesses. He understands where each person is vulnerable, and he attacks there. Without God's protection, we make ourselves vulnerable to temptation and, even worse, give in and sin. We need the cover of prayer, like a spiritual umbrella, to protect us from Satan's schemes.

3. Prayer persists (Matt. 26:44-46). Jesus prayed the same prayer three times that critical night. Why? He knew what He had to do, but He was also human. He understood the next hours would be painful. He needed God's help and strength.

We cannot just pray for something one time and consider it a closed subject. We need to be persistent in praying, for our faith grows that way. By praying regularly about a need, we show God we want His answer. He may choose to answer our prayer fairly quickly. On the other hand, He may change our minds as we continue in prayer and help us realize that what we are praying for is not really good for us right now.

4. Prayer strengthens (Matt. 26:47-50). Judas and the soldiers came to arrest Jesus in the garden. Judas greeted Jesus as "master" and kissed Him. Jesus called Judas friend even as he betrayed Him. How could he do that? How could He honestly address this betrayer in this way?

It is only through God's strength and help that Jesus was able to speak and act in love. This kind of strength is beyond human understanding.

We too can have this kind of strength no matter what is happening in our lives. Strength comes through close communion with our Lord through prayer.

Prayer was vitally important to Jesus during this crucial night. He kept in close communication with the Father and thus gained strength for His ordeal.

How much more do we, who are only human, need to keep in close touch with God?

—*Judy Carlsen.*

World Missions

Engaging in intensive and agonizing prayer is all too uncommon in our day, even on mission fields. This is regrettable, given the challenging task that God has given us—that of evangelizing our world.

Prayer is speaking to God. It is a means of seeking guidance and of becoming empowered for carrying out our life mission. It is also a means of attaining the wisdom (Jas. 1:5) that is so vitally needed in our spiritual battles.

John Hyde, Presbyterian missionary to India, was one who learned the effectiveness of fervent prayer. "Hyde's ministry centered in itinerant outreach to remote villages. Learning several local languages, he became one of rural India's powerful preachers. His spiritually minded, revival-oriented messages were also sought after for Indian missionary conferences" (Douglas, ed., *Who's Who in Christian History,* Tyndale).

Despite Hyde's accomplishments, he became discouraged by the lack of converts. Gradually he turned to "vigilant, persistent prayer. Thus began an intense prayer life that soon formed his greatest work. Remarkably, as Hyde spent sometimes forty or more hours on his knees, significant numbers of conversions began to come."

Hyde, who has commonly been referred to as "praying Hyde," went on to form the Punjab Prayer Union, "an effort to emphasize prayer among missionaries and converts in India."

A number of large-scale spiritual revivals have been spawned through prayer. Perhaps none has had a greater impact than the Great Revival of 1907 in Korea, which ignited a fire that still flickers in some parts of that country.

Robert Alexander Hardie, a Southern Methodist medical missionary, is believed to have provided the spark that kindled the revival flames. "He had been commissioned to lead a week-long Bible study and prayer time for a group of missionaries who desired a spiritual refreshing. During the meeting, Hardie himself was overwhelmed by the powerful movement of the Holy Spirit. Not only the missionaries, but also other Korean Christians . . . were shaken by the visible breaking down of a person who suffered, according to his own words, the agony of confessing his own failures" (Park, *The Urban Face of Mission,* Presbyterian and Reformed).

Before long, a renewal movement was spreading across the entire nation. At one gathering, "those who were present uniformly report (ed) that it was as if a tornado had swept through that place, leaving none unaffected."

Many Koreans were touched in dramatic ways. One observer, Dr. George Heber Jones, reported that people mortgaged their homes, sold their crops, and then bought inferior supplies to live on. Some women cut off their hair and sold it, and also sold their wedding rings, to help pay for the spread of the gospel.

Jones also told of a farmer who sold his only ox to help pay for a chapel. "He and his brother hitched themselves in place of the ox and dragged the plow through the fields that year" (Glover, *The Progress of World-wide Missions,* George H. Doran).

It is remarkable to see God responding to heartfelt pleas. The Father's answer may require a willingness to bear a cross. Countless people have already done that all over our world, with gratifying results.

Talking to God is an awesome privilege. It also involves a risk. Yielding oneself fully to God can have unforeseen consequences!

—Albert J. Schneider.

The Jewish Aspect

In the concentration camps of the Nazis, the Jews wondered why their prayers were not heard. They cried out to God and practiced, as best they could, the rabbinic Judaism that had been handed down to them. In agony they requested deliverance and recited from their prayer books, but few were rescued and millions perished.

To this day they wonder why heaven was sealed and why God was silent. Some—who can say how many—became atheists. In fact, the nation of Israel today is largely a secular state, not a religious one.

The Holocaust is a topic still on the lips of Jews. The museum in Washington, D.C., keeps it before the public, as they want it to be. A missionary to the Jews told me that the question that rivets their attention is, Why did God allow the Holocaust?

Perhaps part of the answer is found in the passage before us today. Jesus prayed, "Let this cup pass from me" (Matt. 26:39), and although God heard Him, He allowed Jesus to suffer torture and death. God was working out His purpose. Jesus referred to it as "thy will" (vs. 42). God's will takes precedence over the suffering of any individual, even His only begotten Son.

All national leaders, including Jewish ones, have decided not to conform to God's will, even as Jesus decided to conform to it; consequently, the Jewish nation has continued going through national suffering and agony, seeking their own righteousness. They have suffered more than most because of the evil and irrational anti-semitism that has stained the pages of history. That amid all of this hatred they have been preserved as a people is a testament to God's providence.

God's will involved Jesus' tasting death for every person. He bore our sins in His body on the cross. We receive His righteousness when we believe in Him. He died for us freely; that was grace. We avail ourselves of that finished work when we believe; that is faith. Without His suffering, it would not be possible.

The Holocaust removed Europe as the world center of the Jewish people and led to the establishment of the State of Israel. All prophetic passages are going to be fulfilled, including those that speak of God's blessings on the Jews. God is working His purpose in the suffering of all His chosen people, both Jews and Gentiles. We watch His working with awe. Will we be a part of His plan or not?

God's will for us is to preach the gospel to every person (Mark 16:15), and that includes Jews! Will we do that? It might involve some hardship and suffering, some ridicule and taunting. Will we do it anyway? What His will is is not the question anymore. We know what the Great Commission is and what is involved.

There is no middle ground. If we are not part of God's plan, we are automatically part of the world's plan and program. Judas made that choice and came with the soldiers and mob carrying swords and staves. We are either for God or against Him.

Why not decide today that we are going to be partners with Christ and reach out to the Jews with the gospel of salvation? Let us learn how to do it. We can study the Bible, get to know the Jewish culture, make friends for Christ's sake, and introduce them to Him. He has promised to guide us, empower us, and be with us to the end of the age. What seems impossible with us is possible with God. We can pray each day, "Lord, Your will be done. Guide me to some Jewish person to whom I can witness."

—Philip J. Lesko.

Guiding the Superintendent

When faced with a difficult decision, what do you do? Do you pray?

Though we may sense what God wants us to do in a particular situation, not all decisions are clear-cut. In those times we may struggle to know God's will.

Christ knew what the Father wanted Him to do. Nevertheless, the Son of God found Himself agonizing in prayer concerning God's will. If that was true for Him, it will be true for us as well.

DEVOTIONAL OUTLINE

1. Troubled deeply (Matt. 26:36-38). After the Last Supper, Christ and His disciples made their way to the Garden of Gethsemane, just east of the temple. Moving farther into the garden with His inner circle of apostles, Christ instructed them to watch and pray with Him.

Even the Son of God sought the emotional support of fellow humans when facing a difficult decision. As the prospect of the cross loomed before Him, Christ declared, "My soul is exceeding sorrowful, even unto death" (vs. 38). "As perfect Man, He felt the awful burden of sin, and His holy soul was repelled by it" (Wiersbe, *Bible Exposition Commentary*, Victor).

2. Testing determined (Matt. 26:39-44). The "cup" that Christ found difficult to anticipate was the prospect of dying for the sins of mankind. Never before had He felt the weight of guilt that is so common to us. Now, however, He was about to bear the sins of the whole world (II Cor. 5:21; I Pet. 2:24).

As Jesus considered what was about to occur, He asked whether there was another way to fulfill God's plan of redemption. Since He wanted to submit to the Father's will above all else, though, He concluded His prayers with a commitment to obey Him. So it should be with us when struggling with a problem or difficult decision.

Coming back to the disciples, Jesus found them asleep. It was not intentional that they failed to remain awake; it was simply the weakness of their human flesh.

Two more times the Master returned to the place of prayer and repeated His request to the Father. Each time, Jesus concluded His prayer by expressing a willingness to surrender to the Father's plan (cf. Acts 2:23; 4:27-28). It is imperative that we pray similarly.

3. Traitorous disciple (Matt. 26:45-50). Fully convinced that salvation could not be realized other than through the cross, Christ returned to His disciples with a renewed determination to obey the Father (cf. Heb. 5:7-9). In the meantime, the traitorous Judas was leading officers and servants of the high priest to the garden to arrest the Lord Jesus.

Jesus may well have looked like an average Jewish man, and thus He would have to be pointed out by Judas; otherwise, the officers might arrest the wrong man and their plot would be foiled.

Though a common greeting among Jews, the irony of a kiss being used to identify God's Son casts a striking light on Judas's treachery.

CHILDREN'S CORNER

Stress the fact that Christ had to die on the cross even though He recoiled from the thought. For Him, pleasing His Father was more important than getting out of a painful ordeal. Children should know that God will not always take away pain and sorrow. But He will be with them and bring them through it.

—John A. Owston.

LESSON 5　　　　　　　　　　　　　　　　　　APRIL 2, 2023

Scripture Lesson Text

MATT. 27:38 Then were there two thieves crucified with him, one on the right hand, and another on the left.

39 And they that passed by reviled him, wagging their heads,

40 And saying, Thou that destroyest the temple, and buildest *it* in three days, save thyself. If thou be the Son of God, come down from the cross.

41 Likewise also the chief priests mocking *him,* with the scribes and elders, said,

42 He saved others; himself he cannot save. If he be the King of Israel, let him now come down from the cross, and we will believe him.

43 He trusted in God; let him deliver him now, if he will have him: for he said, I am the Son of God.

44 The thieves also, which were crucified with him, cast the same in his teeth.

45 Now from the sixth hour there was darkness over all the land unto the ninth hour.

46 And about the ninth hour Jesus cried with a loud voice, saying, Eli, Eli, lama sabachthani? that is to say, My God, my God, why hast thou forsaken me?

47 Some of them that stood there, when they heard *that,* said, This *man* calleth for Elias.

48 And straightway one of them ran, and took a spunge, and filled *it* with vinegar, and put *it* on a reed, and gave him to drink.

49 The rest said, Let be, let us see whether Elias will come to save him.

50 Jesus, when he had cried again with a loud voice, yielded up the ghost.

51 And, behold, the veil of the temple was rent in twain from the top to the bottom; and the earth did quake, and the rocks rent;

52 And the graves were opened; and many bodies of the saints which slept arose,

53 And came out of the graves after his resurrection, and went into the holy city, and appeared unto many.

54 Now when the centurion, and they that were with him, watching Jesus, saw the earthquake, and those things that were done, they feared greatly, saying, Truly this was the Son of God.

NOTES

Crucified for Sinners

Lesson Text: Matthew 27:38-54

Related Scriptures: Psalm 22:1-18; Isaiah 53:3-12; Luke 23:32-47

TIME: A.D. 30   PLACE: Golgotha

GOLDEN TEXT—"We have seen and do testify that the Father sent the Son to be the Saviour of the world" (I John 4:14).

Introduction

The crucifixion was the greatest demonstration of God's love and grace, but it was also the greatest example of human depravity and injustice. In dying for us, Jesus suffered unimaginable pain. Matthew's description of the crucifixion helps us sense the awful abuse that Jesus endured.

As Jesus died, however, God made it clear that something momentous had happened. He tore in two the inner veil of the temple between the holy place and the Holy of Holies. Although only seen by priests, it was a powerful demonstration that the barrier between God and human beings had been breached. God was pleased with the sacrifice of His Son.

LESSON OUTLINE

I. ABUSE OF JESUS—Matt. 27:38-44

II. ABANDONMENT OF JESUS—Matt. 27:45-50

III. ACKNOWLEDGMENT OF JESUS—Matt. 27:51-54

Exposition: Verse by Verse

ABUSE OF JESUS

MATT. 27:38 Then were there two thieves crucified with him, one on the right hand, and another on the left.

39 And they that passed by reviled him, wagging their heads,

40 And saying, Thou that destroyest the temple, and buildest it in three days, save thyself. If thou be the Son of God, come down from the cross.

41 Likewise also the chief priests mocking him, with the scribes and elders, said,

42 He saved others; himself he cannot save. If he be the King of Israel, let him now come down from the cross, and we will believe him.

43 He trusted in God; let him deliver him now, if he will have him: for he said, I am the Son of God.

44 The thieves also, which were crucified with him, cast the same in his teeth.

Crucified among criminals (Matt. 27:38). Matthew 26 and 27 trace the sad series of events that brought Jesus to the cross. Jesus was betrayed by Judas, arrested by an armed force sent by the Jewish leaders, illegally convicted by the Jewish court, and then condemned to death by the intimidated governor. He was subjected to abuse, taunting, beating, and total injustice as He died on the cross.

The Roman soldiers who were to execute Jesus took Him outside the city to a place called Golgotha. There they nailed Him to a cross, for He was to suffer the horrific death by crucifixion.

{Jesus was not the only man condemned to die that day. Along with Him were two others. They are called "thieves" (vs. 38). The term Matthew used to describe them most likely refers to individuals guilty of political rebellion against the Roman government.}Q1 It may well have been that Barabbas was scheduled for execution that day because he also was a robber, or insurrectionist (cf. John 18:40). He was released by Pilate at the insistence of the multitude, and Jesus may have taken his place on the cross (Matt. 27:15-26).

In any case, the fact that Jesus was crucified among criminals fulfilled Isaiah's ancient prophecy that the Messiah would be "numbered with the transgressors" (Isa. 53:12). The holy Son of God had to die as though He were a common criminal.

Scorned by spectators (Matt. 27:39-40). The Romans chose public places for crucifixions. They wanted this terrible display of death to deter other people from crime. Golgotha was located along one of the major roads that came into Jerusalem. As Jesus hung on the cross, many people passed by and saw Him.

No doubt word about Jesus' arrest and conviction had passed quickly through the city. Among the charges brought against Jesus was that He had said that He was able to destroy the temple and to rebuild it in three days (26:61). The Jewish council failed to understand that He was speaking of His own death and resurrection by referring to the temple of His own body (cf. John 2:19-21). As news spread through the crowd, they too misunderstood what Jesus had meant.

{The spectators were scornful to Jesus. They knew that He had claimed to be the Son of God; so they called on Him to save Himself by coming down from the cross.}Q2 Little did they realize that they were echoing the words of Satan (Matt. 4:3, 6) as they challenged Jesus to prove His deity.

In reality, this was a final temptation that Jesus had to resist as He accomplished the will of God. Had He come down from the cross, the whole plan of salvation would have failed. To bring salvation to sinful humans, Jesus had to die on the cross as God's perfect Substitute for sinners.

Mocked by religious leaders (Matt. 27:41-43). Joining with the scornful spectators, the religious leaders mocked Jesus. Included in this group were representatives of the full range of the Jewish religious establishment. The chief priests belonged to the powerful Sadducean families. The scribes were the scholars of the Old Testament law, and most of them were Pharisees. These, along with the elders, who were esteemed tribal and family heads, made up the Sanhedrin, the Jewish council. Although these groups had many disagreements, they all joined forces in deriding Jesus as He suffered on the cross.

Rather than speak directly to Jesus, as those who passed by did, the religious leaders talked to one another. Doubtless, however, they made sure to speak loudly enough so that He could hear their taunts as He hung on the cross.

{The leaders took words that Jesus had spoken and threw them back in His face. Jesus had claimed to save others, but He could not save Himself. He had claimed to be the King of Israel; if He came down from the cross, they would believe Him, they said. He called Himself the Son of God, but where was God when Jesus needed His help?}Q3

Throughout His ministry Jesus was opposed by the religious leaders. Even as He was dying for the sins of the world, they insisted on mocking the Saviour. They did not recognize and respond to His love for them.

Insulted by thieves (Matt. 27:44). The final voices in the choir of abuse against Jesus came from the two thieves, or insurrectionists. Even in the pain of their crucifixion, they too insulted Jesus. As Luke 23:39 relates, one of the criminals railed at Jesus, saying, "If thou be Christ, save thyself and us." The other criminal, however, had a change of heart and asked Jesus to remember him when He came into His kingdom (vss. 40-43).

ABANDONMENT OF JESUS

45 Now from the sixth hour there was darkness over all the land unto the ninth hour.

46 And about the ninth hour Jesus cried with a loud voice, saying, Eli, Eli, lama sabachthani? that is to say, My God, my God, why hast thou forsaken me?

47 Some of them that stood there, when they heard that, said, This man calleth for Elias.

48 And straightway one of them ran, and took a spunge, and filled it with vinegar, and put it on a reed, and gave him to drink.

49 The rest said, Let be, let us see whether Elias will come to save him.

50 Jesus, when he had cried again with a loud voice, yielded up the ghost.

Suffering in darkness (Matt. 27:45). {Jesus was placed on the cross at the third hour (Mark 15:25), or nine o'clock in the morning. After He had suffered there for three hours, supernatural darkness descended upon the land until three o'clock in the afternoon.}Q4

This could not have been a solar eclipse, because the Passover was always held at the full moon, making an eclipse impossible. Instead, it was a supernatural darkening of the skies by God, comparable to His plague on Egypt (Ex. 10:21-23). This was a visible indication of God's judgment on sin (cf. Amos 8:9). In the eerie daytime darkness, Jesus suffered on the cross as He bore the sins of the world.

Suffering in loneliness (Matt. 27:46-47). Although there was a crowd watching His crucifixion, Jesus felt alone and abandoned. No doubt the three hours of darkness only intensified His feeling of loneliness. Quoting the words of Psalm 22:1, Jesus cried out, "My God, my God, why hast thou forsaken me?"

Theologians have long struggled to fully understand what these words mean. {How could God the Father forsake God the Son? In bearing the sins of the world, Jesus became sin for us (II Cor. 5:21). He was made a curse for us (Gal. 3:13). In a way that defies human understanding and surpasses human language, Jesus as the Sin Bearer was alienated from fellowship with God the Father.}Q5 To be our Substitute, He had to endure the unspeakable pain of being forsaken by His Father. There is no way that we can appreciate the full import of what this meant for Jesus.

"Eli," which means "my God" (Matt. 27:46), sounds much like the name of the great Old Testament prophet Elijah. Some of the bystanders thought that Jesus was calling out to Elijah to help Him. Because Elijah had been taken to heaven without dying (cf. II Kgs. 2:11), many of the Jews believed that he came to assist godly people in need. They did not realize that Jesus' cry was not for a prophet to aid Him but was a reflection of His loneliness as He was forsaken by God the Father.

Suffering in ridicule (Matt. 27:48-49). {Hearing Jesus' cry, one of the people, most likely one of the soldiers, filled a sponge with sour, vinegary liquid and lifted it to Jesus to give Him a drink. This beverage was the common drink of soldiers and poor people; so it was readily available. This was an act of individual kindness to Jesus as He suffered intensely.}[Q6]

The rest of the crowd, however, was not nearly so compassionate. They did not manifest even the minimum of human sensitivity toward one in great pain. {In their hostile opposition to Jesus, they told the person who had been kind to Him to stop. With scornful skepticism they said, "Let us see whether Elias (Elijah) will come to save him" (vs. 49). Even in the presence of Jesus' excruciating pain, they insisted on ridiculing Him.}[Q7] They sought to halt the one person who offered some help, and they only added to Jesus' suffering by their sarcastic words.

Suffering in death (Matt. 27:50). Crucifixion was a horrible form of execution calculated to prolong the agony of death. It was not unusual for people to hang on the cross for many hours and even for a few days. The Romans used this cruel form of execution as a public deterrent to rebellion against their rule.

Typically, crucifixion resulted in profound exhaustion. Jesus, however, was in control of His faculties even when on the cross. At the ninth hour, around three o'clock in the afternoon, He cried again with a loud voice. This was not the feeble whimper of a defeated victim but rather the triumphant cry of the Victor: "It is finished" (John 19:30).

Jesus had willingly laid down His life as the sacrifice for human sins. That accomplished, He voluntarily yielded up His spirit, or "ghost" (Matt. 27:50). His death was not a tragedy in which Jesus was defeated by evil men; it was His conscious, intentional triumph over sin. His suffering was God's means to bring us salvation.

ACKNOWLEDGEMENT OF JESUS

51 And, behold, the veil of the temple was rent in twain from the top to the bottom; and the earth did quake, and the rocks rent;

52 And the graves were opened; and many bodies of the saints which slept arose,

53 And came out of the graves after his resurrection, and went into the holy city, and appeared unto many.

54 Now when the centurion, and they that were with him, watching Jesus, saw the earthquake, and those things that were done, they feared greatly, saying, Truly this was the Son of God.

The torn veil (Matt. 27:51a). Although Jesus had been crucified as though He were a common criminal, several events at the time of His death testified to the truth that He was indeed the Son of God. At Jesus' death the veil in the temple was torn from the top to the bottom. That the tear began at the top of the massive curtain suggests that God Himself was responsible.

The temple veil had barred the way to the Holy of Holies, which represented the presence of God. In the Old Testament system, only the high priest could enter the Holy of Holies, and then only on the Day of Atonement with the blood of the atonement offering for the nation.

{Hebrews 10:19-20 develops the significance of the torn veil. By His death, Jesus opened up direct access to God. Instead of going through the Old Testament priesthood, Christians now can enter boldly into the presence of God through the blood of Jesus.}[Q8]

The opened tombs (Matt. 27:51b-53). When Jesus died, the earth was shaken by a powerful earthquake. Rocks were torn apart as God's mighty power was displayed. In ancient Israel, tombs were usually caves hewn in the stone, with rocks placed over the entrances. It was not surprising, therefore, that the earthquake caused many tombs to open.

{What was astonishing, however, was that after Jesus' resurrection, the bodies of many believers were resurrected. They came out of their graves, went into Jerusalem, and appeared to many people there.}[Q9] What an incredible sight that must have been!

The Bible says no more about what happened to these resurrected believers. It is therefore pointless to speculate about whether they died again or were taken to heaven directly. What was significant about their appearance was that it demonstrated that Jesus' death was vitally connected with the eternal life of God's faithful.

This was a miracle, for it required power far beyond the human realm. To those who were willing to accept it, the resurrection of these people was undeniable proof that Jesus was Lord over death. Through His own death on the cross, Jesus brought eternal life to those who had and would put their trust in God.

The convinced centurion (Matt. 27:54). The Roman centurion and his band of soldiers had no doubt performed numerous crucifixions. Jesus' death, however, was vastly different from all others they had witnessed. They heard the bystanders and the religious leaders mock Jesus because He claimed to be the Son of God (vss. 40, 43). {As they watched the way in which Jesus died and as they experienced the earthquake, they became terrified. They could only conclude that Jesus truly was the Son of God.}[Q10]

Earlier, when Jesus had walked on the Sea of Galilee and calmed the storm, His disciples had come to the same conclusion. They had said in reverence, "Of a truth thou art the Son of God" (Matt. 14:33). Now, at His death, the hardened Roman soldiers were forced by the facts to the same conclusion. Their testimony was a fitting contrast to the scornful attitude of the Jews.

—*Daniel J. Estes.*

QUESTIONS

1. Who was crucified alongside Jesus?
2. How did the people who were passing by use Jesus' words to scorn Him?
3. How did the religious leaders mock Jesus?
4. For how long did Jesus suffer in darkness?
5. Why was Jesus forsaken by God the Father?
6. How did one man demonstrate compassion to Jesus in His pain?
7. How did the spectators ridicule Jesus' cry to the Father?
8. How did the rending of the temple veil symbolize the significance of Jesus' death?
9. What happened when the earthquake opened many graves?
10. How did the Roman soldiers respond to Jesus' death?

—*Daniel J. Estes.*

Preparing to Teach the Lesson

There is no truth more precious to Christians than that God's Son died for sinners. Jesus' death on the cross paid the penalty for our sins and secured eternal life for all who trust in Him. His teachings and miracles would have been in vain if Jesus had not died for us.

TODAY'S AIM

Facts: to review Matthew's account of the crucifixion of Jesus Christ.

Principle: to reaffirm the fact that Jesus' death gave us life.

Application: to give students a deeper appreciation for what Christ has done for them at Calvary.

INTRODUCING THE LESSON

Crucifixion illustrates the depravity of man. It was one of the cruelest methods of execution ever devised. The Phoenicians originated the barbaric practice. It was adopted by the Romans and used extensively by them.

A person condemned to be crucified would usually be forced to carry the crossbeam of his cross to the execution site. The victim was nailed to the cross with his knees slightly bent so that he would have to seesaw up and down in order to breathe. Death would come slowly with excruciating pain. Along with the pain came the shame of being made a public display.

Jesus, the Son of God, submitted to such treatment for us. We review the details of His atoning death in this week's lesson.

DEVELOPING THE LESSON

1. Mocking at the crucifixion (Matt. 27:38-44). Matthew calls the two who were crucified with Jesus "thieves." Luke refers to them as "malefactors" (23:33), which means that they were criminals. Many crimes were punishable by death in those days. Roman authorities hoped that cruel public executions would help them maintain order in highly volatile places like Judea.

Jesus' detractors came by to look on and to add insult to injury by taunting Him.

They mocked Jesus as a temple destroyer. (Refer to John 2:19-22, where Jesus spoke of His body as a temple.) He did not look like a temple destroyer or builder as He hung on the cross. The crowd also remembered Jesus' claim to be the Son of God and the King of Israel. A man dying by crucifixion did not fit their concept of these titles either.

The chief priests, the scribes, and the elders all came by to join in the coarse mocking of the crowd. It would seem beneath the dignity of such officials, but this was a moment of victory for them. They were the very people who had conspired to kill Him. They claimed that they would believe in Him if He would come down from the cross. That was nonsense, of course, since they had not accepted His previous miracles.

The most unlikely mockers of all were the two who were being crucified with Jesus (Matt. 27:44). Read Luke's account of the malefactor who became penitent (Luke 23:39-43).

2. Agony at the crucifixion (Matt. 27:45-49). Mark states that the crucifixion began at the third hour, or 9:00 A.M. (15:25). According to our text (Matt. 27:45), darkness prevailed from the sixth hour (noon) until the ninth hour, or 3:00 P.M. This was a time of intense physical suffering for Jesus.

Jesus' suffering was more than physical. The words of Jesus in verse 46 are a quotation of Psalm 22:1. "Jesus sensed a separation . . . He had never known, for in becoming sin the Father had to turn judicially from His Son" (Walvoord and Zuck, eds., *The Bible Knowledge Commentary,* Victor). Refer to Romans 3:25-26.

Onlookers misunderstood Jesus' cry to be a call for Elijah (Matt. 27:47). In response to the cry, one man offered Jesus vinegar on a sponge. Although Jesus had rejected the earlier offer of vinegar mingled with gall to deaden pain (vs. 34), He accepted this offer of vinegar (John 19:28-30). Perhaps the offer was made so that the man might hear Jesus more plainly. The others, however, continued to mock (Matt. 27:49). Even in His suffering, not much compassion was demonstrated toward Jesus.

3. Aftermath of the crucifixion (Matt. 27:50-54). Jesus "yielded up the ghost." Take your students to John 10:17-18. Jesus gave up His life voluntarily.

List the things that happened when Jesus died (Matt. 27:51-54). The veil of the temple was ripped from top to bottom; an earthquake occurred; and the centurion acknowledged Jesus as the Son of God. Note that the dead saints arose after Jesus' resurrection.

Discuss the implications of the temple veil being ripped in two. Previously, the veil had separated the Holy of Holies from the holy place, where the ordinary priests performed their religious activities. Only the high priest had access to God's presence and only on the Day of Atonement. Jesus' death made God accessible to all who trust Him (cf. Heb. 10:19-22).

Since all true believers in the Lord are and always have been forgiven and declared righteous by Christ's sacrifice for sin (Rom. 3:24-26), when Jesus died, the Old Testament saints were justified. Jesus, being the "firstfruits" (I Cor. 15:23) of the resurrection, was the first to be raised; then many of the Old Testaments saints arose from the dead (Matt. 27:52-53).

The Roman centurion had never before seen such phenomena as accompanied Jesus' crucifixion. We wonder what became of that Roman.

ILLUSTRATING THE LESSON

The illustration pictures the primary truth of this lesson—Jesus' death gives us life.

CONCLUDING THE LESSON

Jesus died in the company of criminals, who joined religious leaders, soldiers, and the nearby general population in mocking Him at the scene of the crucifixion. He suffered excruciating physical pain, as well as the emotional and spiritual pain of being separated from His Father in heaven. After He died, the temple veil was ripped and the earth shook.

Why did Jesus die on the cross? He died for us. He died to pay the penalty for our sins.

ANTICIPATING THE NEXT LESSON

Our next lesson shows us why we can have unshakable hope. Jesus' resurrection proved His victory over death and the prince of darkness.

—*Bruce A. Tanner.*

PRACTICAL POINTS

1. It was entirely appropriate that our Saviour died the death of a criminal, since He was dying for violators of God's law (Matt. 27:38).
2. We must not allow mockery to shake our faith; it is merely an attempt by the wicked to justify their own unbelief (vss. 39-44).
3. The suffering Christ endured should remind us of the depth of our sin before God (vss. 45-46).
4. The most heartfelt expressions of God's people will often be ridiculed and mocked by the enemies of Christ (vss. 47-49).
5. Jesus' life was not taken from Him; He freely gave His life so that we can have everlasting life (Matt. 27:50; cf. John 10:15-18).
6. Christ's death guarantees the believer both free access to God and future resurrection unto eternal life (Matt. 27:51-54).

—Jarl K. Waggoner.

RESEARCH AND DISCUSSION

1. Why did Jesus suffer the great indignities He experienced on the cross (Matt. 27:38-44)?
2. What accounts for the hateful behavior of those who witnessed Jesus' crucifixion? How is such hatred of Christ exhibited today?
3. What does a knowledge of Psalm 22 contribute to our understanding of Jesus' suffering and death?
4. Why is it important doctrinally to note that Jesus willingly gave His life on the cross (Matt. 27:50)?

—Jarl K. Waggoner.

ILLUSTRATED HIGH POINTS

Passed by reviled him (Matt. 27:39)

A church located in the heart of the city received permission to hold open-air meetings in the city park.

The first meeting was disrupted by shouting, whistling, and other disturbances. A group of Christians sang, others gave testimonies, and the pastor preached a short message. During the message, the shouting increased to the point that it was difficult for the pastor to be heard.

"Take your religion back to your church!" a man shouted.

"Who are you to tell us how to live?" called another.

When the invitation was given, however, two young men came forward and said they wanted to be saved.

This was the Son of God (vs. 54)

George was a wealthy and successful businessman. He married his high school sweetheart, bought a beautiful home, and seemingly had everything he desired.

George's business put him in contact with people who drank and partied. Before long, he started drinking. That led to parties, more drinking, and finally, drugs. After many warnings, his wife left him. He went bankrupt and lost everything. He was without family or friends.

One night while walking the streets of the city, George heard a familiar song. It was a hymn his mother used to sing as she worked around the house. He walked into an open doorway to see a group of young people. He sat down and listened. That night he got saved.

After his conversion, George said to the group, "I have many times used God's name in cursing, but I never really knew Him. I now believe that God's Son died for me."

—V. Ben Kendrick.

Golden Text Illuminated

"We have seen and do testify that the Father sent the Son to be the Saviour of the world" (I John 4:14).

"The value of the cross of Christ is dependent upon *who* died on that cross. It was not just a man who died for us, but it was the Son of God" (Mitchell, *Fellowship,* Multnomah). There is conclusive evidence of this.

To whom does the "we" in the golden text refer? It "certainly refers to all those, especially the apostles, who had direct knowledge of Jesus' earthly life; but it probably ought not to be limited to them" (Gaebelein, ed., *The Expositor's Bible Commentary,* Zondervan).

There indeed was eyewitness testimony to the life, death, burial, and resurrection of Jesus Christ. The word "sent" also indicates that Jesus was a historical person.

Christ really lived in time and history. Those things that took place as described in our Scripture lesson, as well as in the other Gospels, were historical and real.

This being said, we still must consider the possibility that "the first person plural in verses 7-13 is . . . meant to include the readers." (Walvoord and Zuck, eds., *The Bible Knowledge Commentary,* Victor). All believers testify about Jesus.

Although no one has "seen God at any time" (I John 4:12), the believer does, in a sense, see by faith. Through the eye of faith he sees that Christ died on the cross of Calvary for his sins and has provided salvation. He sees because of the indwelling Holy Spirit, who is given to those who believe (cf. vs. 13). He sees in the presence of other believers evidence of the love of God (cf. vs. 7). He sees in himself and others the change that comes by faith in Christ (cf. Rom. 5:1; 8:1).

Because the Holy Spirit in us gives us this seeing experience, we are to "testify" to the truth of the gospel. "But when the Comforter is come, whom I will send unto you from the Father, even the Spirit of truth, which proceedeth from the Father, he shall testify of me: and ye also shall bear witness, because ye have been with me from the beginning" (John 15:26-27).

The Comforter confirms in the believer the reality of the saving work of Christ just as surely as if he had been standing with the centurion and saying, "Truly this was the Son of God" (Matt. 27:54).

The value of Christ's death is found in who He was and is—the Son of God. He was the only one who could save us. God's righteousness required a perfect sacrifice, or payment, for our sins. Jesus of Nazareth was the only perfect one; thus, "he is the propitiation for our sins: and not for ours only, but also for the sins of the whole world" (I John 2:2; cf. II Cor. 5:21).

This truth, the answer to human need, must be shared. God is "not willing that any should perish, but that all should come to repentance" (II Pet. 3:9).

Jesus' mission was "to seek and to save that which was lost" (Luke 19:10). His death provided the means of salvation to all who believe (cf. Heb. 9:12). He commissions all believers to tell everyone this good news! "To wit, that God was in Christ, reconciling the world unto himself, not imputing their trespasses unto them; and hath committed unto us the word of reconciliation" (II Cor. 5:19). Each new believer brings His mission closer to fulfillment.

—Richard P. Voth.

Heart of the Lesson

Heart of the Lesson is hardly an adequate title for this week's feature. It should be called, instead, "Heart of the Bible." The entire purpose for Christ's coming is contained in these few verses.

1. The doubters (Matt. 27:38-44). It took only a few days for the crowd's enthusiastic reception of Jesus to wear off. Their aspirations for a successful rebellion against Rome unrealized, the people were easily beguiled by the Jewish leadership into demanding Jesus' death by crucifixion (vss. 1, 20).

Word of the sign that Jesus had promised to the Jewish leaders must have spread rapidly. It was mentioned at His trial (Mark 26:61) and used to taunt Him while He hung on the cross (27:40). It is easy but cruel to take remarks out of context and use them against a person when he is suffering.

Notice that three groups of people were mocking Jesus—the passersby, the Jewish leaders, and the thieves who were being executed with Him. This was indeed a day of great cruelty. Are we—and should we be—willing to speak out on behalf of people who are being persecuted for their beliefs?

Observe the hypocrisy of the Jewish leaders as they swore belief if Jesus would come down from the cross (Matt. 27:42). When He did something far better in emerging from the tomb, they sought to suppress the evidence (28:12-15).

2. The despair (Matt. 27:45-49). Much has been written about the suffering of Jesus and other crucifixion victims. These accounts affect us deeply—and rightly so; but they only touch the surface of what took place on the cross.

What do you own, what relationship do you enjoy, the loss of which you would dread more than extreme pain? Is there something you fear more than the experience of severe pain? These are unpleasant thoughts, but they give some insight into Jesus' experience on the cross.

If He had been given the above mental exercise, Jesus might have identified the relationship with His heavenly Father as His most prized possession and the touch of sin as the thing He feared most. The atonement demanded that He bear the guilt of sin. The experience of this demanded that He be separated from His Father.

In George Orwell's *1984,* the state broke people's wills by subjecting them to the thing they feared most. Under this type of stress, prisoners asked that others be made to suffer instead.

3. The display (Matt. 27:50-54). Jesus did not yield to the pressure to deliver Himself. He endured the atoning experience in full consciousness and brought it to conclusion with a shout of triumph. Any suffering we are called upon to endure will never be this extreme, but we should try, with God's help, to follow Jesus' example.

How would the events described in these few verses have affected you as an average citizen or as a member of the Jewish leadership? Think of the lightning and the earthquake, to say nothing of the appearance of dead saints from earlier generations. What thoughts occurred to those who first saw damage in the temple? Would people in either of these groups have had second thoughts?

The nearest witnesses, the executioners, were moved by what they saw (Matt. 27:54). May the same be said of us as we contemplate Christ's sacrifice for us.

—*Ken Schafer.*

World Missions

One of the most reassuring teachings about God is this one: "God is no respecter of persons" (Acts 10:34)—all are sinners (Rom. 3:10, 23). All deserve His judgment (1:18-19), yet "the Father sent the Son to be the Saviour of the world" (I John 4:14). Jesus died for us—not just for some of us but for every one of us. Salvation is thus available to anyone who desires to turn to God for the forgiveness of his sin.

I was reminded of this theological truth while visiting various ministries in New York City during the summer of 1996. Within a period of one week, I saw God working in many ethnic communities—the Bronx, Harlem, Chinatown, and Greenwich Village.

One particular ministry that touched my heart was located in Harlem. The church began in 1920 as a neighborhood Bible study led by a young woman. She provided Bible training to converts who were denied membership in an exclusive uptown church. In fact, the current pastor's family came to know Jesus Christ through this woman.

The congregation worships in a renovated junior high school that occupies an entire city block. They purchased the school from the city of New York at public auction after the city reduced the price from $1,000,000 to $300,000. They paid half the amount, and the city provided the church a mortgage for the other half.

Since the building had stood vacant for eight years, every piece of sellable material had been stripped by vandals. In addition, sixteen inches of water and heating oil had flooded the basement. For one year, the congregation worked together to prepare the building for renovation.

Today, the building houses a beautiful sanctuary where the church's congregation of two thousand worships during two morning worship services. They also have a large fellowship hall that is used by the congregation for special events. We expect to find a sanctuary and a fellowship hall in a church, but what continues to impress me are the other facilities in the building.

First, there are two gymnasiums and a fitness center for the young people of the neighborhood. They serve as great opportunities to reach the young for Jesus Christ.

Second, there is a rehabilitation center for men. The center provides for men off the street with physical, emotional, and spiritual needs. They are given a place to live, responsibilities, and a place to worship with a group of people who love them.

Third, there is a crisis center. People who are destitute or in need can come to receive food, clothing, and counseling. A prerequisite for everyone asking for help is a visit with a counselor. The church does more than just hand out food and clothing. They are committed to helping people care for themselves.

I praise God for Christians who, like God, are no respecter of persons. One woman's determination to rise above social prejudice and her desire to disciple a small group of converts in 1920 has resulted in a ministry that has literally touched thousands of people in Harlem.

While we are enjoying eternity together, while we walk upon the streets of gold beside the crystal sea, I suspect that many people will have stories like this to share about the faithful efforts of believers to spread the gospel and show the love of Christ to a lost world. How thankful we should be for the grace of God!

—Herbert W. Bateman, IV.

The Jewish Aspect

Today's study is appropriately titled "Crucified for Sinners." Believers who make that statement are in a way accepting responsibility for His death. Throughout history, there has been a tendency to single out the Jewish people alone as the responsible party for Jesus' death.

A Jewish community activist in my city asked me to be a part of a commission of religious leaders he was organizing. He hoped the commission would lay to rest once and for all the charge against the Jewish people that they had murdered Jesus. I accepted the invitation.

A Mormon official offered the opinion that the evidence pointed only to Roman guilt.

A Catholic nun held that crucifixion was not a Jewish form of capital punishment. She seconded the opinion that the Romans were exclusively to blame.

Three Protestant clergymen spoke warmly of Jewish humanitarian principles and labeled the charge against the Jewish people as ridiculous.

When my opportunity to speak came, I quoted the apostle Peter's message in which he laid the responsibility for the death of Jesus collectively on Herod, Pontius Pilate, the Gentiles, and the people of Israel (Acts 4:27). Peter went on to say that the rulers and the people could do only what God determined would be done (vs. 28).

I offered the conclusion that the whole human race is guilty of the murder of Jesus Christ, not simply those present in Jerusalem in those dark days. The good news is that this murderous act is precisely what God had determined to use to provide salvation.

The commission dissolved, for no one produced evidence clearing anyone of complicity in the death of Jesus. The Jewish activist was disappointed, but I pointed out to him that it truly is wrong to charge the Jews alone with a crime for which we all share guilt. It was another opportunity to invite my friend to experience the soul-cleansing blood of the Lamb.

The conduct of the Jews at the cross was representative of the enmity of a fallen world toward the Saviour. The passersby reviled Him (Matt. 27:39-40). The Jewish leaders mocked Him (vss. 41-43). Even the criminals executed with Jesus "cast the same in his teeth" (vs. 44).

The Jewish leaders' conception of Jesus' identity should have been jolted by the supernatural phenomenon that occurred in relation to His crucifixion. From noon until three o'clock, darkness covered the land (Matt. 27:45). At the moment when He yielded His spirit to God, there was a violent earthquake that split the rocks (vs. 54).

For the Jews, however, the rending of the temple veil may have been the most startling event in a day filled with the unusual. The veil was sixty feet long and thirty feet wide. It was as thick as the width of the palm of one's hand. (Edersheim, *The Life and Times of Jesus the Messiah,* World).

One day the Jews will ask the Messiah, "What are these wounds in thine hands?" His gracious reply will be, "Those with which I was wounded in the house of my friends" (Zech. 13:6). That will be a very special moment not only for the Jews but for all believers.

—Lyle P. Murphy.

Guiding the Superintendent

Jesus could have called thousands of angels to take Him away. Instead He chose to accept the insults, the beatings, the torture, and the hatred of the angry observers near His cross. What monumental self-control it took to suffer such shame and agony in order to rescue pitiful sinners like us!

DEVOTIONAL OUTLINE

1. Verbal abuse (Matt. 27:38-44). Jesus' so-called trials were over, and His excruciating execution had begun. Who would be so vile as to insult and taunt a dying man? The two robbers, who were undergoing the same punishment, did. One *might* excuse them, since they were suffering, but what motive might the passersby have had for taunting Him?

More than that, who would expect the high-society, religious leaders to act so wickedly, contrary to their own religion? The distinguished administrators of the temple, the highly educated teachers of the Jewish law, and the elders—old men—were acting like jeering children. Worst of all, their ridicule of this bloodied and mutilated man centered on Jesus' trust in God.

2. Vexing appeal (Matt. 27:45-50). The crowd should have recognized that the unusual darkness, which lasted from noon until three o'clock, was related to the suffering of Jesus. Instead, they continued their mocking. It would not be wise to assume that the gibes thrown at Jesus did not affect Him. Their main taunt—that His Father had turned His back on Him—was true! At about three o'clock, Jesus cried out in agony, "My God, my God, why hast thou forsaken me?"

Jesus' words were misunderstood by some of the onlookers. They thought He was calling for Elijah. One of the bystanders ran and put a sponge full of vinegar on a stick and raised it to Jesus' lips, possibly to give Him some relief. Others, however, sneeringly said that they should leave Him alone and see whether Elijah would actually come to save Him.

Jesus then cried out in a loud voice and died. It seemed that His enemies had won.

3. Victorious aftermath (Matt. 27:51-54). At the moment of Jesus' death, the curtain that hid the Holy of Holies was ripped in two. What a glorious turn of events this was after such hideous circumstances—Jesus had opened the way for sinners to have fellowship with God! A violent earthquake split the rocks, opening the tombs of many righteous people, who walked out of them alive! What better proof could anyone want of Jesus' claim to be the Son of God?

The Jewish leaders were oblivious to what had transpired. The Roman centurion and his men, however, were terrified by the earthquake and other unusual phenomena and declared that Jesus had most assuredly been the Son of God!

CHILDREN'S CORNER

Children can be encouraged to thank Jesus for what He did and to ask for God's forgiveness based on Jesus' sacrifice.

Many children are looking for a role model to look up to. Notwithstanding the weakling many assume Jesus to be, this lesson shows Him to be a courageous hero. So Jesus is both a role model for the children to follow and a forgiving Saviour when they fail Him, like the disciples did. He will not cast them away; they must simply trust Him.

—*Todd Williams.*

Scripture Lesson Text

JOHN 20:1 The first *day* of the week cometh Mary Magdalene early, when it was yet dark, unto the sepulchre, and seeth the stone taken away from the sepulchre.

2 Then she runneth, and cometh to Simon Peter, and to the other disciple, whom Jesus loved, and saith unto them, They have taken away the Lord out of the sepulchre, and we know not where they have laid him.

3 Peter therefore went forth, and that other disciple, and came to the sepulchre.

4 So they ran both together: and the other disciple did outrun Peter, and came first to the sepulchre.

5 And he stooping down, *and looking in,* saw the linen clothes lying; yet went he not in.

6 Then cometh Simon Peter following him, and went into the sepulchre, and seeth the linen clothes lie,

7 And the napkin, that was about his head, not lying with the linen clothes, but wrapped together in a place by itself.

8 Then went in also that other disciple, which came first to the sepulchre, and he saw, and believed.

9 For as yet they knew not the scripture, that he must rise again from the dead.

10 Then the disciples went away again unto their own home.

19 Then the same day at evening, being the first *day* of the week, when the doors were shut where the disciples were assembled for fear of the Jews, came Jesus and stood in the midst, and saith unto them, Peace *be* unto you.

20 And when he had so said, he shewed unto them *his* hands and his side. Then were the disciples glad, when they saw the Lord.

NOTES

Risen from the Dead!
(Easter)

Lesson Text: John 20:1-10, 19-20

Related Scriptures: Psalm 16:1-11; Luke 24:1-12;
I Corinthians 15:12-19; Ephesians 1:15-23

TIME: A.D. 30   PLACES: near Jerusalem; Jerusalem

GOLDEN TEXT—"Then the same day at evening, being the first day of the week, when the doors were shut where the disciples were assembled for fear of the Jews, came Jesus and stood in the midst, and saith unto them, Peace be unto you" (John 20:19).

Introduction

This morning many churches have a sunrise service. For some the early morning is warm and balmy, but for others it is chilly and a little uncomfortable. Some churches have a breakfast ready for those who attend that early service. The entire scene has been traditional for many churches for decades and leaves fond memories in the hearts of those who attended when they were young. It is a unique and special way to remember the resurrection of our Lord, who died on the cross but did not remain in the burial tomb.

Resurrection Sunday is probably the most significant day on the Christian calendar. When Jesus rose from the dead, He proved once and for all that He really is the Son of God and Saviour of mankind. Because of His resurrection, all of us who have received Him personally can be sure of our own resurrection one day.

LESSON OUTLINE

I. THE UNEXPECTED EMPTY TOMB—John 20:1-5

II. THE GRADUALLY EXPANDED UNDERSTANDING—John 20:6-10, 19-20

Exposition: Verse by Verse

THE UNEXPECTED EMPTY TOMB

JOHN 20:1 The first day of the week cometh Mary Magdalene early, when it was yet dark, unto the sepulchre, and seeth the stone taken away from the sepulchre.

2 Then she runneth, and cometh to Simon Peter, and to the other disciple, whom Jesus loved, and saith unto them, They have taken away the Lord out of the sepulchre, and we know not where they have laid him.

3 Peter therefore went forth, and that other disciple, and came to the sepulchre.

4 So they ran both together: and the other disciple did outrun Peter, and came first to the sepulchre.

5 And he stooping down, and looking in, saw the linen clothes lying; yet went he not in.

The discovery (John 20:1). {While John focused on Mary Magdalene in his Gospel, the other authors tell us she was not alone in going to the tomb on that first day of the week.}[Q1] Matthew 28:1 says "the other Mary" went with her. Mark 16:1 includes Mary the mother of James as present. This is probably who Matthew refers to. Mark also mentions Salome, who was the mother of James and John and the wife of Zebedee (mentioned in Matthew 27:56). Luke simply says "they" (24:1), namely, "the women" (23:55) but later includes Joanna and "other women" (24:10).

It was now Sunday morning. The women had come with the intention of anointing the body of Jesus with the proper burial spices (Luke 24:1). They may have wanted to complete a task they thought unfinished due to the rushed burial before the beginning of the Sabbath (John 19:38-42), or this may simply have been an extra act of devotion. {We know that Mary Magdalene had been a loyal follower of Jesus for a long time because He had cast seven demons out of her (Luke 8:2).}[Q2] John said she arrived while it was still dark. Matthew 28:1 refers to the beginning of dawn.

The last the women had seen, the tomb had been closed with a large stone over the entryway. According to Mark 16:3, they were having a discussion on the way to the tomb that morning: "And they said among themselves, Who shall roll us away the stone from the door of the sepulchre?" We understand their concern when Mark mentions that "when they looked, they saw that the stone was rolled away: for it was very great" (vs. 4). Their discovery of the open entryway was both a surprise and a relief at first, being so unexpected.

Matthew explains why the stone was rolled away: "And, behold, there was a great earthquake: for the angel of the Lord descended from heaven, and came and rolled back the stone from the door, and sat upon it" (28:2). John does not indicate that Mary saw the angel at this time. {She must have arrived first, taken an initial look, and then left immediately to tell the disciples before the other women arrived.}[Q3] (John 20:14 says she returned later and was the first one to see Jesus alive when He made a special appearance to her there.)

The report (John 20:2-3). Mary immediately ran to find Simon Peter and John ("the other disciple, whom Jesus loved" [cf. 19:26]). Her initial evaluation of the situation was that someone had taken the body of Jesus to another location. Even though Jesus had often spoken of the fact that He would rise from death, she had no firm grasp of that, so she had no thoughts about that possibility now.

The other women who followed Mary to the tomb entered it and found Jesus' body gone and two angels present who announced His resurrection (Luke 24:4-7). These women also hurried off to report these things to the disciples (vss. 9-10). {However, according to Luke, the women's words seemed to the disciples "as idle tales, and they believed them not" (vs. 11).}[Q4] {But it did not take long for Peter to decide to look into their story (vs. 12), and John decided to go too (John 20:3).}[Q5] They would naturally be concerned if the body of Jesus had been removed and taken somewhere else. These two were the most likely candidates for checking things out: the leader of the group and the one whom Jesus loved.

It is interesting to note that even the disciples were not prepared for Jesus' resurrection. They had fled in fear earlier and apparently were still in hiding. The fact that they initially considered the women's report idle words reveals their forgetfulness about what Jesus had said regarding His rising from the dead. The Greek word translated "idle tales" in Luke 24:11 speaks of nonsense or an incredible story, something almost beyond belief. When the women reported that Jesus' body was missing, the disciples never seemed to consider the possibility of resurrection.

It is difficult to understand how people in today's culture perceive the truth of Jesus' resurrection. It is not uncommon to hear people refer to Jesus' coming again, even though they do not believe in Him. Yet there are many who mock this teaching and think we believers are foolish to think something like this could ever happen. The truth of Jesus' resurrection gives us assurance that we too have a life beyond this one and will one day live forever. It is true that all believers in this age who die will be resurrected.

The follow-up (John 20:4-5). {The two disciples were off on a footrace. While Peter, the older one, left first, John, the youngest of all the disciples, not surprisingly soon overtook him and arrived at the tomb ahead of Peter. What might be a little surprising is that John did not enter the tomb right away but merely leaned over and looked in.}[Q5] We are not told whether he was fearful or just hesitant because of the unique and unexpected situation he was facing. For whatever reason, he waited until Peter arrived.

"Though John's youthful legs carried him more swiftly to the grave, once he was there he looked in, but he waited for Peter's arrival before entering the cave. None of the possible natural explanations for the missing body were of any comfort. If Jesus' body had been stolen or moved by the religious leaders, the disciples would have reasons to worry about their own fate" (Barton et al., *Life Application Bible Commentary,* John, Tyndale).

What was going on in the minds of these two men? The fact that they ran indicates some kind of excitement on their part. They had no idea what they were going to find when they arrived. Surely the women were accurate in their report. After all, they would not lie about such a serious thing as this. So what were they to expect when they got to the tomb? Why go there if the body was already gone? And what could they do about it if that was confirmed upon their arrival?

When John looked into the tomb, he saw the linen clothes in which Jesus had been buried. This is one of the evidences that His body had not been stolen, for no thief or person moving a body to another location would have taken time to unwrap it. This should have been an immediate reassurance to John that something other than that had occurred. There was no evidence of any type of crime, and the graveclothes were lying there empty. They were lying there looking like Jesus must have simply passed through them!

THE GRADUALLY EXPANDED UNDERSTANDING

6 Then cometh Simon Peter following him, and went into the sepulchre, and seeth the linen clothes lie,

7 And the napkin, that was about his head, not lying with the linen clothes, but wrapped together in a place by itself.

8 Then went in also that other disciple, which came first to the sepulchre, and he saw, and believed.

9 For as yet they knew not the scripture, that he must rise again from the dead.

10 Then the disciples went away again unto their own home.

19 Then the same day at evening, being the first day of the week, when the doors were shut where the disciples were assembled for fear of the Jews, came Jesus and stood in the midst, and saith unto them, Peace be unto you.

20 And when he had so said, he shewed unto them his hands and his side. Then were the disciples glad, when they saw the Lord.

Seeing the burial clothes (John 20:6-7). When Peter arrived, he did a typical "Peter thing." He never hesitated to act or speak and often got himself in trouble because of it. So when he got to the tomb, he walked right in without hesitation. {There he saw what John had seen when he peered in from the outside: the linen wrappings were neatly lying there in the place where Jesus' body had been. Now there were two eyewitnesses to the fact that the clothes had been left behind without a body in them.

Peter also noticed the piece of cloth that had been wrapped around Jesus' head. It was not with those that had been around His body but rather was folded neatly and laid in a place by itself. The whole scene was obvious proof that Jesus had risen from death.}Q6 The body wrappings were in place instead of being piled off to the side somewhere in disarray. They were there as if Jesus' body had simply slipped out of them. The headpiece looked as if He had taken it off and carefully folded it before laying it back down.

"Whether motivated by shame or just acting according to character, Peter plunged into the darkness. We assume one of the men carried some kind of lantern or torch. The text says that Peter saw what John had seen and in addition, the burial cloth. But the word changes to one with a slightly different meaning, perhaps best translated as 'noticed' rather than 'looked at'" (Gangel, *Holman New Testament Commentary: John*, Broadman & Holman).

It was obvious that there had been nothing rushed about the resurrection. The folded headpiece, which looked like a deliberate act, gave the appearance of unhurried activity on the part of Jesus before He left the tomb. We should be aware that the stone had not been rolled away to let Jesus out but rather to let people in to see the empty tomb and the other evidences of His resurrection. It would soon be obvious that He was not limited to movement through open doors (John 20:26).

Believing the evidence (John 20:8-10). Matthew 20:17-19 says, "And Jesus going up to Jerusalem took the twelve disciples apart in the way, and said unto them, Behold, we go up to Jerusalem; and the Son of man shall be betrayed unto the chief priests and unto the scribes, and they shall condemn him to death, and shall deliver him to the Gentiles to mock, and to scourge, and to crucify him: and the third day he shall rise again." While Jesus said this on several occasions, the disciples somehow failed to grasp His words.

Later, the disciples became so focused on what Jesus was facing in His crucifixion that the promise of His resurrection to follow was completely forgotten or ignored. {John finally understood when he followed Peter into the empty tomb. When he saw the whole scene, including the headpiece lying there by itself, he finally grasped the truth of what Jesus had said about the resurrection. He believed as he looked upon the empty tomb.}Q7 Up to that point in time, the disciples had not comprehended the truth about the resurrection.

"So three of Jesus' followers saw the empty tomb, but John was not finished with his report. He wanted his readers to know that after Peter entered the tomb, John himself finally found enough courage to follow him. Now we have yet another use of the English verb saw and yet a third Greek word appearing in the original text. This time John uses a word that means 'to perceive with understanding.' That is why our text reads that John *saw and believed"* (Gangel). It must have been an exciting moment!

We wonder what John said to Peter when he realized what had happened. In those few moments, their minds grasped a truth that would change their lives and ministry from that day on. Did they go back and explain to the other disciples at this time? All we read is that following this discovery, the disciples went to their own homes. But it was a time of discovery that would lead to the spreading of the gospel to all the known world.

Showing the wounds (John 20:19-20). {It was still the same day when Jesus made this appearance to His disciples, but it was now evening.}^{Q8} This is reiterated in the statement that it was the first day of the week. The disciples had met and were in hiding because they feared the Jewish leaders who had seen to Jesus' crucifixion. It would not have been hard to imagine that they might also try to get rid of Jesus' followers, especially those who had been in training with Him. So they gathered together behind closed doors.

Suddenly, Jesus was standing there among them. His new resurrection body no longer had the limitations His body had before. Apparently this sudden appearance terrified the disciples, for Jesus immediately spoke words of peace to them.

{Jesus further reassured them by demonstrating that His was a material body. He had them look at His hands and side to see the wounds there.}^{Q9} {He wanted them to know for certain that they were not looking at a ghost or anything to be feared.}^{Q10} This was immediately reassuring, and their emotions were soon those of gladness.

"The historical fact of the resurrection and its theological meaning will become the centerpiece of apostolic preaching in the Book of Acts. Perhaps from impetus provided by Peter and John, New Testament preachers claimed that the Savior is forever alive—a dramatic truth of the heart of the gospel to this very day. Our living Lord has conquered both sin and death. We can function in spite of trouble and heartache, knowing the ultimate victory is his and ours" (Gangel).

—*Keith E. Eggert.*

QUESTIONS

1. On which of the women who went to Jesus' tomb on resurrection morning did John focus?
2. Why was she so loyal to Jesus?
3. What did Mary immediately do after she arrived at the tomb?
4. What was the disciples' initial response to what the women told them?
5. Who decided to check out their story, and what did they do when they arrived at the tomb?
6. What did these men find at the tomb?
7. What was it that led to John's belief in the resurrection?
8. When after His resurrection did Jesus appear to His disciples?
9. How did He reassure them that He was in a material body?
10. Why did Jesus want His disciples to be assured in this way?

—*Keith E. Eggert.*

Preparing to Teach the Lesson

All over the world this Sunday, Christians are celebrating the resurrection of Jesus Christ. In our lesson this week, we look at the details of that first Resurrection Sunday.

TODAY'S AIM

Facts: to study the details of the resurrection of Jesus on that first Easter Sunday.

Principle: to show that Jesus is the living Word of God.

Application: to emphasize that Jesus' resurrection from the dead calls us to follow Him unreservedly.

INTRODUCING THE LESSON

Imagine someone declaring that he is back from the dead. It seemed a preposterous claim concerning a simple peasant from Nazareth, and many found it hard to believe. Some were skeptical, but the evidence was undeniable.

The idea of someone rising from the dead *is* hard to believe. Many have claimed to rise from the dead, but only Jesus rose from the dead never to die again; and He did so in such a manner that it cannot be denied. Many saw Him crucified and then saw Him again alive after He returned from the grave. Our lesson this week is a reminder to all of us that our God did something no other so-called god or deity did for the world. Jesus was unique in that He died willingly because He loved us so much, and then He came back to show us that He is indeed the living Word of God.

The bodily resurrection of Christ is one thing that sets Christianity apart from the religions of the world. His resurrection also gives His followers assurance of forgiveness and of their own future resurrection. So important is it to the Christian faith that Paul said, "If Christ be not raised, your faith is vain; ye are yet in your sins" (I Cor. 15:17).

DEVELOPING THE LESSON

1. The body of Jesus missing (John 20:1-2). It was still dark in the early hours of that resurrection morning when Mary Magdalene came to the tomb. This tells us something of the devotion to Jesus that Mary had. When she got there, she found to her surprise that the stone at the mouth of the grave was already rolled away. She thought that something bad must have happened and ran to tell Simon Peter and John, the disciple "whom Jesus loved."

Mary's report to Peter was one of fear and concern. She told Peter that someone had stolen the body of Jesus and placed it somewhere else. It is important to show the class that this response from Mary came despite the many times that Jesus had told His disciples that He would indeed rise again. They had forgotten that truth, however. In our search to believe, we can sometimes miss the obvious, as these followers of Jesus did. Encourage the students to take Jesus, the living Word, seriously.

2. The disciples see and believe (John 20:3-10). There is nothing as convincing as seeing something for oneself. Peter and the other disciple, John, ran to the tomb and saw the evidence for themselves. They saw the linen cloth lying there. Peter went inside the tomb while John waited at the door. Peter noticed that the cloth that had covered Jesus' face was folded up and set to the side. It was as if Jesus' body had simply passed through the graveclothes.

This was a very solemn moment for the disciples. They saw, and at least John believed (vs. 8). Jesus was indeed risen, and here was proof. The Scriptures that talked about Jesus rising from the dead suddenly made sense. They were indeed true. Jesus, the Living Word, was alive indeed! It was a moment of realization. Help the class to see that each of us must come to that moment of enlightenment with the help of God's Spirit. We do not worship a dead deity but the living Jesus.

Emphasize to the students that without the resurrection, we are lost to an eternity without God. This is what our celebrations of the risen Lord mean to us. If Jesus had not risen from the grave, there would be no foundation for us to believe in Him. The resurrection of Jesus gives credibility to our faith.

3. The Living Word appears to His disciples (John 20:19-20). If any of his readers were still not convinced of the truth of the risen Lord Jesus, John reported another encounter of Jesus with His disciples that shows us again that He is alive. In the evening of that Resurrection Sunday, Jesus gave His disciples another opportunity to believe in Him.

The disciples were still unsure of all the reports that they were hearing about Jesus being alive. They were also afraid of the Jewish leaders who had instigated Jesus' crucifixion, so they were gathered together behind locked doors. It was at this time of uncertainty that Jesus showed up again, right there in their midst, to assure them that everything would be all right for them. He gave them a blessing of peace in their time of anxiety. Then He gave them another proof that He was alive. He showed them His hands and His side, which were publicly pierced at His crucifixion.

The response of the disciples was one of sheer joy. They needed no more convincing. Jesus Himself was in their midst. He was alive, and their believing in Him was validated again. Jesus had not let them down. Help the class to see that when we truly understand through the eyes of faith that our Lord Jesus is alive, it makes all the difference in the world in the way we live. The disciples were never the same again. They received boldness and power after Jesus' resurrection.

When we truly grasp the truth about the living Word of God, our lives are transformed and freed from anxiety and fear. The event of the resurrection changes everything for us.

ILLUSTRATING THE LESSON

We rejoice because Jesus is alive today. He is our living Word.

CONCLUDING THE LESSON

Leave the class with the challenge that joy can replace our fears and anxieties, if only we take that simple step of believing in the One who has shown Himself to us in so many ways. He gives us reason to believe in Him.

ANTICIPATING THE NEXT LESSON

Next week we will see first how Jesus helped the disciples understand that His crucifixion fulfilled prophecy. Then we will consider His final instructions and ascension to heaven.

—A. Koshy Muthalaly.

PRACTICAL POINTS

1. Those who serve God with great love will be first to witness His greatest wonders (John 20:1).
2. Those who love Christ are eager to be witnesses to His resurrection and salvation (vss. 2-4).
3. Some people believe after much contemplation; others believe right away (vss. 5-8).
4. No matter how well we know the Bible, God always brings forth fresh truths as we reread and meditate upon it (vss. 9-10).
5. In the midst of our worst fears and troubles, Jesus is with us, offering us His peace (vs. 19).
6. To be in the presence of Jesus is the highest joy (vs. 20)!

—*John Lody.*

RESEARCH AND DISCUSSION

1. Mary Magdalene was the first to visit Jesus' tomb, early that morning. Using commentaries and harmonies of the Gospels, can you discover the actual order of events on that first Easter morning?
2. Are you enthusiastic about Christ's resurrection this Easter season? How can you personally be an enthusiastic witness?
3. Read the four Gospel accounts of Christ's resurrection. Share with your Sunday school class the new insights impressed upon you.
4. God's comfort for you is meant to also comfort others (cf. II Cor. 1:4). How has God comforted you in the midst of your fears and trials?

—*John Lody.*

ILLUSTRATED HIGH POINTS

And believed (John 20:8)

Many years ago Irwin H. Linton, a Washington, D.C. lawyer who wrote the book *A Lawyer Examines the Bible* (Baker), spoke in our Bible college chapel service. He said he liked to talk to lawyers about the gospel because they are trained to recognize evidence. This does not mean that lawyers are rushing to receive Christ, but we can be confident that our faith can be defended.

One lawyer who honestly examined the evidence for the resurrection was Simon Greenleaf, a Harvard Law School professor who contributed greatly to the development and expansion of that school back in the middle 1800s. He is the author of *A Treatise on the Law of Evidence,* a classic legal volume.

Dr. Greenleaf believed the resurrection was false and wanted to expose it as a myth. But after honestly examining the evidence, he wrote a book declaring that the evidence would yield only one verdict: Jesus Christ rose from the dead as He said.

Peace be unto you (vs. 19)

A perusal of Web sites on the Internet reveals many good, sound presentations of the gospel. Some are scholarly defenses of the claims of Christ.

Josh McDowell wrote *Evidence That Demands a Verdict* (Campus Crusade). This is a book on apologetics designed to give Christians the tools they need to make a reasonable defense of their faith. At the same time, however, he also pointed out the great value and importance of walking faithfully with Christ and being quick to share a clear, simple testimony of how we came to trust in Christ as our personal Saviour.

—*David A. Hamburg.*

Golden Text Illuminated

"Then the same day at evening, being the first day of the week, when the doors were shut where the disciples were assembled for fear of the Jews, came Jesus and stood in the midst, and saith unto them, Peace be unto you" (John 20:19).

In John's account of Jesus' resurrection, it is Mary Magdalene who first witnesses the risen Lord. Before that happened, she had run and told Peter and John that she had found Jesus' tomb empty, they merely surveyed the empty tomb and went back home without actually seeing Jesus.

But Mary went back to stand before the entrance of the tomb, weeping for the loss of her Lord's body. As she wept, she looked into the tomb and saw two angels. After a moment, she turned and saw Jesus, although without recognizing Him at first.

Jesus spoke her name and thereby revealed who He was to her. Then He told her to go and tell the other disciples that He would soon ascend to the Father. So she obediently and joyfully did what He asked her to do.

Our golden text takes place on that same evening of resurrection Sunday. The disciples had hidden themselves away behind closed doors because they feared that the Jewish leaders were still pursuing them, even after having their Master crucified.

Into this atmosphere of intense trepidation, Jesus Himself suddenly appears in their midst, greeting them in peace. The disciples were evidently in great need of peace at that moment, and Jesus' resurrection presence brought them just the joy and peace they so lacked.

The resurrection of Christ is the vindication of all His redemptive work on behalf of all who trust Him as Lord and Saviour. It is God's stamp of approval on our salvation from sin.

Without the resurrection, our faith is meaningless. As Paul writes, "If Christ be not risen, then is our preaching vain, and your faith is also vain. . . . If in this life only we have hope in Christ, we are of all men most miserable" (I Cor. 15:14, 19).

Yet this is precisely what modern skepticism advocates. It contends that we must jettison all supernatural elements, including the resurrection, and live merely to follow Christ's moral example.

But what would be the value in following Christ's example if His redemptive work were a failure? If we pursued such a course, we would be no better than a hoard of lemmings who blindly follow their deluded leader into suicidal death and oblivion.

Belief in the bodily resurrection of Jesus Christ is essential to saving faith. Let no one persuade you otherwise.

It was precisely their confident witness of Christ's bodily resurrection that enabled the apostles and early disciples to endure persecution and even death rather than deny their faith in Christ. Because they knew for certain that Christ had risen from the dead, they knew also that they themselves would one day be raised from the dead unto eternal life with Christ.

"For I delivered unto you first of all that which I also received, how that Christ died for our sins according to the scriptures; and that he was buried, and that he rose again the third day according to the scriptures" (I Cor. 15:3-4).

—John Lody.

Heart of the Lesson

The Apostle Paul said, "And if Christ be not risen, then is our preaching vain, and your faith is also vain" (I Cor. 15:14). Shortly thereafter, Paul wrote, "And if Christ be not raised, your faith is vain; ye are yet in your sins" (vs. 17). The resurrection of Jesus Christ is an essential part of the gospel account. In a sense, Christ's resurrection was the stamp of approval from God the Father. If Christ had not lived the perfect life in thought, word, and deed and if He had not suffered unto bloodshed, even death on a tree, there would be no resurrection and thus no forgiveness of sins.

Mary Magdalene, Peter, and the beloved disciple were some of the first to observe Christ's empty tomb, proving the resurrection. In John 20:1-10, 19-20, there are three things we will consider.

1. The disciples' thoughts prior to Jesus' resurrection (John 20:1-7). Throughout Jesus' earthly ministry, He made it abundantly clear that He had to die upon a cross, only to be raised three days later. "Destroy this temple, and in three days I will raise it up" (2:19). Mark 8:31 says, "And he (Jesus) began to teach them, that the Son of man must suffer many things, and be rejected of the elders, and of the chief priests, and scribes, and be killed, and after three days rise again."

Despite the Lord's teaching, His disciples were still unable to put that teaching together with the fact that He must be crucified and resurrected from the dead. They desired a messiah who, without suffering, would establish political and military dominance. They never understood that Messiah would suffer, die, be buried in a tomb, and rise in three days to establish His rule, which was not political or military. After His resurrection, it was a different story, however.

2. A testimony to the truth of Jesus' words (John 20:8-10). "Then went in also that other disciple, which came first to the sepulchre, and he saw, and believed." What must it have been like to be a witness to the empty tomb? Although Jesus preached of this miraculous event, now it had finally happened. The hour occurred when His body was no longer in the tomb. And what was the disciples' response? It was belief! However, this is not all that there was to this story. It is one thing for Jesus' body to be gone and quite another thing for Him to appear to others. This would be the ultimate proof that He had indeed risen from the dead, just as He had said He would do.

3. Jesus' appearance (John 20:19-20). Shortly after the verification of Jesus' missing body, the disciples experienced an event that further verified what Jesus and the Scriptures taught. It was the resurrected Jesus Himself. "Peace be unto you," He said as He appeared in their midst. Their response was exceeding gladness.

You should be exceedingly glad that Jesus, as your Lord and Saviour, resurrected from the dead. As a result, not only have you been granted the forgiveness of your sins, but you have also received the righteousness of Christ and a reconciled relationship with God the Father. Moreover, your "own" resurrection is promised. One day you will have a glorified body, which will be incorruptible and undefiled, reserved for you. Praise be to God for His goodness!

—Leon Brown.

World Missions

The message hit home for me when the evangelist asked, "If you were God, how would You feel about a world that highlights the birth of Your Son, the Saviour, with a fat man in a red suit and then observes His resurrection from the dead with a rabbit that lays chocolate eggs?"

Satan has done a masterful job of diverting man's attention from the fact of the resurrection and its immense importance to our salvation. Even the word "Easter" is believed to come from the name of a pagan goddess.

At first, the resurrection was hard for the disciples to grasp. This was because "they knew not the scripture, that he must rise again from the dead" (John 20:9).

Typically, children do not stagger in unbelief as do most adults. Children have no problem with a stone rolled away from the sepulchre, angels in white, and a Saviour nailed to a cross but now very much alive. Similarly, children often know that heaven is very real and that salvation is wonderful.

Christians have seen the need to reach children for Christ. One Child Evangelism Fellowship (CEF) worker began his presentation of their work by asking how many in the audience were saved as children. A good many hands were raised. He then asked how many were saved after age twenty-five. The number was much lower. Yet most of our evangelistic effort and funding is directed to winning adults!

J. Irwin Overholtzer gave his life to winning children to Christ. He wrote, "As far as we know open-air evangelism of children began in 1924 in Sacramento, California." This was the first organized undertaking we know of as Child Evangelism Fellowship, which works across North America and through much of the world (*Open-Air Evangelism Teacher Training,* International Child Evangelism Fellowship).

Overholtzer was a dynamic children's worker. He related one visit to Chicago in 1934 when he happened upon twelve boys playing in the water of a broken hydrant. Four of the boys had been led to Christ in a visit to the neighborhood a month before. The four urged the others to pause in their water play.

"They gathered around me as I told them the Story of Stories," Overholtzer reported. Each was led to trust in Christ. One boy, Dickson, clung to the evangelist. Dickson insisted he follow him home in order to lead Dickson's sister to Christ. She was so bashful, however, that Overholtzer gave up on the little girl. Dickson said, "I will lead her to Christ."

Overholtzer and his young disciple Dickson led two more to the Lord. The great evangelist said his records for that date showed eighty-eight decisions for the Saviour.

Readers who may be interested in the array of CEF ministry aids and materials can contact the organization at cefonline.com. And Child Evangelism Fellowship is just one of many ministries focused on reaching children. There is a wealth of resource material out there that can provide your church or Sunday school with help in reaching and making strong disciples of the children around you.

The important thing is to keep our eyes open to the opportunities the Lord gives us to minster to these little ones who are so close to His heart. He told His apostles (and He tells us), "Suffer the little children to come unto me, and forbid them not: for of such is the kingdom of God" (Mark 10:14).

—Lyle P. Murphy.

The Jewish Aspect

Why was it so hard for the disciples, including the women who followed Jesus, to believe that He would be raised from the dead? How does talk of the resurrection of Jesus sound to Jewish ears in our time?

Resurrection is a Jewish concept. No writings prior to the Old Testament speak of a kind of afterlife that fits with the idea of resurrection.

For example, a culture that is famous for its strong belief in the afterlife is Egypt, a nation that was contemporary with ancient Israel and that had an influence on the thinking of Israelites for a certain period of history. Yet the Egyptian concept of afterlife is very different from the biblical concept of resurrection.

Egyptian beliefs included festival celebrations of the dying and rising of Isis and Osiris. Yet, as N. T. Wright explained, these were symbolic of winter and spring, the dying and new life of the crops each year. Egyptian burial customs and texts discovered by archaeologists reveal that they held a less gloomy idea of the underworld than some other cultures but that the dead lived only incompletely in a shadow world after death (*The Resurrection of the Son of God,* Fortress).

Resurrection is a concept that comes from the Old Testament. While there were various hints in the early parts of the Bible, the most clear texts come from the Prophets. Jesus taught that the idea of resurrection was evident from the statement "I am . . . the God of Abraham" (Exod. 3:6; cf. Mark 12:26). There are other earlier hints of an undefined belief in the afterlife, such as the expression "gathered to his people" (Gen. 25:8), and similar terms.

Resurrection, however, is a return to bodily life in the physical world. The first text that clearly defines this promise is Isaiah 26:19: "Thy dead men shall live, together with my dead body shall they arise." The clearest Old Testament statement about resurrection is probably Daniel 12:2, which says, "Many of them that sleep in the dust of the earth shall awake, some to everlasting life, and some to shame and everlasting contempt."

Yet the strange fact about the resurrection of Jesus is that none of His followers believed in it until afterward and when He appeared to them. This was despite the fact that Jesus foretold His resurrection many times (cf. Matt. 16:21; 17:9, 22-23; Mark 8:31; 9:31). Still, on the morning the empty tomb was discovered, the disciples were hiding in fear and disbelief (John 20:19), and the women were coming to anoint His body for permanent burial (Luke 24:1).

What was so hard for the followers of Jesus to believe and understand? Why is it that in John 20:9, the Apostle John had to report plainly, "For as yet they knew not the scripture, that he must rise again from the dead"?

The problem with the resurrection of Jesus was not that the disciples failed to believe in the concept of resurrection. Rather, the resurrection of Jesus did not follow the commonly held belief that all the dead will be raised at the end of the age. Indeed, this teaching is implied in Old Testament texts such as Isaiah 26 and Daniel 2. It was also the understanding of Martha, the sister of Lazarus, who said of her dead brother, "I know that he shall rise again in the resurrection at the last day" (John 11:24).

The resurrection of Jesus pointed to others still to come. It was a new idea to digest, and it required a faith adjustment.

—Derek Leman.

Guiding the Superintendent

Death cannot keep his prey—
 Jesus, my Savior!
He tore the bars away—
 Jesus, my Lord!

With forgivable poetic license, hymn writer Robert Lowry ("Christ Arose") put into verse a truth that absolutely thrills the heart of every believer: Jesus lives! There were no bars to tear away, just a stone to be moved; and as others have noted, it was moved from the tomb not to let Jesus out but to let seekers in. Christians celebrate His resurrection not only on Easter but also on every Lord's Day—in fact, on every day of the year.

DEVOTIONAL OUTLINE

1. The surprise (John 20:1-2). In a culture where family members often stayed away from a burial site for several days of mourning, it is not surprising to note it was a friend of Jesus who made the first appearance at His tomb. It is surprising, however, to find it was a woman, for in Jewish culture the witness of a woman was not always accepted. The fact that John recorded the event as it was instead of making up a more acceptable story underscores its reality.

Mary Magdalene herself was surprised to find the tomb unsealed and open, and she hastened to report the news to Simon Peter.

Some today deride Christianity as being anti-women, but a fair reading of the Bible, along with knowledge of the cultural mores of the day, shows Jesus (and the Bible as a whole) elevated women far above the practices of that day and of many contemporary societies today.

2. The search (John 20:3-10). It seems best to attribute Peter and John's haste to get to the tomb not to any doubt about Mary's report but to a desire to find out what had happened. They surely knew Jesus' attitude toward women, and they themselves knew the female disciples of the Lord. If they had not believed Mary, they would not have raced to the tomb.

John, the beloved disciple, outran Peter and was the first to observe the empty tomb with the graveclothes still there. Had the body been stolen, as some suggested then and still do today, the graveclothes would surely have been taken with the body.

Upon his arrival, Peter preceded John into the tomb and noted the orderly way the graveclothes were displayed. Then John entered, and at that point he believed Jesus had been resurrected. Such knowledge must have come more from evidence observed, for it is stated it did not come from knowledge of the Scriptures. At that point, they returned to their homes, apparently to think through and try to make sense of what they had seen.

3. The certainty (John 20:19-20). That evening the disciples met behind closed doors rather than in an open and public place so as not to attract the attention of the authorities. Once they were assembled, the resurrected Jesus appeared in their midst. To show them He was really alive, He spoke and invited close scrutiny. For the first time in many hours, there was collective joy in the small band of disciples.

CHILDREN'S CORNER

Lead children to accept the trustworthiness of the written Word of God. In this day of having Bible apps on our phones and other devices, it is still good for teachers to hold up a printed Bible as they teach and make clear they are telling nothing but truth that comes straight from the Word of God.

—Darrell W. McKay.

LESSON 7   APRIL 16, 2023

SCRIPTURE LESSON TEXT

LUKE 24:36 And as they thus spake, Jesus himself stood in the midst of them, and saith unto them, Peace *be* unto you.

37 But they were terrified and affrighted, and supposed that they had seen a spirit.

38 And he said unto them, Why are ye troubled? and why do thoughts arise in your hearts?

39 Behold my hands and my feet, that it is I myself: handle me, and see; for a spirit hath not flesh and bones, as ye see me have.

40 And when he had thus spoken, he shewed them *his* hands and *his* feet.

41 And while they yet believed not for joy, and wondered, he said unto them, Have ye here any meat?

42 And they gave him a piece of a broiled fish, and of an honeycomb.

43 And he took *it,* and did eat before them.

44 And he said unto them, These *are* the words which I spake unto you, while I was yet with you, that all things must be fulfilled, which were written in the law of Moses, and *in* the prophets, and *in* the psalms, concerning me.

45 Then opened he their understanding, that they might understand the scriptures,

46 And said unto them, Thus it is written, and thus it behoved Christ to suffer, and to rise from the dead the third day:

47 And that repentance and remission of sins should be preached in his name among all nations, beginning at Jerusalem.

48 And ye are witnesses of these things.

49 And, behold, I send the promise of my Father upon you: but tarry ye in the city of Jerusalem, until ye be endued with power from on high.

50 And he led them out as far as to Bethany, and he lifted up his hands, and blessed them.

51 And it came to pass, while he blessed them, he was parted from them, and carried up into heaven.

52 And they worshipped him, and returned to Jerusalem with great joy:

53 And were continually in the temple, praising and blessing God. Amen.

NOTES

Proofs of the Resurrection

Lesson Text: Luke 24:36-53

Related Scriptures: Acts 1:1-4; I Corinthians 15:3-8; I John 1:1-4

TIME: A.D. 30   PLACE: Jerusalem

GOLDEN TEXT—"These are the words which I spake unto you, while I was yet with you, that all things must be fulfilled, which were written in the law of Moses, and in the prophets, and in the psalms, concerning me" (Luke 24:44).

Introduction

There are many who feel that all religions are essentially the same.

While we realize that there may be similarities between various religions, Christians know there are also vast differences. Most of these come down to the Person of Christ.

Most world religions have high regard for Jesus. They believe He is a great teacher, a prophet, or even some manifestation of deity.

The Bible makes clear that Jesus is far more than the above. During His ministry, He claimed He was sinless (John 8:46), God's Son (9:35-37), and the way to the Father (14:6). When He was worshipped (9:38), He accepted it. But although He was a masterful teacher and a compassionate healer, the one thing that especially validated Jesus' claims was His rising from the dead. Hence, the resurrection was at the heart of all apostolic preaching.

LESSON OUTLINE

I. **SKEPTICAL DISCIPLES**—
Luke 24:36-43

II. **SCRIPTURES FULFILLED**—
Luke 24:44-47

III. **SPIRIT PROMISED**—
Luke 24:48-49

IV. **SAVIOUR ASCENDS**—
Luke 24:50-53

Exposition: Verse by Verse

SKEPTICAL DISCIPLES

LUKE 24:36 And as they thus spake, Jesus himself stood in the midst of them, and saith unto them, Peace be unto you.

37 But they were terrified and affrighted, and supposed that they had seen a spirit.

38 And he said unto them, Why are ye troubled? and why do thoughts arise in your hearts?

39 Behold my hands and my feet,

that it is I myself: handle me, and see; for a spirit hath not flesh and bones, as ye see me have.

40 And when he had thus spoken, he shewed them his hands and his feet.

41 And while they yet believed not for joy, and wondered, he said unto them, Have ye here any meat?

42 And they gave him a piece of a broiled fish, and of an honeycomb.

43 And he took it, and did eat before them.

Afraid (Luke 24:36-37). Earlier in this chapter, two disciples had an unusual encounter with Jesus on the Emmaus road. After the Lord had revealed Himself to them, "he vanished out of their sight" (vs. 31). Quickly returning to Jerusalem, the two reported this to the others, who were meeting behind locked doors "for fear of the Jews" (John 20:19). They no doubt worried that the fate that had befallen their Master might be meted out to them as well.

As this week's text begins, the two disciples were continuing to relate to the others the events that had occurred, particularly that they had recognized Christ in the breaking of bread (Luke 24:35). {Just then, Jesus appeared in their midst. Since He did not enter through the door, it is apparent that His glorified body was not subject to the same limitations all of us experience in our earthly bodies.}Q1

With regard to our own resurrected bodies, we can assume that like the glorified, resurrected body of the Lord Jesus, our new bodies will not be subject to current limitations. While there will be continuity with our previous body (I Cor. 15:35-54), there will also be discontinuity. The new body will be strong, spiritual, heavenly, and no longer subject to pain, disease, sorrow, or death (Rev. 21:4).

Greeting the disciples in a typical Jewish fashion, the Saviour said, "Peace be unto you" (Luke 24:36). They felt anything but peace, however; "they were terrified and affrighted" (vs. 37).

Keep in mind that this was still the very day Jesus had risen. They had not anticipated the events of the past few days, but this was not because the Lord had not given them ample warning. {For whatever reason, the disciples were unable (or unwilling) to process the information Christ had given concerning both His death and His resurrection. Consequently, they thought they were seeing a ghost—a mistake they had made on another occasion (Mark 6:49).}Q2

Admonished (Luke 24:38-39). Knowing their thoughts, Christ asked them why they were troubled in mind and heart. Had they actually listened more carefully to the things the Lord had been telling them the previous six months, they would not have been so surprised when it came to pass.

{Challenging the disciples to examine His hands and feet, Christ wanted them to be fully convinced that what they were seeing was real.}Q3 He was no apparition, but a person with a real body of "flesh and bones" (vs. 39). As alluded to earlier, we can assume that our own resurrected bodies will be similar. There is one thing we can be sure of—the resurrection of Christ was literal, physical, and bodily.

Assured (Luke 24:40-41). Having challenged the disciples to examine His body, the Lord permitted them to make sure that the wounds in His hands and feet were real. If He had been just a spirit, such examination would have been impossible, for, as He said, "A spirit hath not flesh and bones, as ye see me have" (vs. 39).

This seems to have convinced the disciples, and joy filled their hearts upon seeing the risen Lord. Even so, they still found it astonishing. The truth of the resurrection was difficult for them to grasp.

According to John, Thomas was absent from this particular meeting and was unwilling to believe the testimony of the others. He therefore declared, "Except I shall see in his hands the print of the nails, and put my finger into the print of the nails, and thrust my hand into his side, I will not believe" (20:25). About a week later, Jesus appeared again and challenged Thomas to examine the evidence himself. Apparently the sight of the Lord was convincing enough, for Thomas exclaimed, "My Lord and my God" (vs. 28).

Affirmation (Luke 24:42-43). {To further affirm that a literal resurrection had occurred, Jesus asked the disciples for something to eat. Surely a ghost would neither need nor have the ability to eat earthly food.}Q3 They responded by giving Him some fish and honey. Eating it in their presence gave further proof of His actual resurrection.

Since these men were to be given the task of taking the gospel to the world, they had to be absolutely sure that what they were preaching was true. The fact that they boldly proclaimed the resurrection and were willing to die in the effort is itself convincing proof of what they preached. To be sure, many will die for false causes that they believe to be true; few, if any, will die for what they know to be false!

According to the account of this meeting in John, Jesus told the disciples that they were being sent as the Father had sent Him (20:21). He also breathed on them, promising that they would receive the Holy Spirit (vs. 22), perhaps anticipating what would occur on Pentecost. They were also given power to grant forgiveness (vs. 23) through the gospel they would preach.

SCRIPTURES FULFILLED

44 And he said unto them, These are the words which I spake unto you, while I was yet with you, that all things must be fulfilled, which were written in the law of Moses, and in the prophets, and in the psalms, concerning me.

45 Then opened he their understanding, that they might understand the scriptures,

46 And said unto them, Thus it is written, and thus it behoved Christ to suffer, and to rise from the dead the third day:

47 And that repentance and remission of sins should be preached in his name among all nations, beginning at Jerusalem.

Minds opened (Luke 24:44-45). The disciples had to be convinced of the resurrection through visible, tangible proof. But had they listened to Jesus more carefully, they would have known that these things had been foretold by Him in concert with the prophetic testimony of the Old Testament.

Most of us have probably been taught to divide the Old Testament into four sections: Law, History, Poetry, and Prophecy. However, this was not the way the Scriptures were divided in Christ's time—or in a modern Hebrew Bible.

{The Old Testament was divided into three sections in the Jewish Scriptures: Law, Prophets, and Writings. These three sections contain twenty-four books, which are the same as the thirty-nine books of our Old Testament.}Q4 The difference has to do with the fact that a Hebrew Bible often combines books that are divided in our Old Testament. As an example, all twelve Minor Prophets (Hosea through Malachi) were written on one scroll and seen as one book.

{In a Hebrew Bible, the Law contains

the same first five books of the Pentateuch found in our Bibles. The Prophets include the prophetic books (minus Daniel) and a number of historical books. The Writings begin with Psalms and include a variety of books, some coming from later biblical history.}Q5

When Christ said that the Law, Prophets, and Psalms were fulfilled in Him, He was declaring that everything in the Scriptures was pointing to Him. From our perspective, this means that when we read the Old Testament, we can anticipate finding Jesus there. This will include prophecies, promises, types, and figures. Some commentators in the early centuries of the church went in for fanciful, allegorical interpretations of simple historical narratives. Christ *is* found in the Old Testament, but only where He is intended to be found!

{It is one thing to hear and read the Scriptures; it is quite another to understand them. Christ therefore opened the disciples' minds to comprehend the Scriptures—an absolute necessity for those who were going to carry this message to the ends of the earth (Acts 1:8).}Q6

On the one hand, the Bible can be understood by all, as anyone might understand any other written document. But to fully comprehend the message that is contained therein, divine illumination is necessary. This was seen on Pentecost when Peter preached the Word, but the Spirit convicted hearts (Acts 2:37). Similarly, Paul preached the gospel in Philippi, and the Lord opened the heart of Lydia so "that she attended unto the things which were spoken of Paul" (16:14).

Mission outlined (Luke 24:46-47). Reinforcing what He had already said, the Lord Jesus emphasized that the Scriptures foretold both His sacrificial death and His resurrection on the third day.

While the term "gospel" can mean any of the accounts of the four evangelists (Matthew, Mark, Luke, or John), it can also be applied to the entire Christian message found in the New Testament. In a nutshell, however, the gospel has to do with the death, burial, and resurrection of Christ. This is the way Paul frequently used "gospel" in his letters. As he wrote to the Corinthians, "I declare unto you the gospel which I preached unto you, . . . how that Christ died for our sins according to the scriptures; and that he was buried, and that he rose again the third day according to the scriptures" (I Cor. 15:1, 3-4).

Christ may have given the Great Commission on several different occasions in slightly different forms (cf. Matt. 28:18-20; Mark 16:15-16). The account in Luke is essentially the same, apart from the fact that repentance stressed.

{People may sometimes get the impression that Christ's death and resurrection automatically provides forgiveness for humanity. This, of course, is not true. Only as people turn from sin and turn to God—that is, truly repent—can they expect to be pardoned from sin.}Q7 To be sure, repentance does not earn salvation; it is itself, in fact, a gift of God's Spirit.

SPIRIT PROMISED

48 And ye are witnesses of these things.

49 And, behold, I send the promise of my Father upon you: but tarry ye in the city of Jerusalem, until ye be endued with power from on high.

While all of us are to bear witness to the truth of the Bible and even present our personal testimonies of what the Lord has done for us, we are not witnesses in the sense that the original apostles were. They could give eyewitness testimony concerning both the miracles and the teachings of Christ. Seeing the risen Lord and being able to examine His wounds put them in a unique category of believers.

When a replacement was later sought for Judas, one of the qualifications was that the man had to have seen the risen Lord (Acts 1:22).

We, of course, fall into a different category of believers. As Jesus said to Thomas, "Because thou hast seen me, thou hast believed: blessed are they that have not seen, and yet have believed" (John 20:29).

{The disciples needed spiritual power to carry out their mission, so the Saviour urged them to stay in Jerusalem and wait for the coming of the Spirit (Acts 2:1-4).}Q8 On the night before the crucifixion, Christ had given His disciples necessary teaching concerning the coming Holy Spirit (John 14—16), though at the time they most likely failed to comprehend it. With the arrival of the Spirit, however, they would be guided into all truth (14:26; 15:26; 16:13).

SAVIOUR ASCENDS

50 And he led them out as far as to Bethany, and he lifted up his hands, and blessed them.

51 And it came to pass, while he blessed them, he was parted from them, and carried up into heaven.

52 And they worshipped him, and returned to Jerusalem with great joy:

53 And were continually in the temple, praising and blessing God. Amen.

Final blessing (Luke 24:50-51). If we had only Luke's Gospel, we might get the impression that Jesus ascended to heaven immediately after the resurrection. The other Gospels detail additional appearances of Christ, even in Galilee (Matt. 28:7; John 21:1-14). {And Acts informs us that Christ was "seen of them forty days" (1:3). This probably means He appeared intermittently over a forty-day period, after which He ascended (vss. 9-11).}Q9

As with the other Gospels, Luke compressed time as he related a few resurrection appearances. Although we do not consciously notice it, this occurs when we watch a news broadcast. Highlights are given, sometimes covering a considerable length of time. History books do the same when a war covering several years is recounted in a few pages.

Followers' return (Luke 24:52-53). That the disciples "worshipped him" indicates that they were now fully convinced of Jesus' identity.

{Naturally, they worshipped in the temple, the Jewish place of worship.}Q10 Luke's Gospel begins in the temple, and it concludes in the same place.

—*John Alva Owston.*

QUESTIONS

1. What do we know about Christ's body after His resurrection?
2. Why did the disciples think they had seen a spirit?
3. What things did Jesus do to convince His followers that they were not just seeing a ghost?
4. What is meant by the Law, Prophets, and Psalms?
5. How is the Hebrew Bible both like and unlike our Old Testament?
6. Why was it important that the minds of the disciples be opened to understand the Scriptures?
7. What is repentance? Why is it necessary for us to repent?
8. What were the apostles to wait for in Jerusalem?
9. How long did Christ make appearances to His disciples?
10. What was one thing the disciples did while waiting in Jerusalem?

—*John Alva Owston.*

Preparing to Teach the Lesson

As we study the Scriptures, it is important to understand that everything the prophets spoke about Jesus' death and resurrection was fulfilled. Our God is One who keeps His word. Our lesson this week shows us how Jesus fulfilled in every detail what the prophets had foretold about Him.

TODAY'S AIM

Facts: to demonstrate how Jesus showed Himself to His disciples to prove that what the prophets had said about Him was true.

Principle: to confirm that when God gives us His promises, He keeps His word.

Application: to affirm that we can always trust what God says to us because He keeps His promises.

INTRODUCING THE LESSON

There is no other book in the world like the Bible. It is full of prophecy that has been fulfilled down through the ages and continues to be fulfilled. It is interesting that other holy books do not have such extensive and detailed prophecies in them. The Bible is unique in this. In our lesson this week, we see how the prophets of old pointed forward in time to the coming of the Messiah and the things that He had to undergo. These things were fulfilled just as they said. God keeps His word and so can be trusted.

DEVELOPING THE LESSON

1. Why do you doubt? (Luke 24:36-40). Whenever God is working in strange and unusual ways that stretch our faith and put it to the test, there are always some who are slow to believe. It appears that this was the case when the two disciples on the way to Emmaus reported back to the others about having met with the risen Jesus (vs. 35). As if to strengthen their argument, we find Jesus appearing before them at that very moment, offering them a greeting of peace.

Help the class understand that in a time of confusion, the Lord's peace is what we need. This time it came in the reassuring presence of the risen Saviour and in the fulfillment of what the prophets had foretold for centuries. But not everyone reacted positively. Luke tells us that some thought He was a ghost! Jesus reassured them. One can surmise that it was His voice (though Luke does not mention this) that they could not forget. It had a way of calming their fears.

Jesus, in His usual manner, asked them why they had doubted. He then showed them His hands and His feet as proof that He was the same Person that had been crucified. He asked them to touch Him and see, for spirits (ghosts) do not have physical bodies as He did. He was alive indeed. Help the class to feel the emotion as the disciples began to see that this was the same Jesus who had been with them. They still were not fully convinced.

Being able to touch and to feel, along with seeing Jesus, was not quite enough tangible proof just yet for the disciples that He was the risen Lord. Ask your students what kind of proof people need to risk putting their trust in the Messiah.

2. What the prophets said is true (Luke 24:41-49). There were still some among the disciples who needed an extra dose of assurance. Jesus sensed this and asked for something to eat. Since spirits do not have physical bodies, they do not eat. Jesus had a transformed physical body and could eat like everyone else. They gave Him a piece of broiled fish, and He ate it before them. They now realized for certain that He was real!

Jesus then took the opportunity to reiterate that all that was spoken about Him by the prophets, Moses, and the psalms had to be fulfilled. Just as He did on the way to Emmaus, Jesus opened up the Scriptures and explained that He was indeed the One they spoke about. He helped them understand the significance of the prophetic words about the Messiah: that He would suffer, die, and rise again after three days.

Then Jesus challenged the disciples to go in the authority of His name and take His message to all nations, starting with Jerusalem. His people, the Jews, needed to hear the message first, for they were the ones who had been promised the Messiah. Then Jesus expanded the message to all, offering all people forgiveness of sins because of what He had done on the cross. The disciples were witnesses to this. He told them to stay in Jerusalem until they received the power of the Spirit, whom He would send from heaven.

Point out that Jesus proved over and over again to His disciples that He was the fulfillment of everything the Bible says about the Messiah. Now He was there in the flesh, risen from the dead. They had seen Him, and they had received a commission from Him to spread the news that He is to be trusted and followed.

3. Jesus returned to heaven (Luke 24:50-53). Having finished what He had come to do, Jesus took His disciples to Bethany, where He blessed them with uplifted hands. He was then caught up to heaven. They watched Him go up. They worshipped Him and were filled with great joy.

When the disciples returned to Jerusalem, they continually gathered in the temple and praised God for what they had experienced. Have the students discuss how they might have reacted if they had seen the risen Saviour with their own eyes. Was the joy of the disciples in keeping with their experience? We all should want to have joy in Him.

ILLUSTRATING THE LESSON

The entire Old Testament pointed to the Messiah, and Jesus was the fulfillment of what those Scriptures had foretold.

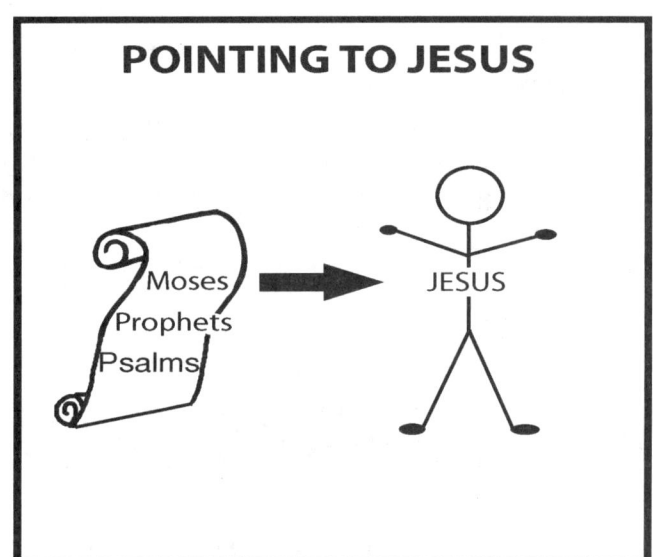

CONCLUDING THE LESSON

How much proof does one need before one can trust Jesus as the Messiah? Challenge the class to see that Jesus is indeed who He said He was and is. Luke has given us more than enough proof that we should believe in Him. Jesus is the fulfillment of what God put in Scripture centuries before. The world does not have to search for a Messiah anymore. He has already come. Challenge the class to put their faith in the One who will not let them down.

ANTICIPATING THE NEXT LESSON

Next week we explore further the wonderful teachings of Jesus. He is the Bread of Life.

—A. Koshy Muthalaly.

PRACTICAL POINTS

1. If we think all our doubts would be resolved if we could just *see* Jesus, look at the Eleven (Luke 24:36-38)!
2. Jesus shows incomparable patience in overcoming our doubts (vss. 39-43).
3. When we get rattled by the seemingly unexpected, Jesus carefully reminds us of the mission (vss. 44-48).
4. The promise of the Father comes to those who obediently wait for it in faith (vs. 49).
5. Although Jesus is not physically with us now, we are continually surrounded by His presence and joy (vss. 50-53).

—Kenneth A. Sponsler.

RESEARCH AND DISCUSSION

1. How does the fact that the disciples thought they were seeing a ghost attest to the reality of the resurrection (Luke 24:37)?
2. Was the risen Jesus actually hungry when He asked for food (vs. 41)? What was His likely purpose in making the request?
3. Since Jesus' explanation of the Scriptures was not recorded for us, how can we be enlightened as the Eleven were (vss. 44-45)?
4. How well have we been doing in the preaching of repentance and remission from sin in Jesus' name throughout the world (vs. 47)?
5. How was Jesus' ascension—a departure from His people—in reality a great blessing for them (vss. 51-53)?

—Kenneth A. Sponsler.

ILLUSTRATED HIGH POINTS

Peace be unto you (Luke 24:36)

"Have a good day!" is a sincere wish, but nobody can *make* it happen.

A good day is every day lived doing the will of God. Jesus greeted His disciples with the typical "Peace be unto you." He had just risen victorious over sin and death, with the power to confer eternal peace, making it a truly good day for believers.

Terrified and affrighted (vs. 37)

The disciples knew nothing about roller coasters, but their emotions took a monster ride that first Easter Sunday.

First, they were devastated by the death of Jesus. There was possibly a glimmer of hope when they heard from the women about the empty tomb.

There was confusion when Peter and John checked the tomb and then sheer terror when Jesus suddenly appeared where the apostles and others had gathered in Jerusalem. Then He spoke, inviting them to touch Him. They did not fully understand, it was all so wonderful, but finally they believed, and the emotional roller-coaster of a day ended with their joyful worship.

The promise of my Father (vs. 49)

It has been written, "A man apt to promise is apt to forget." We can attest to the truth of this statement by observation and experience. We regret the many times we fully intended to do something but realized later that it had slipped from our mind.

"God is not a man, that he should lie" (Num. 23:19); so when He makes a promise, it is certain that He will fulfill it. The Holy Spirit's coming, promised in Joel 2:28-31, confirmed by Jesus in John 14:16, 26, did indeed happen in Acts 2.

—David A. Hamburg.

Golden Text Illuminated

"These are the words which I spake unto you, while I was yet with you, that all things must be fulfilled, which were written in the law of Moses, and in the prophets, and in the psalms, concerning me" (Luke 24:44).

Jesus fulfilled all of God's promises, and in the lives of believers He is always faithful to do what He promised to do. However, we sometimes make claims on His promises that we do not have a right to make. Three questions help us understand the issues involved in claiming God's promises.

1. Is it a promise for me?
2. Are there any conditional parts to the promise?
3. Do I understand there may be a difference between God's timing and my own?

Consider the first qualifying question: Is it a promise for me? According to Romans 15:4, all Scripture is written for believers. We receive instruction and information from every passage. However, there are promises in the Word of God that were not written directly to us. First Samuel 11:9 reads, "To morrow, by that time the sun be hot, ye shall have help." A believer who is having a difficult time in his life might claim such a verse as a definite promise of God for himself. However, the promise was made at a specific time for a particular reason. Not every promise in the Bible can be applied directly to our lives. This promise does teach us principles about God, but it is illegitimate for someone today to claim such a promise as applying specifically to himself as an individual.

The second qualifying question forces us to determine whether conditions are given along with the promise. When Jesus promised that God would give believers whatever they asked for, He attached a condition: "If ye abide in me, and my words abide in you, ye shall ask what ye will, and it shall be done unto you" (John 15:7). The promise is for believers, so we have a right to claim it, but its fulfillment comes after we meet the conditions Jesus gave. People should never consider God unfaithful in keeping His promises when the real unfaithfulness is their own.

The final question believers must ask when considering God's promises concerns the issue of time. Am I expecting God to fulfill His promise on my timetable, or His? The prophet Habakkuk had to learn that distinction. "The vision is yet for an appointed time, but at the end it shall speak, and not lie: though it tarry, wait for it; because it will surely come, it will not tarry" (Hab. 2:3).

Humans are constrained by time; God is not. That is why the apostle Peter wrote that a thousand years is as a day and a day is as a thousand years in God's sight (II Pet. 3:8).

God has an unchangeable plan, and He works out "all things after the counsel of his own will" (Eph. 1:11). He needs no one's advice. Each event in His plan will happen at His appointed time. We must not conclude that God is unfaithful simply because He does not fulfill His promise at the time we would prefer. His timing is always perfect.

The old saying is true: You cannot break God's promises by leaning on them. He will always fulfill His promises. It is essential, however, that we have a biblical understanding of these promises.

—Joseph E. Falkner.

Heart of the Lesson

Promises! Promises! Everybody makes them, from children wanting parental permission to politicians wanting votes. Everyone makes them, but not everyone keeps them. We have all had feelings hurt or been otherwise disappointed when someone broke a promise to us. Is there anybody who actually keeps all his promises? Of course the answer is yes, and that person is Jesus.

1. The promise of resurrection (Luke 24:36a). The very fact that Jesus appeared bodily in the midst of an assembly of His disciples was proof positive that He was not dead. No longer was His body lying lifeless in a dark tomb, for He was standing before them and speaking to them. Jesus had foretold it (cf. Luke 9:22), and it had come to pass.

Every religious leader throughout history has died, but only one has been resurrected. Sadly, many sincere people have chosen to follow dead leaders. The good news we share with others is the news of Christ's resurrection. In fact, the resurrection is the very heart of the gospel, for apart from the resurrection we have no good news and no hope. There is but one gospel, and it is the story of Christ.

2. The promise of peace (Luke 24:36b-43). Our Lord's first word to His startled disciples was "peace." Peace with God and peace with one's fellow man are impossible apart from Christ, but God-given peace was promised in Luke 2:14 by the angels of the Lord in their birth announcement of Christ.

Believers in Christ are no longer enemies of God but are now friends, even family. We continually see lives changed because of Christ and His resurrection power: where there was strife, there is now peace; racist attitudes disappear; and broken family ties are mended. All of this is a foretaste of God's coming kingdom, wherein peace will reign because the Prince of Peace will be in charge. All who trust in Christ share in this hope based on God's promise.

3. The promise of understanding (Luke 24:44-48). Jesus repeated His previous teaching regarding the Old Testament promises about Himself and opened the minds of the disciples to understand. This began the fulfillment of His words found elsewhere. John 12:16 tells us that once Jesus was glorified, His disciples would remember and understand what had not been plain earlier. Jesus told them that understanding would come later (13:7).

At this point in Luke, Jesus had not yet been fully glorified by ascending to heaven; yet the time was near, and so the promise of understanding the gospel was coming to pass. All disciples, both then and today, have the mission of taking this news to the ends of the earth.

4. A promise renewed (Luke 24:49-53). The promise of power from "on high" was reiterated by Christ. The disciples would learn shortly that the "power" was the Spirit of God. They would also learn that this power would not only change them but also work in and through them to change countless others.

The power of the Spirit is present in all believers today. So let us live confidently, as those who are fully trusting Christ as we await the fulfillment of all His promises. He has made promises, and He will keep them.

—Darrell W. McKay.

World Missions

Irene Hanley was a Jewish woman who went everywhere telling others of Jesus the Messiah. She came to Christ after resisting the pleas of a former high-school teacher, the same teacher who at one time had confirmed her own unbelief in the existence of God. She was now a Christian and wanted her friend Irene to become one also (Hanley, *Israel, O My People,* Vineyard International Publishing).

Her friend was faithful to visit almost every Saturday for eight years. This brought conviction to Irene. She knew she needed what her friend possessed.

Finally, one morning Irene began to question herself. "What if the school teacher is right? What if there really is a God? What if Jesus is His Son? Then, if there is a God and if there is a Jesus, there must be a heaven and a hell."

Soon, she fell on her knees and cried, "O God, if You are real, give me faith to believe. O God, if Jesus is Your Son, give me faith to believe this too." Right then, Christ forgave her sin! She was born again.

Irene Hanley's conversion marked the beginning of a lifelong ministry. Through mission trips, talks with rabbis, visits to hospitals, and radio evangelism, this woman touched hearts that only eternity will reveal.

God is faithful to keep His promises. From the beginning of the Bible, God promised that the Messiah would come (Gen. 3:15). After His coming, Satan would be defeated. In God's timing, Jesus came to accomplish this mission. When He comes again, it will be as the victorious King. This good news drives the work of missions forward; because of what Christ has provided, victory is sure.

When Jesus appeared to the disciples after His resurrection, three factors influenced their continued faithfulness to Him. These same three factors also influence the work of worldwide missions.

First, the followers of Christ were assured of His resurrection. At first they were fearful of the unknown. In fact, when Jesus appeared to them in the upper room, they thought they were seeing a spirit (Luke 24:37).

Satan brings all kinds of hindrances to the work of God. He causes fear through opposition and resistance to the gospel and by planting doubt about God's ability to meet every need. One missionary couple was concerned about their children's social development. In the country where they served, young people were very aggressive to marry missionary children in hopes of being able to reach America.

The good news is the reassurance of Jesus: "Why are ye troubled? and why do thoughts arise in your hearts? Behold my hands and my feet, that it is I myself" (vss. 38-39). This guarantee of His resurrected presence drives the work of God.

Second, their eyes were enlightened to a proper understanding of their calling (vss. 44-48). Jesus helped them understand how He fulfilled the Scriptures. This knowledge was not to be kept to themselves. In fact, He said that "repentance and remission of sins should be preached in his name among all nations." This is the main message of missions.

Jesus reminded His disciples of the third influencing factor: the power of the Holy Spirit. He said, "Tarry ye in the city of Jerusalem, until ye be endued with power from on high" (vs. 49). God keeps His promise by enabling His servants to be witnesses. He gives the promises; let us believe and act upon them.

—*James O. Baker.*

The Jewish Aspect

What a marvelous reunion! Jesus stood in the midst of His closest followers. He had come to them and invited them to touch His scars and see that His sufferings were evident. He topped it off by eating food. This was an appeal to sight, to the sound of His voice, and to touch. All this was to prove that He was alive indeed!

The high point of the reunion was the repetition of earlier teaching on the prophecies of the Lord's ministry and works recorded by Moses, the prophets, and the psalmists (Luke 24:44). Those Old Testament messianic prophecies center on the Lord's right to David's kingdom and throne. This is the heart of the message Jews need to hear today.

Old Testament scholar J. Barton Payne explained, "In the Old Testament, the term *mashiah* [Messiah] may be employed in reference to all of those who possess spiritual gifts, for example (Ps. 105:15), the founding patriarchs of the Hebrew people. But this title comes at an early point to be applied in particular to the person of Israel's future Deliverer" (*The Theology of the Older Testament,* Zondervan).

There are literally thousands of Old Testament passages that are prophetic of Jesus and no other person. How shall we marshal the three hundred or more that speak directly of His messiahship?

The Apostle Paul provided exactly what we need. On a missionary journey, he entered the synagogue at Thessalonica (Acts 17:1-2). As a rabbi, he was welcome to present a Bible message. In doing so, he set forth propositional truths under two headings. First, he set forth the truth that the Old Testament teaches a suffering Messiah. Paul said that "Christ (Messiah) must needs have suffered, and risen again from the dead" (vs. 3).

Zechariah is rich in messianic "nuggets." Zechariah 9:9 speaks of the entrance of the Messiah into Jerusalem on the day we now call Palm Sunday. The same prophet told us that the purchase price for the betrayal of the Messiah would be thirty pieces of silver (11:12).

Isaiah tells us of Messiah's torture at the hands of His enemies (50:6). Exact details of His horrible death on the cross are related in Psalm 22:12-18. Isaiah 53:6 tell of His death for us: "The Lord hath laid on him the iniquity of us all." Death could not hold Him according to Psalm 16:8-11. He would be raised from the grave in triumph!

Messianic prophecy has some very special words for the Jews. There will yet be a special reunion when "they shall look upon [Him] whom they have pierced" (Zech. 12:10).

Paul's second propositional truth is that Jesus, by His life, works, and miraculous powers and by His death, burial, and resurrection, fulfilled every prophecy and proved His messiahship (Acts 17:3).

We can imagine that Paul reminded his Jewish audience about Adam, Eve, and Satan's arraignment before God after man's fall into sin (Gen. 3:9-19). God revealed that it would be the seed of the woman that would bring salvation (vs. 15). Isaiah relates that the Seed, Immanuel, God with us, would be virgin born (7:14). Micah 5:2 tells us Bethlehem would be the Messiah's birthplace. Isaiah tells us of His royalty and His special gifts for leading His people (9:6-7).

Paul summed up the evidence, saying, "This Jesus, whom I preach unto you, is Christ (Messiah)" (Acts 17:3). "And some of them believed" (vs. 4).

—*Lyle P. Murphy.*

Guiding the Superintendent

From the time of the Apostle Paul on to the present day, Christians have insisted that belief in the resurrection of Jesus Christ must be central to one's faith (I Cor. 15:3-8). We have just come off another celebration of this great event.

So why is it so important? During His earthly life, Jesus Christ made many promises. If there had been no resurrection, all those promises would have been worthless. Because He did rise from the grave after three days, all those promises are promises kept. Our lesson this week looks at five of the key promises the resurrected Lord made to His original followers and to all who claim Him as Saviour.

DEVOTIONAL OUTLINE

1. I bring peace (Luke 24:36-37). We only have to pick up a current newspaper to see that the world we live in is not at peace. Many politicians and many religious leaders promise peace, but none can deliver. Jesus Christ is different. Just as the grave could not stop Jesus, so nothing today can stop Him from bringing peace.

2. I am alive (Luke 24:38-43). When the postresurrection Jesus first appeared to His disciples, they thought He was a ghost. They were very frightened. He had them examine His body, His feet, His hands, and His wounds. He also ate a meal with them to prove His claim.

This turned their fears to joy. Christians do not worship a dead carpenter. They worship the resurrected Lord Jesus Christ.

3. I fulfill all the Old Testament prophecies (Luke 24:44-46). His death and resurrection were part of God's eternal plan that was revealed in the Old Testament. Not only did Jesus keep the promises He made during His three years of ministry, but by His resurrection He also was able to fulfill all the prophecies of the Old Testament that pertain to His suffering and resurrection. If there had been no resurrection, believers today would not have a reliable Bible to follow, for the Bible would be filled with lies.

4. I have a task for you (Luke 24:47-48). Christians should not be idle people. The resurrection of Jesus Christ gives all of us a great responsibility. That task is telling the world about Jesus and what happened on the cross and in the grave. The message He left is that people need to repent of their sins and accept God's forgiveness.

5. I will be with you (Luke 24:49-53). The fifth promise from Jesus Christ was very specific. He promised to send the Holy Spirit to equip His followers with power.

In the tradition of the high priests, Jesus lifted His hands and pronounced a blessing on the people. The disciples, in turn, worshipped Him. In essence, this is the great promise found throughout the Scriptures (for example, in Exodus 3:12)—the promise of God's presence.

When Jesus makes a promise, be assured that it will be carried out. His resurrection is the guarantee.

CHILDREN'S CORNER

What a great lesson this is to help children understand the importance of keeping one's promises! Even though most of them have felt the disappointment of broken promises many times, they can be encouraged that Jesus always keeps every one of His promises. Further, He will help the children keep the promises they make as they trust Him and rely on His strength.

—*Martin R. Dahlquist.*

LESSON 8 APRIL 23, 2023

Scripture Lesson Text

JOHN 6:22 The day following, when the people which stood on the other side of the sea saw that there was none other boat there, save that one whereinto his disciples were entered, and that Jesus went not with his disciples into the boat, but *that* his disciples were gone away alone;

23 (Howbeit there came other boats from Tiberias nigh unto the place where they did eat bread, after that the Lord had given thanks:)

24 When the people therefore saw that Jesus was not there, neither his disciples, they also took shipping, and came to Capernaum, seeking for Jesus.

25 And when they had found him on the other side of the sea, they said unto him, Rabbi, when camest thou hither?

26 Jesus answered them and said, Verily, verily, I say unto you, Ye seek me, not because ye saw the miracles, but because ye did eat of the loaves, and were filled.

27 Labour not for the meat which perisheth, but for that meat which endureth unto everlasting life, which the Son of man shall give unto you: for him hath God the Father sealed.

28 Then said they unto him, What shall we do, that we might work the works of God?

29 Jesus answered and said unto them, This is the work of God, that ye believe on him whom he hath sent.

30 They said therefore unto him, What sign shewest thou then, that we may see, and believe thee? what dost thou work?

31 Our fathers did eat manna in the desert; as it is written, He gave them bread from heaven to eat.

32 Then Jesus said unto them, Verily, verily, I say unto you, Moses gave you not that bread from heaven; but my Father giveth you the true bread from heaven.

33 For the bread of God is he which cometh down from heaven, and giveth life unto the world.

34 Then said they unto him, Lord, evermore give us this bread.

35 And Jesus said unto them, I am the bread of life: he that cometh to me shall never hunger; and he that believeth on me shall never thirst.

NOTES

The Bread of Life

Lesson Text: John 6:22-35

Related Scriptures: Exodus 16:4-18; Isaiah 55:1-7; John 6:1-13

TIME: A.D. 29   PLACE: Sea of Galilee

GOLDEN TEXT—"Jesus said unto them, I am the bread of life: he that cometh to me shall never hunger; and he that believeth on me shall never thirst" (John 6:35).

Introduction

In *Mere Christianity,* C. S. Lewis concluded a discussion of Jesus' claims with these words: "I am trying here to prevent anyone saying the really foolish thing that people often say about Him: 'I'm ready to accept Jesus as a great moral teacher, but I don't accept His claim to be God.' That is the one thing we must not say. A man who was merely a man and said the sort of things Jesus said would not be a great moral teacher. He would be either a lunatic—on a level with the man who says he is a poached egg—or else he would be the Devil of Hell. You must take your choice. Either this man was, and is, the Son of God; or else a madman or something worse."

This week's text is about Jesus' claim to being the Bread of Life. As always, Jesus' claim came within the context of a normal conversation, but it stirred up a lot of controversy and discord among would-be followers. Few who heard understood what He really meant.

LESSON OUTLINE

I. WHERE IS JESUS?— John 6:22-27

II. WHAT SHALL WE DO?— John 6:28-31

III. MAY WE HAVE THIS BREAD?— John 6:32-35

Exposition: Verse by Verse

WHERE IS JESUS?

JOHN 6:22 The day following, when the people which stood on the other side of the sea saw that there was none other boat there, save that one whereinto his disciples were entered, and that Jesus went not with his disciples into the boat, but that his disciples were gone away alone;

23 (Howbeit there came other boats from Tiberias nigh unto the place where they did eat bread, after that the Lord had given thanks:)

24 When the people therefore saw

that Jesus was not there, neither his disciples, they also took shipping, and came to Capernaum, seeking for Jesus.

25 And when they had found him on the other side of the sea, they said unto him, Rabbi, when camest thou hither?

26 Jesus answered them and said, Verily, verily, I say unto you, Ye seek me, not because ye saw the miracles, but because ye did eat of the loaves, and were filled.

27 Labour not for the meat which perisheth, but for that meat which endureth unto everlasting life, which the Son of man shall give unto you: for him hath God the Father sealed.

Missing Jesus (John 6:22-23). At the beginning of chapter 6 we read of Jesus feeding the multitude near the city of Bethsaida. When He perceived soon after this that there was a movement to make Him king, He immediately left to be by Himself (vs. 15). {Toward evening His disciples boarded a boat and set out across the sea toward Capernaum (vs. 17). Jesus joined them later by walking to them on the water (vss. 18-21). The next day the people started to search for Him around Bethsaida, knowing that He had not sailed with His disciples when they left.

It soon became a source of confusion to them, for they had seen the disciples get into the one small boat and leave and had seen Jesus remain behind.}^Q1 In fact, they had probably seen Him leave their midst and head for the mountain, where He went to pray. They expected to find Him the next morning; yet they could not find Him anywhere, despite the fact that no other boat had departed from there in the meantime. Other boats had arrived, but the one bearing the disciples had been the only one to leave.

{One of the things that always concerned Jesus was the propensity of the people to hope He had come to be the one who would deliver them from the dominion of Rome.}^Q2 Their concept of the coming Messiah was much more political than spiritual, so Jesus avoided making announcements about Himself or allowing the people to elevate Him in a way that would detract from His message. His going to the disciples during their sea journey to Capernaum was a lesson for them, but it also helped Him avoid the misguided crowds.

John mentioned parenthetically that the arriving boats had come from Tiberias to Bethsaida, where the people had eaten bread after Jesus gave thanks for it. Jesus had given thanks before the distribution of the bread, making it a prayer of faith. To John this prayer had been most important, so he made special effort to refer to it here.

Seeking Jesus (John 6:24-25). {We are not told why the boats came from Tiberias, but we wonder whether word of the miracle of the feeding of the crowd had spread that far and others were now coming to see Jesus too. When the people looking for Jesus at Bethsaida could not find Him anywhere, they got into these boats and headed for Capernaum.}^Q3 Perhaps a discussion took place between those in Bethsaida and those who arrived from Tiberias, and it was decided they would travel together to Capernaum to try to find Him.

John 6:24 specifically states that the people were "seeking for Jesus." He had made such a huge impact on them by feeding the crowd that they were determined to see more of Him. Remember that five thousand (vs. 10) was only the number of men, so the estimated numbers of those fed vary greatly from ten to more than twenty thousand people. It was no small group that had witnessed Jesus' miracle. How many were still around the next morning looking for Him we are not told, but it could very well have been a significant number.

Sure enough, Jesus was there in

Capernaum! Upon finding Him, the people had just one question. When did He get there? We would logically assume that they also asked *how* He got there; in fact, there were probably several questions being asked at one time. They knew He had not gone with the disciples, and they knew He had retreated from the crowd on purpose, but they had no idea how He had made it from Bethsaida to Capernaum over night when there had been no other boat available. Their minds were filled with questions.

We find the answers, of course, in the immediately preceding section. When He came to the disciples on the water, they were frightened until He identified Himself. Then when they had taken Him into their boat, they were immediately at their destination.

Hearing Jesus (John 6:26-27). When Jesus began any statement with "Verily, verily, I say unto you," He was about to say something especially important. Four times in this one discourse Jesus started a statement that way (vss. 26, 32, 47, 53). They needed to pay special attention to what He was about to say in each case. {Here, He was about to expose their motives for looking for Him, because He knew their hearts. He knew they were seeking Him to see what further physical provisions He would give them.}Q4

John MacArthur explained, "Jesus' point [was] that the crowds which followed Him were motivated by superficial desires of food rather than any understanding of the true spiritual significance of Jesus' person and mission" (*The MacArthur Study Bible, Word*). It was not even the miracles He performed that they wanted but rather the free food! The miracles John recorded were signs proving Jesus was the Son of God, the Messiah, but they missed that whole point.

{Jesus told them they needed to be looking for spiritual food instead.}Q5 Gangel wrote, "The Lord cut through all the sham of their pretended interest. As he did with Nicodemus, he answered a question they did not ask. Like many modern North Americans, they displayed materialistic and greedy attitudes, working for food that spoils but not for food that endures to eternal life. . . . Like some believers today, they followed Jesus for what they could get out of him" (*Holman New Testament Commentary: John,* Broadman & Holman).

Jesus explained that spiritual nourishment, as opposed to physical, will endure forever. This kind of nourishment comes only from the Son of God, the One the Father has authorized to give it to those who believe in Him.

WHAT SHALL WE DO?

28 Then said they unto him, What shall we do, that we might work the works of God?

29 Jesus answered and said unto them, This is the work of God, that ye believe on him whom he hath sent.

30 They said therefore unto him, What sign shewest thou then, that we may see, and believe thee? what dost thou work?

31 Our fathers did eat manna in the desert; as it is written, He gave them bread from heaven to eat.

Asking what to do (John 6:28-29). {Apparently the listeners thought Jesus meant there were certain things they needed to do in order to have such spiritual nourishment. They had the idea that they would gain salvation by earning it. If they could just prove themselves worthy of being accepted by God, they would be all right.}Q6 That is still a common attitude today. There are many who believe that when they face God and their works in life will be examined, if their good ones outweigh the bad ones, they will get into heaven.

{Jesus responded by telling them

the only work expected of them was to believe in Him. This is not work in the sense we usually think but rather a matter of responding to God's offer of salvation through His Son.}^Q7 There is no activity that can merit salvation and eternal life. In John 5:24 Jesus had already said, "Verily, verily, I say unto you, He that heareth my word, and believeth on him that sent me, hath everlasting life, and shall not come into condemnation; but is passed from death unto life."

Jesus had been sent by God the Father in order to provide salvation for people. The plan originated with the Father and was carried out through His Son. The only requirement for receiving the salvation being offered was belief. It is simply a matter of believing that Jesus is the Son of God and that His death has provided all the payment needed for us to inherit eternal life.

Asking for a sign (John 6:30-31). {These Jews evidently understood that Jesus was claiming to be the Messiah when He said what He did about believing in the One whom God had sent. To them the implication was clear: Jesus was saying He had been sent by God, so they asked for a messianic proof of some kind.}^Q8 The irony is that they had just seen Him miraculously multiply five loaves of bread and two small fish in order to feed thousands of people! How could they not see that a sign had already been given? Why ask for something else?

These people were attempting to minimize what Jesus had done by comparing it with what Moses, by God's power, had done in the wilderness. Moses, they said, had provided manna for the Israelites for the bulk of forty years. Jesus had merely fed several thousand once. If He really was the Messiah, surely He could do better than that! Surely He could do better than Moses! The people even quoted Scripture to support their point (John 6:31; cf. Ps. 78:24).

The people might also have been comparing the fact that Moses had provided bread from heaven, while all Jesus did was give them earthly loaves. One Jewish tradition said that the Messiah would rain bread from heaven when He came, thus taking care of all their human needs for food. All of this was a distraction, because Jesus was not the kind of Messiah they expected. In spite of the fact that He was performing miracles, they still had preconceived ideas of what the Messiah would be like, and He would have to fulfil their expectations!

We hear many ideas about Jesus today that are far from the truth, and Satan uses those ideas to keep people from coming to Christ for salvation. How important it is that our understanding about Jesus come from God's Word and not other people's ideas or opinions!

MAY WE HAVE THIS BREAD?

32 Then Jesus said unto them, Verily, verily, I say unto you, Moses gave you not that bread from heaven; but my Father giveth you the true bread from heaven.

33 For the bread of God is he which cometh down from heaven, and giveth life unto the world.

34 Then said they unto him, Lord, evermore give us this bread.

35 And Jesus said unto them, I am the bread of life: he that cometh to me shall never hunger; and he that believeth on me shall never thirst.

The Bread of God (John 6:32-33). {Jesus quickly informed them that they were thinking incorrectly; it was God, not Moses, who had sent the bread, or manna, from heaven.}^Q9 When the manna was first provided, Moses pointed out that it had come from God. The first time it came, the Israelites saw it as the morning dew disappeared: "And when the children of Israel saw it, they said one to another, It is manna: for they wist not what it was. And Moses said unto them, This is the bread which the Lord hath given you to eat" (Ex. 16:15).

The contrast Jesus made (John 6:32) was between the bread that came from heaven during Moses' day and "the true bread" that was now available to them. The Father had sent the bread in Moses' day, but He had now sent a different kind of bread, and it was in a Person. The biggest difference between these breads is that the one sent during Moses' day satisfied physical needs only; the "true bread," however, would satisfy spiritually and eternally.

Jesus then said plainly, "The bread of God is he which cometh down from heaven, and giveth life unto the world" (vs. 33). The phrase "bread of God" is synonymous with the "true bread from heaven" mentioned in verse 32, and it now points even more clearly to Jesus Himself. "The Jews wanted a daily supply of physical bread. God had given them His Son as the true heavenly bread to meet their daily spiritual needs. The present tense indicates the continual supply" (Barton et al., *Life Application Bible Commentary,* John, Tyndale).

The Bread of Life (John 6:34-35). It is obvious from this request from the Jews that they did not comprehend what Jesus was saying about Himself. They asked Him to give them this bread and to keep giving it to them from that time on. They thought that if they could have the bread that Jesus was talking about given to them, their life would be much easier.

"This dialogue began with the crowd seeking Christ and then seeking a sign, but listeners soon began to seek the 'true bread' that Jesus talked about. However, like the woman of Samaria, they were not ready for salvation. She wanted the living water so that she would not have to keep going to the well. The crowd wanted the bread so they would not have to toil to maintain life. People today still want Jesus Christ only for the benefits He is able to give" (Wiersbe, *The Bible Exposition Commentary,* Victor).

{Jesus finally had to make clear statements for them, and He began by identifying Himself as the Bread of Life. These people needed to know that He was not referring to physical bread but to the spiritual sustenance He could give them if they received Him into their lives.}Q10

The same analogy is intended in Jesus' reference to never thirsting. Both the hunger and the thirst He mentioned are spiritual longings that can be satisfied only through a personal relationship with God through Jesus.

—Keith E. Eggert.

QUESTIONS

1. What was confusing to the people the morning after the disciples had left Bethsaida by boat?
2. What misguided ideas of the people did Jesus continually encounter?
3. What enabled the people to go to Capernaum to seek Jesus?
4. What did Jesus say was the real reason the people were seeking Him?
5. What kind of food did Jesus tell them they should be looking for?
6. What did the people misunderstand about salvation?
7. How did Jesus describe the work they should do?
8. Why did they ask for a sign?
9. What did Jesus say about the bread that they said Moses gave?
10. Who is the real Bread of Life, and what does He provide?

—Keith E. Eggert.

Preparing to Teach the Lesson

People today hunger for something that is genuinely satisfying, but too many look in all the wrong places. John shows us how Jesus satisfies our hunger, for He is also the Bread of Life.

TODAY'S AIM

Facts: to elaborate on Jesus' explanation to His disciples about being the Bread of Life.

Principle: to establish that as the Bread of Life, Jesus offers spiritual and eternal life.

Application: to encourage all to turn to Jesus, who will completely satisfy every need.

INTRODUCING THE LESSON

I come from a land where begging is visible everywhere one turns, much as it was where Jesus lived. The poor are everywhere one goes, and one sees adults and even little children begging for some food just to satisfy their hunger. Many of those who read this lesson are not likely to face hunger in that way. When one is really hungry, it really hurts. In our lesson this week, we see Jesus as the one who can satisfy our most desperate needs as the Bread of Life.

DEVELOPING THE LESSON

1. The crowds seek Jesus (John 6:22-25). The people who had been miraculously fed by Jesus (vss. 5-13) went looking for Him the following day. They knew the disciples had left by boat the previous day, leaving Jesus behind; so they were perplexed by His absence. They did not know Jesus had walked out on the sea to His disciples during the storm in the night and had then taken them to Capernaum. When boats arrived from Tiberias, the crowd boarded them and set off for Capernaum, where they found Jesus.

Get the class to see how eager and anxious the people were to see Jesus. They had seen His miracles, and now they were back for more. Jesus thrilled them with His words and His actions as no one else had done before. Ask the students how long and under what circumstances they would be prepared to wait for Jesus to answer their deepest needs. Help them to compare their own eagerness with that of the crowds who longed to see Jesus again. Stress that it is worth it to patiently wait for Jesus to meet their needs.

2. Eternal needs come first (John 6:26-29). Here we see that Jesus scolded the people for seeking after physical food. This was not wrong in itself, but they had disregarded seeking after the eternal things that they needed much more. Help the class see that seeking physical food is not wrong in itself, but it must be our priority to seek the things of God, which satisfy for all eternity. Jesus admonished the crowd because they sought Him only to obtain physical food.

There was a higher calling for the people. They were to seek Jesus for the heavenly food that they needed. Jesus showed them that they needed to put eternal life and the things of God ahead of physical food and the things of this world. He showed them that that was the sole purpose for His being sent to this earth—to provide eternal life for all. Yet they had to choose to believe in Him.

Help the class realize that eternal things are more important than the physical things of this transient world. Jesus came so that we all might have abundant spiritual and eternal life (John

10:10). This might be a good place to challenge your students to receive Jesus if they have not yet done so. God promises to meet all our needs, even the physical ones. But He does not want us to miss out on being with Him in eternity. He is the eternal Bread of Life, but we have to receive Him by individual choice.

3. Jesus is the Bread of Life (John 6:30-35). The challenge here is to get the students to understand what Jesus is saying. In order to benefit from Jesus, one has to choose to believe in Him as the only one who can satisfy us. When the people asked for a messianic sign from Jesus, they said that Moses had provided manna in the wilderness. They were saying that Jesus had to show them something comparable to that to prove Himself.

Get the class to think through why people often want a physical sign before believing. Remind the class that God does not always give us physical signs but calls us to follow Him in the darkness and to trust Him. Help the class see that God gave His people manna from heaven for physical food, while Jesus gave Himself as the Bread of Life for spiritual food for us. Jesus reminded the people that it was not Moses who provided manna for them but God Himself, the same One who now provides the Bread of Life.

This remark of Jesus certainly caught their attention. They suddenly realized that Jesus was telling them that the manna of old and what Jesus was offering came from the same source. They now wanted to know more. They wanted to know how they could get this spiritual food for themselves every day.

In John 6:35, Jesus made a very profound statement. He said that He is indeed the Bread of Life. Anyone who puts his trust in Him will never be hungry or thirsty again. Jesus is the only one who can satisfy our deepest hunger and thirst. He was not talking about our physical needs but our spiritual ones. He told His hearers that this kind of satisfaction comes only from believing in Jesus and trusting Him.

Help the class understand that Jesus was really calling the people to believe in Him and trust in Him. Remind them that when we trust our Lord Jesus, we will find all we need for a fulfilling life. We will lack for nothing.

ILLUSTRATING THE LESSON

Jesus is the Bread of Life for all who will believe and receive Him.

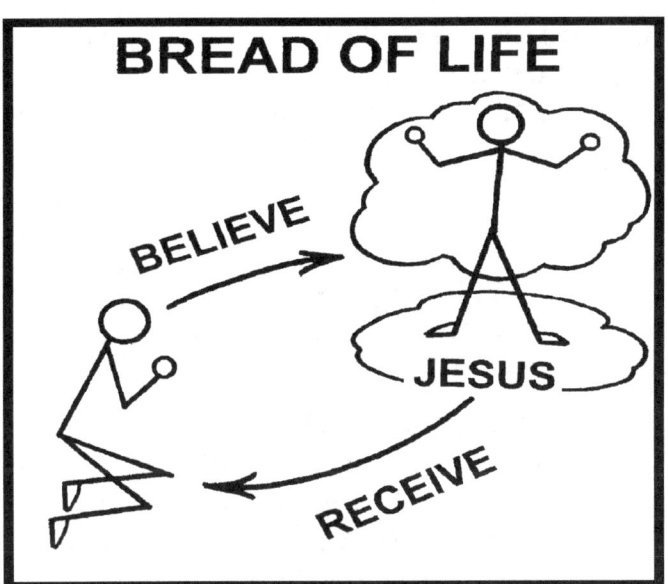

CONCLUDING THE LESSON

Remind the class that believing in Jesus is the first step to experiencing all the blessings that our Lord Jesus has to offer us. When we turn to Him, the Bread of Life, we will not be spiritually destitute again. When we believe in Him, He will satisfy us completely.

ANTICIPATING THE NEXT LESSON

Next week we see how the Bread of Life is also the Light of the World.

—A. Koshy Muthalaly.

PRACTICAL POINTS

1. Fallen humans are prone to seek material rather than spiritual satisfaction (John 6:22-26).
2. If we come to Jesus for any other reason than to worship Him as Lord and Saviour, we are at enmity with God's plan (vs. 27).
3. Believing the gospel seems too simple and trivial to the unbelieving heart (vss. 28-31).
4. Unbelievers give glory to men rather than God (vs. 32).
5. Jesus Himself provides all we need to sustain the abundant Christian life (vs. 33).
6. Unbelievers hear the living words of Jesus Christ but are without understanding (vss. 34-35).

—*John Lody.*

RESEARCH AND DISCUSSION

1. Research and discuss the priority of the spiritual realm over the material realm in the Christian life. How is such a priority to be lived out on a daily basis?
2. What are the proper motives for making a profession of faith? Is a profession that is caused by wrong motives always false?
3. If believing the gospel is such a simple act, why do so many resist the call to believe? What are current religious ideas that can tend to complicate salvation with human additions?
4. Contrast Jesus' intended meanings with the crowd's understanding of Him (or lack thereof).

—*John Lody.*

ILLUSTRATED HIGH POINTS

When camest thou hither? (John 6:25)

The people were confused. Jesus was in Capernaum, but how did He get there?

They would never have imagined that Jesus walked on the water (John 6:19). Even when we think we have thought of everything, we often leave out God and His solution. Let us always remember that God is the God of the impossible (cf. Luke 1:37).

The true bread of life (vs. 35)

Years ago as a student in Bible college, I was given an assignment to preach at a rescue mission.

I preached the gospel the best I could and was thrilled when two men came forward. We went into a back room, where I reviewed the plan of salvation to make sure they understood.

Halfway through, they interrupted and asked whether they could get some food and a bed for the night. I realized then they were similar to the crowd in John 6. They wanted food but were not interested in bread that satisfies the soul.

I am the bread of life (vs. 35)

The online encyclopedia Wikipedia pointed out that bread has a significance beyond nutrition. It mentioned the Lord's Prayer, with the phrase "Give us this day our daily bread" (Matt. 6:11), as well as bread being used in the Eucharist, or communion.

Bread also has become (along with "dough") a euphemism for money.

The encyclopedia mentioned some other ways bread is used around the world, but it neglected to refer to the most important one of all—Jesus, the Bread of Life.

—*David A. Hamburg.*

Golden Text Illuminated

"And Jesus said unto them, I am the Bread of Life: he that cometh to me shall never hunger; and he that believeth on me shall never thirst" (John 6:35).

Our golden text for this week happens to be the final verse of our lesson text. It also happens to be the initial verse of the main portion of Jesus' fourth discourse recorded in John's Gospel, the "bread of life" discourse.

John's Gospel is organized around seven major discourses prior to the narrative of Christ's final week (cf. 3:1-36; 4:1-42; 5:19-47; 6:22-65; 7:1-52; 8:12-59; 10:1-42; 13:1—17:26). The "bread of life" discourse is significant because it features the first of seven occurrences of Jesus speaking the phrase, "I am" (cf. 6:35; 8:12; 10:7, 11; 11:25; 14:6; 15:1), claiming full divinity for Himself with the Father by alluding to the name of God first revealed to Moses (cf. Ex. 3:14).

John's Gospel also features seven miracles (cf. 2:1-11; 4:46-54; 5:1-9; 6:1-14; 6:15-21; 9:1-8; 11:1-46). Note that two of these miracles, Jesus' feeding of the multitude and walking on water, occur just prior to the "Bread of Life" discourse.

Of obvious relevance to this week's text is Jesus' feeding of the multitude, since it supplies the subject matter for Jesus' dialogue with the crowd of people who had followed Him from the site of that miracle, on the eastern shore of the Sea of Galilee, to the synagogue in Capernaum (cf. 6:1, 24, 59).

The crowd that now followed Jesus were there because they expected Him to give them all another free meal. When they finally found Him, they asked a question that sounded innocent enough, "Rabbi, when camest thou hither?" (vs. 25). But Jesus, knowing their true intentions, rebuked them for their unbelief in spite of witnessing such a great miracle. He exhorted them to work for food that gives eternal life rather than for food that perishes with the physical body.

As their dialogue with Jesus continued, the crowd's thinking remained fixed on earthly things, so their misunderstanding of Jesus escalated. At one point, they actually had the audacity to demand another miracle from Him before they would believe what He was saying (cf. vs. 30)! They wanted Him to rain manna down on them as Moses had done. It would seem that their lust for free food knew no bounds!

It was at this lowest point of spirituality for His audience that Jesus revealed to them that He Himself was the Bread of Life that they so desperately needed. The person who puts trust in Jesus will never lack for spiritual nourishment, for He is the never-ending source of heavenly food, the very Word of God (cf. John 1:1, 14; Matt. 4:4).

Jesus is still the Bread of Life for us today, though so many still do not understand this. His flesh and blood were given as a sacrifice that still stands as the saving atonement that takes away God's righteous wrath against our sins. Yet in our fallenness, we still chase after foods that can never satisfy—both physical and spiritual.

But the voice of the Holy Spirit still cries out to each succeeding lost generation, "Ho, every one that thirsteth, come ye to the waters, and he that hath no money; come ye, buy, and eat; yea, come, buy wine and milk without money and without price" (Isa. 55:1).

—*John Lody.*

Heart of the Lesson

God has created us with physical and spiritual needs. We have both physical needs (food, clothing, and shelter) and spiritual needs (forgiveness, reconciliation, justification, and more). Often, however, our focus shifts to emphasize our physical needs over and against our spiritual ones. Finances, shelter, and clothing sometimes eclipse our desire for the gospel of Jesus Christ—that gospel that tells us that Christ is the Bread of Life.

1. They were seeking Jesus for the wrong reasons (John 6:22-27). In verse 26, Jesus revealed to the crowds why they sought Him. "Verily, verily, I say unto you, Ye seek me, not because ye saw the miracles, but because ye did eat of the loaves, and were filled." Jesus' statement referred to a miracle He had performed earlier. He turned five barley loaves and two fish into multiple loaves and fish (vss. 1-13), thus satisfying the hunger of the people. Astonished by His miracle, the crowd responded by saying, "This is of a truth that prophet that should come into the world" (vs. 14).

2. They were shown that which they must seek (John 6:28-35). Jesus perceived that this response was unsatisfactory. Their physical needs were met, but their spiritual needs remained. The people failed to notice that the miracle pointed to the Miracle Worker—namely, Messiah. All they walked away with was a brief amazement at a miracle and a full belly. There was more to this story than fish and loaves, nonetheless. Eternal life was at stake.

The people needed to remove their focus from their physical needs and turn instead to their spiritual needs. Just as the Israelites needed more than manna from heaven, so the people standing before Jesus needed more than bread for sustenance. Their most pressing need was to believe in the One the Father sent (vs. 29). "For the bread of God is he which cometh down from heaven, and giveth life unto the world" (vs. 33).

Have you tasted of this bread? Have you experienced the life-giving power of the bread come down from heaven? The apostle John said, "If we confess our sins, he is faithful and just to forgive us our sins, and to cleanse us from all unrighteousness" (I John 1:9). The forgiveness of sins and eternal life with Jesus Christ are for all those who believe in the Lord for their spiritual sustenance, knowing that "neither is there salvation in any other: for there is none other name under heaven given among men, whereby we must be saved" (Acts 4:12). It is the name of Jesus Christ. Do you believe this?

Jesus helped clarify what those standing before Him needed. Yes, they needed physical food, but they also needed spiritual food. Indeed, Jesus said He was this spiritual food, food that would nourish and strengthen the people. "I am the bread of life: he that cometh to me shall never hunger; and he that believeth on me shall never thirst" (John 6:35). What profound words! Never had a man spoken like this before. Our response to the Lord Jesus should be the grateful embrace of the free offer of spiritual life that Jesus sets before us. Like the people of Jesus' day, we need this bread, and it is the bread come down from heaven, Jesus Christ. "For the bread of God is he which cometh down from heaven, and giveth life unto the world" (vs. 33).

—*Leon Brown.*

World Missions

Have you heard of the Orphan Movement? Some years ago, it was the subject of two separate articles and a magazine's lead-in editorial. *Christianity Today* for July 2010 informs us of evangelicals' growing attention to adoption. According to the magazine, adoption was the sixth most pressing issue of 2009. Many changes have occurred since then, but interest in adopting internationally remains high.

It is important to grasp that "international adoption is not simply a nice thing to do. It's not a celebrity trend. [Instead, it] is adding a child to your family. It's making a lifelong commitment to another human being" ("11 Things To Know About International Adoption" adoption.org).

In a very hard-hitting article, Russell D. Moore, vice president of Southern Baptist Seminary, introduces us to his two sons. The parent's description begins with the boys' infant years in a Russian orphanage. In the first of two visits to Russia, the Moores were taken down the hall to the nursery. The squalor and the stench were stifling, but that was not the most alarming sensation.

As Americans, they were accustomed to the bedlam typical of our nurseries. In the Russian orphanage, the silence was deafening. Babies rocked in their cribs, slats gently bumping against the wall. But there was no crying, for as Moore understood, unanswered cries for food, comfort, or love teach the child to rock silently ("Abba Changes Everything," *Christianity Today,* July 2010).

It was hard to leave the boys. As they started down the hall, they heard one of their boys let out a horrifying scream. Nothing could be done for the little fellow or his brother. Under Russian law, the Moores had to fly home and later return to Russia to complete the adoption process (Russia has since that time closed to foreign adoptions).

As he remembered the departing scream, Dr. Moore thought for the first time of the Abba portions of the New Testament. "Abba" means Father or, even more intimately, Daddy. Paul wrote, "Ye have received the Spirit of adoption, whereby we cry, Abba, Father" (Rom. 8:15). Dr. Moore said it so well: "None of us are natural-born children of God."

Orphan care is, by definition, missionary work. A local pastor has two wonderful Haitian children. They were advertised on the Internet in hopes of finding adoptive parents for them. The pastor followed those children until there was no question the Lord wanted them in the family and in His! As the world measures things, the second child cost $10,000 in adoption fees, but the child is well and, best of all, saved.

Dr. Moore's children, safe at home and well cared for, need not worry about hungering and thirsting. Godly parents will find the Lord's provision for them. The exciting thing is to have them know the One who promises that if they come to Him, they will never hunger or thirst (John 6:35). By faith, this can become a reality.

Christian couples suffering childbearing difficulties often turn to adoption. Churches know how to make newborns welcome. But what of the children adopted out of foster care programs? At least three American Christian organizations are undertaking the work of preparing families for adopting children and churches for supporting those families. Christians who adopt are in a special way providing for these children the "Bread of life" (Barnhill, "Churches Adopt Adoption," *Christianity Today,* July 2010).

—*Lyle P. Murphy.*

The Jewish Aspect

Many people, both Jewish and Christian, think that Judaism is completely incompatible with the idea of God dwelling among people. The Christian doctrine of the Incarnation—that God became a man, Jesus—is, of course, not held to be true in Judaism, but not because of any aversion to the idea that God closely relates to His people.

The history of Jewish thought is replete with contradictions to this supposed fact. The Old Testament itself is filled with examples of God's presence, name, glory, wisdom, and word dwelling on the earth. Jewish texts in legal literature such as the Talmud and Midrash (as well as ancient apocalyptic writings and more recent mystical writings, such as the literature of Kabbalah) are filled with expositions of the mystery of God's immanence, His nearness to His people, and His dwelling within creation.

John 6:31-35 provides an example of this common type of Jewish discussion. The substance of the conversation revolves around Jesus' having just fed the crowd miraculously with bread (vss. 10-15).

God promised and delivered on His promise to Israel that He would "rain bread from heaven" (Ex. 16:4) as they fled Egypt in the desert. This miracle has been associated with the wonders worked through Moses, including the plagues, the parting of the sea, and the water from the rock.

The crowd asked Jesus to show them some sign so that they could believe in Him. They quoted from the Scriptures: "As it is written, He gave them bread from heaven to eat" (John 6:31). Psalm 78:24 is probably the verse they were referring to. It speaks of God having "given them of the corn of heaven."

Jesus corrected their understanding by making two changes in the way they recited the verse. Raymond Brown pointed out—and this pattern occurs often in rabbinic writings—that this kind of correction follows a convention: "do not read as so-and-so, but as such-and-such" (*The Gospel According to John I-XII,* Yale University).

In citing Psalm 78:24, the crowd seemed to understand the "he" as referring to Moses as the one who gave the bread. They also read this as a completely past event. Jesus changed their understanding of the words "he" and "given."

Jesus did this by saying, "Moses gave you not that bread from heaven; but my Father giveth you the true bread from heaven" (John 6:32). A reading of Psalm 78 confirms that the bread was given not by Moses but by God. "The Lord" is mentioned in verse 21; and since there is no change of subject in the following verses, He is the subject of the action described in verse 24.

Furthermore, the people read Psalm 78:24 as saying God "had given" (in the past) bread from heaven. Yet the word "given" can also be understood in a continuing sense. If Moses were the giver, it would make sense that the giving was limited to his time. But since God is the Giver, He can give again and again in any period or generation He chooses. Thus, in Jesus' correction, He said "giveth" (John 6:32)—present tense.

Jesus identified Himself through various hints as the Son who was doing the work of the Father. His claim here is that in multiplying bread for the multitude, He had done the same work as God. He was continuing the provision of bread from heaven and, in fact, is the Bread who gives life.

—Derek Leman.

Guiding the Superintendent

Our third and final unit of study this quarter revolves around the invitation of Jesus to come to Him. He presents Himself as the Bread of Life to those who hunger after righteousness; the Shepherd to lost sheep; the Resurrection and the Life to those dead in sins; and the Way, the Truth, and the Life to those seeking the true path.

DEVOTIONAL OUTLINE

1. Seeking Jesus for the wrong reason (John 6:22-26). Almost everyone loves free food, especially when it comes with a surprise. Thousands had enjoyed just that when Jesus multiplied the loaves and fish (vss. 1-13). A miracle and full stomachs were a wonderful way to end the day. Most likely all had slept well.

The problem is that stomachs have a continuing need for food. So the multitude sought to find Jesus the next day, hoping He would once again fill their bellies. It took a boat ride to find Him, but find Him they did—just in time to get a short lecture. Jesus was very plain in His speech, prefacing it with "Verily, verily" (literally, "amen, amen," or "truly, truly") (John 6:26), indicating that what followed was to be listened to very carefully. He then told the people they sought Him for the wrong reason.

Many still seek Jesus today but, sadly, not all with right motives. Some want healing, or help in a failing business, or to be rid of an unpleasant situation without any commitment to Him as Lord.

2. Seeking a sign when they had just had one (John 6:27-33). When Jesus spoke about food that did not perish and the need to believe that He was the Son of God and could give such, the people sought a sign that they might believe. They obviously did not remember the sign of the day before, when Jesus miraculously fed them! They remembered their ancestors had been provided manna in the wilderness for forty years, and they wanted to see Jesus do something equal to this or better.

Jesus told them it was His Father who had provided for their ancestors and that He would provide for them too through His Son, Jesus.

How many times do we fail to see something the Lord is trying to teach us in life?

3. Seek Jesus for the right reason (John 6:34-35). Like the woman at the well who wanted special water from Jesus, these people asked Jesus for the imperishable bread He mentioned. They thought He would just give it to them.

How many people want to go to heaven when they die but want to get the ticket with only head faith and without commitment to Christ?

Jesus then told them plainly they would receive such bread from Him only with a genuine and obedient faith. That is the meaning of Jesus' words here as well as elsewhere in John's Gospel when speaking about faith.

Following Jesus for the right reason is wanting a personal relationship with Him; it is desiring Him to be Master and Lord; it is a commitment to discipleship.

CHILDREN'S CORNER

Lead children to understand that real faith obeys Jesus. This may not be as difficult to teach as it might seem. Adults are the ones who tend to separate faith and obedience. Children seem to know, for instance, that if they trust their parents, they should do what their parents ask of them. It is the same with what Jesus tells us.

—Darrell W. McKay.

LESSON 9　　　　　　　　　　　　　　　　　　　APRIL 30, 2023

Scripture Lesson Text

JOHN 8:12 Then spake Jesus again unto them, saying, I am the light of the world: he that followeth me shall not walk in darkness, but shall have the light of life.

13 The Pharisees therefore said unto him, Thou bearest record of thyself; thy record is not true.

14 Jesus answered and said unto them, Though I bear record of myself, *yet* my record is true: for I know whence I came, and whither I go; but ye cannot tell whence I come, and whither I go.

15 Ye judge after the flesh; I judge no man.

16 And yet if I judge, my judgment is true: for I am not alone, but I and the Father that sent me.

17 It is also written in your law, that the testimony of two men is true.

18 I am one that bear witness of myself, and the Father that sent me beareth witness of me.

19 Then said they unto him, Where is thy Father? Jesus answered, Ye neither know me, nor my Father: if ye had known me, ye should have known my Father also.

20 These words spake Jesus in the treasury, as he taught in the temple: and no man laid hands on him; for his hour was not yet come.

12:44 Jesus cried and said, He that believeth on me, believeth not on me, but on him that sent me.

45 And he that seeth me seeth him that sent me.

46 I am come a light into the world, that whosoever believeth on me should not abide in darkness.

NOTES

The Light of the World

Lesson Text: John 8:12-20; 12:44-46

Related Scriptures: Isaiah 9:2-6; Matthew 5:14-16;
John 1:1-10; I John 5:5-13

TIMES: A.D. 29; 30   PLACE: Jerusalem

GOLDEN TEXT—"I am the light of the world: he that followeth me shall not walk in darkness, but shall have the light of life" (John 8:12).

Introduction

Jesus pleased His Father in all ways, as we have seen this quarter, including in what He taught. The Lord taught the truth about Himself and God in perfect love and perfect accuracy. In particular, the Gospel of John includes seven significant "I am" statements by Jesus, which offer a great deal of insight into who He truly is and what He came to accomplish. Last week's text included the first of these statements, "I am the bread of life" (6:35).

The second of the statements is in the text for this week: "I am the light of the world" (8:12). The others are "I am the door" (10:7), "I am the good shepherd" (vs. 11), "I am the resurrection, and the life" (11:25), "I am the way, the truth, and the life" (14:6), and "I am the true vine" (15:1).

Jesus gives light to a dark world.

LESSON OUTLINE

I. THE OFFER OF LIGHT—
   John 8:12-16

II. THE OFFER OF WITNESSES—
    John 8:17-20

III. THE OFFER OF ESCAPE FROM DARKNESS—JOHN 12:44-46

Exposition: Verse by Verse

THE OFFER OF LIGHT

JOHN 8:12 Then spake Jesus again unto them, saying, I am the light of the world: he that followeth me shall not walk in darkness, but shall have the light of life.

13 The Pharisees therefore said unto him, Thou bearest record of thyself; thy record is not true.

14 Jesus answered and said unto them, Though I bear record of myself, yet my record is true: for I know whence I came, and whither I go; but ye cannot tell whence I come, and whither I go.

15 Ye judge after the flesh; I judge no man.

16 And yet if I judge, my judgment is true: for I am not alone, but I and the Father that sent me.

Jesus' claim (John 8:12). "Life involves conflict between God, who is good, and evil powers. Evil is darkness, shutting out opportunity to see or know good. God is the source of light which exposes evil for what it is. Jesus is that light in person exposing the evil of the world and pointing the way to God" (*Disciple's Study Bible,* Holman). We live in a world under Satan's sway (John 14:30; II Cor. 4:4; Eph. 2:2), though it is under the ultimate control of God. Evil is prevalent everywhere on this globe.

As the description above states, evil is darkness. {We live in a dark world. In many nations the darkness is so great that it is dangerous for Christians to be present, for the forces of evil prevail and control the thinking of the people.}[Q1] The United States can no longer rightly be thought of as a predominantly Christian nation, because living by the principles of God's Word is no longer foremost in the minds of most people. In fact, God's truth is being opposed with increasing vehemence and hostility in much of our society.

{There is only one hope for dispelling this darkness; it is found in the Person of Jesus Christ, the Son of God. He boldly declared, "I am the light of the world: he that followeth me shall not walk in darkness, but shall have the light of life" (John 8:12).}[Q1] Jesus was not claiming to be a light but the Light, which was a claim of deity.

It is likely that Jesus was still at the Feast of Tabernacles (7:2), during which He had used the water-drawing ritual to declare Himself to be the One who could quench spiritual thirst. During this feast, large lamps were lit, and the people held festive dances of celebration. Jesus used this ritual to declare Himself to be the light of the entire world, not just the local area. Jesus exposes sin, dispels darkness, and shines into the world through His children. The forces of darkness cannot stand against this light.

Jesus' knowledge (John 8:13-14). {As usual, the Pharisees challenged Jesus immediately, this time with the accusation that all He had for validating His statement was a false self-witness. Their implication was clearly that they were not about to accept His claim with nothing more than that to consider.}[Q2] If there was no supporting testimony, they claimed they could rightly dismiss His words. It was commonly thought that every person was a liar and therefore needed to have his words verified through at least one other person.

Jesus' response was that He could bear witness to Himself because His words were always the truth. He was not a liar, as they assumed. {In addition, He knew where He had come from and where He was going. They knew nothing about this. While this might not have sounded like very good evidence to His critics, we understand that He was challenging them with facts that they should have known about their Messiah but did not.}[Q3] If they would listen carefully to His words and observe His works, they would recognize Him.

Jesus' origin was heaven and His Father. He would return to His Father in due time; so He understood His destiny. There are times when an individual is the only one who knows the entire truth about a matter. No one else has the facts he does. This is why some of our court cases are so difficult to resolve. Jesus was a true witness because of His comprehensive knowledge about His origin and destiny. Even though the Pharisees thought they knew much about Him, they were actually woefully lacking in knowledge.

It was not Jesus' fault that they could not recognize who He was. The truth had been presented adequately. Nor is it God's fault when a person dies and faces eternity separated from Him. The truth can be known; when a person chooses to ignore it, he will be held responsible when he faces God on Judgment Day.

Jesus' judgment (John 8:15-16). After God rejected Saul as king of Israel, He sent Samuel to the home of Jesse to anoint a new king. Jesse had eight sons. When Eliab, the firstborn, stepped before Samuel, Samuel concluded that he was probably looking at the next king of Israel, perhaps because Eliab was tall and good-looking. God spoke immediately, however, and instructed the prophet about His ways: "The Lord seeth not as man seeth; for man looketh on the outward appearance, but the Lord looketh on the heart" (I Sam. 16:7).

{So it is with judgment. Jesus said the Pharisees judged according to the flesh, that is, by what they could see and hear only. They looked at external things and judged by human standards, with no concept of how God views things.}Q4 Isaiah wrote concerning the coming Messiah, "And he shall not judge after the sight of his eyes, neither reprove after the hearing of his ears: but with righteousness shall he judge. . . . And righteousness shall be the girdle of his loins, and faithfulness the girdle of his reins" (Isa. 11:3-5).

{Jesus said that He would not judge the way they did ("I judge no man" [John 8:15]) but that when the time came for Him to judge, His judgment would be true. The reason was that He would not judge alone; He would be joined by His Father, in whose presence He constantly remained.}Q4 It is important that we realize we cannot fool God by the way we live. Unbelievers who stand before Him will have no way of excusing themselves for not belonging to Him. They will have no excuse for failing to be obedient to Him. He will judge by what He has seen in the heart, not just by our actions.

THE OFFER OF WITNESSES

17 It is also written in your law, that the testimony of two men is true.

18 I am one that bear witness of myself, and the Father that sent me beareth witness of me.

19 Then said they unto him, Where is thy Father? Jesus answered, Ye neither know me, nor my Father: if ye had known me, ye should have known my Father also.

20 These words spake Jesus in the treasury, as he taught in the temple: and no man laid hands on him; for his hour was not yet come.

Bearing testimony (John 8:17-18). The Mosaic law stated, "At the mouth of two witnesses, or three witnesses, shall he that is worthy of death be put to death; but at the mouth of one witness he shall not be put to death" (Deut. 17:6). This was also true of other matters: "One witness shall not rise up against a man for any iniquity, or for any sin, in any sin that he sinneth: at the mouth of two witnesses, or at the mouth of three witnesses, shall the matter be established" (19:15).

{The Pharisees tried to apply this principle to Jesus.}Q5 They were also mockingly reminding Him of what He had said on an earlier occasion: "If I bear witness of myself, my witness is not true" (John 5:31). At that time, of course, He had explained what He meant, but the Pharisees ignored that. {So now Jesus proceeded to point out that the law did require two witnesses for validating truth and that He did indeed have two witnesses. He bore witness regarding Himself, and the Father who sent Him also testified for Him.}Q6

John's Gospel has already established the fact that John the Baptist had come as a witness for Jesus (1:7; 5:33). The Samaritan woman had said, "Come, see a man, which told me all things that ever I did: is not this the Christ?" (4:29). Jesus had also explained that His Father was a witness for Him (5:32, 37). He had pointed out that His works testified for Him (vs. 36). Beyond all these, the Old Testament spoke of Him (vss. 39-40).

There had already been plenty of proof regarding Jesus, but the Pharisees refused to acknowledge it. Sadly, this same type of refusal often occurs today when people are presented with the truth about Christ. The coldness in many hearts and the blindness of many eyes keep people from acknowledging what is obviously the truth about Him.

Knowing God (John 8:19-20). If Jesus was going to claim His Father as His witness, the Pharisees wanted to know where he was. They would like to interview him. They were thinking, as usual, in human terms only; so they asked about His earthly father. {Since they had rejected Jesus' message and claims of deity, they could not understand how God could be Jesus' Father. Jesus replied that the question itself revealed their ignorance. They did not know Him or His Father. If they had known Him, they would have known His Father too.}Q7

All of this was taking place in a very public place referred to as the "treasury" (vs. 20). This was part of the Court of Women, a courtyard in the precincts of the temple where women were allowed. {Considering the intensity of opposition, it would seem that people must have been present who were eager to arrest Jesus and get rid of Him. John explained that even though this was the case, no one laid hands on Him, simply because "his hour was not yet come."}Q8 The implication is that they were ready to act but were divinely restrained from doing so.

The Greek word translated "laid hands on" is *piazō,* meaning to "take hold of" or "seize." It could refer to a neutral action, as in taking someone's hand, but was more commonly used in hunting contexts (as in catching fish) or in the official sense of arresting or taking someone into custody. We know that the Pharisees wanted to arrest Jesus and have Him under their control. But God's plan was not at the point when this was meant to occur. It is good to be reminded that God is in control of every situation.

THE OFFER OF ESCAPE FROM DARKNESS

12:44 Jesus cried and said, He that believeth on me, believeth not on me, but on him that sent me.

45 And he that seeth me seeth him that sent me.

46 I am come a light into the world, that whosoever believeth on me should not abide in darkness.

Believing in God (John 12:44-45). It was now the final week of Jesus' life. He had already made His triumphal entry into Jerusalem (vss. 12-15). He had announced that the light was going to be with them for only a short time more, after which they needed to be certain they walked in light and not in darkness (vs. 35). John reported that even though Jesus had given many evidences of who He was, many people still did not believe in Him (vs. 37). Many others did believe, however, including some of the rulers (vs. 42).

At some point Jesus evidently called out loudly so that everyone in the vicinity could hear clearly. His opening words were "He that believeth on me, believeth not on me, but on him that sent me. And he that seeth me seeth him that sent me" (vss. 44-45). He was assuring the people that anyone who believed in Him was at the same time believing in God, His Father. Anyone who sees Jesus for who He really is also sees God as He really is. Jesus was claiming to be the visible manifestation of God!

Later, Jesus would say to Philip, "Have I been so long time with you, and yet hast thou not known me, Philip? he that hath seen me hath seen the Father; and how sayest thou then, Shew us the Father?" (14:9). Jesus clearly claimed to be God. As such, He was the promised Messiah for whom Israel had been waiting. They needed to believe, that is, have faith, in Him. They had to entrust their entire spiritual well-being to Him if they were ever to be in heaven with God.

So it is with us. Our eternal destiny depends on what we do about Jesus Christ, who came to earth and died for us.

Your spiritual well-being must be entrusted to Him. He is waiting to be your Saviour now if you have never received Him.

Living in light (John 12:46). The emphasis of this lesson has been on Jesus as the Light of the World. We have noted that the presence of evil throughout the world causes the world to be in darkness. We have also noted that Jesus repeatedly referred to Himself as the source of spiritual light in this dark world. {Once again He made His claim: He came as a light into the world, and whoever believes in Him will not walk in darkness. It is a matter of having spiritual understanding as opposed to being ignorant of God's ways.}^Q9

The apostle Paul explained it this way: "But as it is written, Eye hath not seen, nor ear heard, neither have entered into the heart of man, the things which God hath prepared for them that love him. But God hath revealed them unto us by his Spirit: for the Spirit searcheth all things, yea, the deep things of God. For what man knoweth the things of a man, save the spirit of man which is in him? even so the things of God knoweth no man, but the Spirit of God" (I Cor. 2:9-11).

It is sometimes difficult for unbelievers to comprehend the reality of their lack of spiritual understanding. {Many think they have insight into spirituality, but their knowledge is false. That is why it is important to emphasize the most important matter first: believe in the Lord Jesus Christ in order to be saved (Acts 16:31). There is no other requirement. Once this decision has been made, the pathway to spiritual understanding and learning to live in the light has begun.}^Q10

—*Keith E. Eggert.*

QUESTIONS

1. Why is there so much darkness in the world, and what is our hope?
2. Why did the Pharisees challenge Jesus' self-witness?
3. Why did Jesus speak of where He came from and where He was going?
4. How did Jesus say His judgment would differ from that of the Pharisees?
5. What Old Testament basis of testimony did the Pharisees use against Jesus?
6. How did Jesus respond?
7. What did Jesus mean when He said that they knew neither Him nor His Father?
8. Why was no one able to apprehend Jesus?
9. What did Jesus mean when He said that whoever believes in Him would not walk in darkness?
10. What must happen before people can understand true spirituality?

—*Keith E. Eggert.*

Preparing to Teach the Lesson

Last week's lesson looked at Jesus as the Bread of Life that every person needs. In this week's text we find Jesus proclaiming Himself to be the Light of the World.

TODAY'S AIM

Facts: to examine passages in which Jesus proclaims Himself to be the Light of the World.

Principle: to show that Jesus is indeed the Light of the World.

Application: to challenge believers to walk in Jesus' light.

INTRODUCING THE LESSON

When I was a small boy, there was no electricity in our family home. Kerosene lamps and candles were our only source of illumination. Such weak lighting only allows people to walk around without running into things. Reading or doing fine work by kerosene lamp or by candle is very difficult.

When I was about thirteen years old, we were able to have our old farmhouse wired for electricity. What a day it was when the first switch was thrown, flooding the house with wonderful light! One of the first things we did after getting lights was to clean house. Cobwebs that had been unnoticed in the darkness could not hide when the light came in.

This week's lesson proclaims that Jesus is the Light of the World. In His presence, darkness flees and sin is exposed.

DEVELOPING THE LESSON

1. The declaration (John 8:12). Jesus said, "I am the light of the world." What does this mean? Discuss the obvious benefits of light. It is a blessing that we often take for granted until we are deprived of it. Light allows us to see. Sight allows us to move about, do work, and care for others and ourselves. Those who are blind cannot take advantage of light. In Scripture, light is associated with righteousness, while darkness is associated with sin. Read I John 1:5. In John 8:12, Jesus promised that those who followed Him "shall not walk in darkness." What does this mean? Professing Christians living sinful lives contradict their claims of discipleship. Read 3:20. "Talking the talk" is no substitute for "walking the walk."

2. The dialogue (John 8:13-20). Identify the Pharisees as a sect within ancient Judaism that was committed to keeping and teaching the law of Moses, along with their expanded, rabbinical interpretations. Additional information on the Pharisees can be obtained from any Bible dictionary or encyclopedia. The Pharisees were Jesus' main antagonists throughout His earthly ministry.

List the Pharisees' two objections to Jesus as stated in John 8:13. First, the rabbis did not recognize self-testimony. They therefore rejected Jesus' claims about Himself. Second, the Pharisees claimed that Jesus' testimony concerning Himself was not true.

Read John 8:14-18. Ask a volunteer to paraphrase Jesus' rebuttal. He insisted that what He said about Himself was true. If two witnesses were required, He and the Father would be the two witnesses.

Reflect on the question "Where is thy Father?" (vs. 19). Discuss the Pharisees' possible motives for asking such a question. "The Pharisees' next question was doubtless spoken in scorn" (MacDonald, *Believer's Bible Commentary,* Nelson). Perhaps they were even questioning the legitimacy of Jesus' birth. Maybe they were baiting Him to commit what they would have considered blasphemy. It is obvious that Jesus and His opponents were poles apart.

Focus on Jesus' response to the Pharisees' question. What great truth does this response reinforce? The Father and the Son are inseparable. To know one is to know the other. Refer to John 10:30 and 14:7-9. To deny the Son is to deny the Father. Read also I John 2:22-23.

Jesus' encounter with the Pharisees occurred in the temple courts. This was a very public place that was in the domain of His adversaries. Jesus made no effort to tone down His rhetoric or to be diplomatic. Why was Jesus safe? Refer to John 10:18. Jesus was not going to be anyone's victim. No one would hurt Him before His time. Note 12:23, in which Jesus acknowledged, "The hour is come."

3. The deliverance (John 12:44-46). Remind the class that John's purpose in his Gospel was to reveal Jesus as the Son of God. This theme has persisted throughout. Here Jesus again linked Himself to the Father by insisting that to see Him is to see the Father. Read 1:14. What would be the predictable response to such a claim? Remind the students that Jesus' claim of equality with God is the foundation of the gospel.

In John 12:46, Jesus repeated the message of 8:12, declaring Himself to be "a light into the world." Comment on the profound contrast between light and darkness. Darkness cannot exist in the presence of light. God's kingdom of light is absolutely incompatible with Satan's kingdom of darkness. There can be no compromise between light and darkness.

What is the key to deliverance from the darkness? Belief in Christ provides the only deliverance. What is possible for those who believe? Read Philippians 2:15. Our relationship with God through belief in Christ allows us to walk in the light and to reflect His light in a dark world.

ILLUSTRATING THE LESSON

Jesus is the Light of the World! A candle glowing in the darkness illustrates this triumphant announcement.

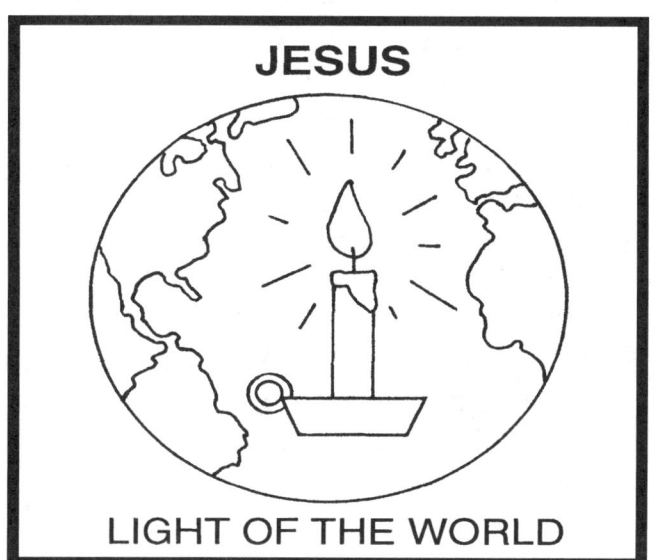

CONCLUDING THE LESSON

Events unfolding in the world today remind us that we are living in a very dark place. Sin is rampant, and the sad results of sin are everywhere to see. Man, with all his science and technology, still wanders in the night without purpose or hope. Two thousand years ago, Jesus announced, "I am the light of the world." He offered hope to a world in despair. Today His great declaration still resonates. Our darkened world needs to see the light that Jesus can provide. Announce boldly that Jesus is the Light. Let His light shine through you!

ANTICIPATING THE NEXT LESSON

One of John's most heartwarming portraits of Jesus shows Him to be the Good Shepherd. He offers guidance and protection to those who are the sheep of His flock.

—*Bruce A. Tanner.*

PRACTICAL POINTS

1. When we have adequate light, whether we are speaking of physical light or spiritual light, we neither stumble nor fall (John 8:12).
2. We should readily accept the truth whenever we find it (vss. 13-14).
3. If we agree with God, we will not misjudge anything (vss. 15-18).
4. Many questions arise simply because we are not fully following God (vs. 19).
5. If we are in God's hands and following His will, we need not fear what people might do to us (vs. 20).
6. We cannot know God except through Jesus, and we cannot come to God except through Jesus (12:44-46).

—Ralph Woodworth.

RESEARCH AND DISCUSSION

1. Are we the light of the world in the same way that Jesus is (John 8:12; cf. Matt. 5:14)?
2. Why did most of the Pharisees find it so difficult to accept Jesus as the Son of God (John 8:13; cf. Luke 7:30)?
3. Earlier Jesus had said that the Father gave Him authority to judge. Why did He say here that He judges no one (John 8:15; cf. 5:27; Acts 10:42; II Tim. 4:1)?
4. How can we be sure a witness is telling the truth (John 8:13-17; cf. 15:27; Acts 22:14-15)?
5. Do you think God has a timetable for all things, including your life (John 8:20; cf. Eccl. 3:1)?

—Ralph Woodworth.

ILLUSTRATED HIGH POINTS

The light of the world (John 8:12)

When a person views a film, the room is darkened. Afterwards, when the lights are turned on or he goes outside, everything seems very bright. It takes a few moments for his eyes to adjust.

Unsaved people live in a dark world. The gospel call is a challenge to come out into the light. The devil cautions, "You had better watch out! If you let others know what you are really like, they will despise you!" But the believer must reply, "I believe Jesus has paid the price for all my sin, including the world of darkness I chose to live in for so long. And I am not going to live there anymore!"

As our spiritual eyes become more accustomed to the light, we can see that there are others who are living daily in the brilliance of Christ's presence. There is much joy for they are free at last from darkness and its deeds.

I am not alone (vs. 16)

An elevator got stuck in a power failure. At first there was some panic among the seven occupants. Then one man remembered a tiny flashlight he carried in his pocket. When he turned it on, fear dissipated.

Ephesians 5:8 says that we are like that flashlight. Just as the flashlight draws power from the batteries, so we draw power from Christ. As light, we destroy darkness, bring relief, and lift spirits.

Sometimes we may be tempted to feel that we should be less outspoken for the Lord, but we forget that it is the nature of light to shine. Jesus pointed out how strange it would be to put a light under a basket. It is fruitless to build a city on a hill and think it will not be noticed (Matt. 5:14-16).

—Ted Simonson.

Golden Text Illuminated

"I am the light of the world: he that followeth me shall not walk in darkness, but shall have the light of life" (John 8:12).

The eighteenth century witnessed what has been called the Enlightenment. It was a time when reason, as well as experience, was credited with advancements in both political and social realms.

With all due respect, true enlightenment comes not from such sources but from the Creator Himself. It is through a belief in and a study of God and His Word that individuals are enlightened in the things that matter most. Someone has said that we call a person educated today if he knows everything about that which will pass away and nothing about that which is eternal.

Our golden text is only one of a number of verses in the Bible, and especially in John's Gospel, to teach that the light we really need is available only from God, who is light Himself (John 1:4; I John 1:5). We need God's light because this world is in moral darkness. God has already given physical light, and He stands ready to give moral and ethical light to the one who recognizes the need and reaches out by faith to the Lord.

God is Light; the Lord Jesus is Light; and the Word of God is Light also (Ps. 119:105). In addition, the Holy Spirit's ministry, in part, is shining light into the dark corners of the heart to expose sin so that we can be convicted and confess it to God. The Spirit also enlightens those who read His Word (cf. I Cor. 2:14).

In our golden text, Jesus goes on to state that those who follow Him will not walk in darkness. He does not mean He will provide a physical light on a dark night. Rather, a disciple of Christ will be given the wisdom he needs to make day-to-day decisions. We have to want spiritual light to receive it, and the promise is that those who are genuine followers of the Lord will understand His Word and be able to apply it to everyday decisions.

There is no need for a believer to make excuses for his sins. He should not plead ignorance about right and wrong, especially if he has the Bible and is serious about hiding it in his heart (cf. Heb. 5:11-14). Paul wrote in Romans 7:7 that he would not have known what lust was if it had not been for the law of God, which says, "Thou shalt not covet" (Ex. 20:17). That is true enlightenment, the kind sorely needed in every heart and in every land today.

It is such a shame that many today are attempting to rid the classroom, the courtroom, and the public square of God and His Word. Many feel that Christianity is only a superstition the masses have adopted and that it stands in the way of social progress and brotherhood.

To spurn God and His Word, however, is the surest way to plunge the world even more deeply into spiritual darkness than it is now. We who are a part of God's church need to be faithful to do several things in the time we have left. First, we must live by the light God has given. Such a life is a positive witness, and it fulfills Matthew 5:14-16 by letting our light shine before others. Second, the church must always preach the Word of God. It is the only message we have that will make the world a better place as individuals repent and come to Christ, who is, as He so plainly stated, the Light of the world.

—Darrell W. McKay

Heart of the Lesson

The morning following the last day of the Feast of Tabernacles, Jesus began teaching in the temple. Extremely large lamps stood within the temple in the Court of Women. The large lamps were a symbol of the pillar of fire God used to light the way for the Israelites' journey in the wilderness.

Jesus testified about Himself at least three times in this week's text. He said, "I am the light of the world" (John 8:12); "I am not alone" (vs. 16); and "I am one that bear witness of myself" (vs. 18).

1. Jesus is the Light (John 8:12). Jesus told the Jews that He is the Light of the World. He lights our way as we sojourn here on earth.

Light enables people to see more clearly. Light has brilliance. It signifies enlightenment and perception. It is related to purity, holiness, and righteousness. Light has the capability to dispel darkness. The world is full of darkness. It has been full of sin and wickedness since the fall of Adam and Eve.

Jesus, the Light of the World, came to earth to light the way for all mankind. He performed many miracles, including giving sight to the blind. He showed mankind the way to the Father and how to be pleasing in His sight. Everyone has an opportunity to be enlightened by the Light of the World. Trusting in Jesus as the Messiah will lead us to everlasting life. Believers have Jesus' assurance of having the everlasting light of life. Rejecting Him will lead to eternal darkness.

2. A witness of the Light (John 8:13-18). Jesus is the Light of the World, and the Father is His witness. There is no better witness than the Father, since He sent Jesus. Jesus was sent to deliver mankind from sin and darkness. Believers who walk in His light are no longer blinded by sin. All who trust in Jesus no longer have to walk in darkness.

Although the Father is Jesus' witness, Jesus did not have to prove anything to anyone. No one can disprove what He says. Whether Jesus had a witness or not, His testimony is still valid. He speaks the truth. Jesus is the Way, the Truth, and the Life (14:6).

The scribes and Pharisees did not want to accept what Jesus said. Jesus reminded them of the Jewish law which states, "At the mouth of two witnesses, or three witnesses, shall he that is worthy of death be put to death" (Deut. 17:6). Jesus Himself was a witness to who He is. The Father was also a witness. Therefore, the Jewish leaders should have accepted Jesus' testimony.

3. Light is enlightening (John 8:19-20). Jesus' light helps us see our condition. We recognize that we need salvation. Jesus, the Light of the World, has power to bring us into His light.

4. Last call for light (John 12:44-46). Can you imagine a loved one staying in a dark house without utilities when he had an opportunity to stay where there were utilities? It would be very difficult to leave a loved one in that condition.

Jesus was compelled to speak out once more to appeal to the Jews. He knew the Jews needed salvation. Jesus was sent to save sinners. He yearned for them to believe in Him. It was difficult for Him to leave the Jews in darkness (cf. Luke 13:34).

The Jewish leaders claimed to know God. How could they know God but not His Son, especially since God sent His Son to them? Do you know Jesus? Do you look to Him? He is the Light of the World.

—Arletta Merritts.

World Missions

The missionary of Christ lives in a glass house, so to speak. He is watched constantly. His every move and action are observed. His daily behavior shows the truth of John 8:12: "He that followeth me shall not walk in darkness."

A missionary is truthful. This is foreign to cultures where lies and deceit are practiced from childhood, where nobody can trust anyone, and where people commonly see how much they can get away with. Then the missionary comes, and they try to take advantage of him. He, on the other hand, is always found to be telling the truth. It has to be shocking. At first people think he is just naive. But, no—it is the light of the gospel shining in a dark place!

The missionary is honest. He does not steal. People steal from him. They take his tools, his clothes—anything they can get away with. He has to barricade his home when he leaves. One tribe in New Guinea had an obsession about counting things and stole things such as beads just to count them. The man of God is different. He always recognizes ownership and protects others' property rather than pilfer it. He shows a light in that darkness.

Love comes through in many ways. The missionary speaks respectfully to the people. He gives medical help such as stitching up wounds, dispensing pills, and giving injections for malaria or other diseases. He learns the language. His wife helps with childbirth. This is the light of Christ being reflected from his heart and his wife's.

The missionaries' relationship is observed. He treats his wife with tenderness as an equal. He does not beat her. He does not make her work like a beast of burden. He does not cheat on her or speak badly of her behind her back. The natives notice this. It is a witness to them of the power of the gospel, the light of life. Native women would like to be treated in the same manner by their men.

The missionary does not drink alcohol. He does not go into drunken rages and fight with the other men. He has self-control and is temperate. He uses only medically-needed drugs. He does not try to get the people to grow marijuana or coca. He tries to help them grow a cash crop, like coffee, but nothing addictive, like betel nut. Why? It is that light!

Traders come with goods to sell, and take advantage of the people. The missionary may be misunderstood at first, and they may expect him to steal goods or mine for gold or set about some commercial enterprise. But it soon becomes apparent that his interest is in learning their language and teaching them out of the Bible. He cares about their souls, and the light begins to dawn.

Other outsiders have come and studied their language and habits and made notations in their little books. Then they left without helping the people much. The missionary stays and helps them a lot. He keeps talking about Jesus. There is a decision to be made. The old gods will have to be abandoned. Is it worth it? Forces are at work. Voices speak pro and con. Hopefully, the truth and the light win out.

The light, by its very nature, exposes the works of darkness: immorality, dishonesty, and oppression. This makes some people angry. They try to retaliate and drive the missionary away. They even kill to prevent change. There is danger in walking in the light. We need to pray for our missionaries that they will have divine protection from the forces of evil. Pray that the light overcomes the darkness.

—Philip J. Lesko.

The Jewish Aspect

John 8:12 records another saying of Jesus that was very appropriate for the occasion. The setting is the temple during the Feast of Tabernacles (cf. 7:2; 8:2). This location is vitally important.

Jesus was standing near the temple treasury when He spoke the words of John 8:12 (cf. vs. 20). The treasury of the temple adjoined the Court of Women (Brown, *The Anchor Bible: John,* Doubleday). This location made His words all the more appropriate as a call to Israel to turn to Him as Messiah and God.

It was in the Court of Women that one of the glorious spectacles of the Feast of Tabernacles occurred. In Sukkah 5:1, the Mishnah describes four giant lampstands that were set up in the Court of Women for the feast (Neusner, *The Talmud of the Land of Israel,* University of Chicago Press).

There is some debate in the Jerusalem Talmud about how tall these lampstands were. Some claimed they were about fifty cubits, or seventy-five feet, high, but others said this height would not have been feasible. They were certainly tall, however, for the priests had to use ladders to fill them with oil and light their wicks. On top of these lampstands were large bowls filled with olive oil and lit with wicks made from the discarded linen robes of the priests (Neusner). It was said that these four lampstands gave such a light that the whole city of Jerusalem reflected it, making the city even more beautiful at night than usual (Brown).

Not only were the lampstands magnificently tall and bright, but they also were the object of a very dramatic and memorable ceremony. Sukkah 5:3 says that pious men and wonder-workers would dance in the Court of Women beneath the light of these lampstands, holding torches in their hand (Neusner).

Light and fire have long been symbols of God's power and revelation to the world. Israel was led by a pillar of fire, which also served to light their way (Ex. 13:21). David called the Lord "my light" (Ps. 27:1), and in Psalm 104:2 God is described as wearing light as a garment. Isaiah speaks of the nations seeing the light of the Lord (9:2) and of Israel being glorified with God's light (60:1).

How appropriate, then, were the words of Jesus, standing right next to the Court of Women in the full light of the four lampstands: "I am the light of the world: he that followeth me shall not walk in darkness, but shall have the light of life" (John 8:12).

The meaning of Jesus' words on such an occasion was multilayered. Jesus was the true glory of Jerusalem, greater than the four lampstands that made the city beautiful at the feast. Jesus was the light that glorified Israel, as promised in Isaiah 60:1, for it is Israel's glory to have brought forth the Messiah and Saviour of the world. Jesus is the light that shines in darkness in "Galilee of the nations" (9:1), a light to the Gentiles (42:6). He is, as John said in the beginning of this Gospel, "the light of men" (1:4). "And the light shineth in darkness; and the darkness comprehended it not" (vs. 5).

Jewish people today ought to know how Jewish the account of Jesus is. Christians who want their Jewish friends to know Jesus ought to know such things as these and share them. By doing so they can bring to Israel "the light of life" (John 8:12).

—Derek Leman.

Guiding the Superintendent

To the titles He claimed, Living Water and Bread of Life, Jesus now added a third—the Light. Like bread and water, light is essential for all life. There is only one sun that provides the earth with all the needed light. If the sun were to stop shining, no life could survive on earth. In the same way, there is only one God who is the source of all light for mankind.

Jesus actually made this great claim during the Feast of Tabernacles, during which four gigantic candelabra burned in the temple. This radiant light recalled the pillar of fire that guided Israel in the wilderness.

Just as the lights from the temple were seen all over the city, so Jesus Christ claimed to be the one light that provides guidance for all mankind. As a light guides the traveler through a dark forest, so Jesus Christ will guide His followers through the darkness of the world of sin, evil, and ignorance.

As the Light, Jesus claimed two things about Himself and His relationship with God the Father.

DEVOTIONAL OUTLINE

1. Know Me, know God (John 8:12-20). Immediately after Jesus Christ claimed to be the Light of the world, the ever-present Pharisees challenged Him by calling Him a liar (vs. 13). Their reasoning was simple—a claim about oneself is of no value without corroborating testimony.

Jesus responded by saying He actually had the two witnesses required by the law. The first was Himself. Light, by its very nature, is its own witness. That is what light does. All one has to do is shine a small light in a dark room, and the evidence is obvious. Since being the light was never in doubt, He could give testimony of Himself.

Jesus quickly identified the second witness—His Father. The Father's witness had been through the words and signs of Jesus (cf. John 5:37-47).

The sparring between Jesus and the Pharisees regarding who speaks for God went on and on. Jesus' point was quite simple: Because they had rejected Him, they had rejected God's light for the world. They claimed to know Scripture, but Jesus turned Scripture back on them.

The claim of Jesus Christ is clear in this passage. He claims to be the only one who can show God the Father to the world. Those who reject Him are in reality rejecting God. You cannot have one without the other.

If one is ever to know God, it will be through understanding Jesus Christ.

2. See Me, see God (John 12:44-46). How sad it is when a person becomes blind! What is even sadder is a person who can see but chooses to remain in darkness. This is the emphasis of Jesus' discussion in John 12.

Fact after fact had been presented to Israel, but they had rejected it all. They refused to see Jesus and thus to see God.

CHILDREN'S CORNER

The blindness that Jesus dealt with in our lesson text came after many years of unbelief. To prevent this long-term problem in your students, show how God can be seen in Jesus Christ. This truth should be stated as simply as possible for children. We know that nobody can see God, but we can "see" Jesus through all the words we read about Him in the Bible. When we believe those words, God shows us in our minds and hearts what He is like.

—*Martin R. Dahlquist*

LESSON 10 — MAY 7, 2023

SCRIPTURE LESSON TEXT

JOHN 10:7 Then said Jesus unto them again, Verily, verily, I say unto you, I am the door of the sheep.

8 All that ever came before me are thieves and robbers: but the sheep did not hear them.

9 I am the door: by me if any man enter in, he shall be saved, and shall go in and out, and find pasture.

10 The thief cometh not, but for to steal, and to kill, and to destroy: I am come that they might have life, and that they might have *it* **more abundantly.**

11 I am the good shepherd: the good shepherd giveth his life for the sheep.

12 But he that is an hireling, and not the shepherd, whose own the sheep are not, seeth the wolf coming, and leaveth the sheep, and fleeth: and the wolf catcheth them, and scattereth the sheep.

13 The hireling fleeth, because he is an hireling, and careth not for the sheep.

14 I am the good shepherd, and know my *sheep,* **and am known of mine.**

15 As the Father knoweth me, even so know I the Father: and I lay down my life for the sheep.

16 And other sheep I have, which are not of this fold: them also I must bring, and they shall hear my voice; and there shall be one fold, *and* **one shepherd.**

17 Therefore doth my Father love me, because I lay down my life, that I might take it again.

18 No man taketh it from me, but I lay it down of myself. I have power to lay it down, and I have power to take it again. This commandment have I received of my Father.

NOTES

The Good Shepherd

Lesson Text: John 10:7-18

Related Scriptures: Psalm 23:1-6; Jeremiah 23:1-6;
Ezekiel 34:10-25; I Peter 5:1-4

TIME: A.D. 29   PLACE: Jerusalem

GOLDEN TEXT—"I am the good shepherd: the good shepherd giveth his life for the sheep" (John 10:11).

Introduction

Jesus' teaching in John 10 makes use of many familiar aspects of first-century Palestine. Jesus talked about a shepherd, his sheep, the fold where they stayed at night, and a hireling, or hired hand. Because shepherds and their flocks were very common sights around Israel, the people listening to Jesus would have had no trouble picturing in their minds everything He mentioned.

Throughout the history of Israel, God's people were portrayed as sheep under the guidance of "shepherds," those who were the leaders of the nation.

It is not complimentary to us when the Scriptures refer to us as sheep, for sheep are quite unintelligent and are easily led astray. Sadly, those characteristics often fit us, because we can so easily forget the importance of living by God's Word and instead decide to live our lives the way we want. But it is good to have God as our Shepherd.

LESSON OUTLINE

I. THE ONLY DOOR—John 10:7-10

II. THE ONLY SHEPHERD—John 10:11-15

III. THE WHOLE FLOCK—John 10:16-18

Exposition: Verse by Verse

THE ONLY DOOR

JOHN 10:7 Then said Jesus unto them again, Verily, verily, I say unto you, I am the door of the sheep.

8 All that ever came before me are thieves and robbers: but the sheep did not hear them.

9 I am the door: by me if any man enter in, he shall be saved, and shall go in and out, and find pasture.

10 The thief cometh not, but for to steal, and to kill, and to destroy: I am come that they might have life, and that they might have it more abundantly.

Ignoring the thieves and robbers (John 10:7-8). In the first paragraph of this chapter, Jesus talked about a shepherd entering the sheepfold to call out his own sheep by name. {It was common for more than one flock to be kept in the same fold overnight, but the flocks could be easily separated because the sheep knew their own master's voice.}^Q1 The shepherd always used the door of the fold for getting and returning his sheep, so anyone trying to get to them by some other way would immediately be exposed as an impostor.

Jesus used that illustration to set the stage for identifying Himself as the Good Shepherd. {However, He first referred to Himself as the Door for the sheep. It was common for a shepherd to get his sheep inside the fold and then lie down across the opening so that they could not leave without his knowledge. At the same time, he became a barrier against any wild animals or thieves that might try to harm his sheep. Jesus is a protector for His sheep, guarding them against the destructive forces of Satan and his demons.

A door is a means of entry. Jesus is the means of entry into the family of God.}^Q2 This statement reminds us that He later said, "I am the way, the truth, and the life: no man cometh unto the Father, but by me" (John 14:6). There is, therefore, no other way to get into the family of God but through Him. He alone has died and paid the penalty for our sins, and it is only through trusting Him as our Lord and Saviour that we can become part of God's family and have our eternal destination with Him settled.

{Jesus repeated the thought found in John 10:1 about thieves and robbers trying to get to the sheep (vs. 8). This is a reference to the Jewish leaders who were leading the people astray. They were taking them away from God instead of toward Him.}^Q3 Still, there were those in Jesus' day who were listening to His message and becoming believers in Him.

Entering the door to good pasture (John 10:9-10). When Jesus repeated His claim that He was the Door, He expanded on it by stating clearly that anyone entering through Him was saved. {When the shepherd took his sheep through the door into the fold, he was putting them in a place of safety and security, where enemies and wild animals could not get them. In this way they were safe, saved from the dangers outside the fold. Jesus' reference to being saved refers to spiritual salvation, where there is safety from Satan and eternal destruction.}^Q4

Later, Jesus spoke of this eternal safety: "My sheep hear my voice, and I know them, and they follow me: and I give unto them eternal life; and they shall never perish, neither shall any man pluck them out of my hand. My Father, which gave them me, is greater than all; and no man is able to pluck them out of my Father's hand" (John 10:27-29). We are guaranteed heaven and salvation from hell when we trust Him as our Lord and Saviour. Furthermore, we are spiritually nourished from then on, as indicated by our finding pasture (vs. 9).

Jesus then made another reference to those who are false teachers, or thieves, who rob people of truth. All they can do is steal, kill, and destroy. In taking away the truth, they lead people toward an eternity apart from God. Jesus, on the other hand, said that He came to give people eternal life and a present life that is meaningful and fulfilling. The word translated "abundantly" is *perissos,* referring to a quality of life that is superabundant and superior in every way to a life without Him.

Diligent obedience to God and His Word can give His children a life of enjoyment with Him. He desires to meet all our needs and bless us in ways beyond our imagination. Hebrews 11:6 tells us that "He is a rewarder of them that diligently seek him."

THE ONLY SHEPHERD

11 I am the good shepherd: the good shepherd giveth his life for the sheep.

12 But he that is an hireling, and not the shepherd, whose own the sheep are not, seeth the wolf coming, and leaveth the sheep, and fleeth: and the wolf catcheth them, and scattereth the sheep.

13 The hireling fleeth, because he is an hireling, and careth not for the sheep.

14 I am the good shepherd, and know my sheep, and am known of mine.

15 As the Father knoweth me, even so know I the Father: and I lay down my life for the sheep.

Self-sacrifice (John 10:11). This is the fourth of seven "I am" statements of Jesus that John included in his Gospel. He now said, "I am the good shepherd: the good shepherd giveth his life for the sheep." Every shepherd faced certain dangers in his occupation. Robbers might appear wielding clubs or knives and attempt to steal his sheep. Wild animals were always lurking about in search of a meal. Good shepherds were willing to lay their lives on the line to protect their sheep. Jesus was certainly willing to do that for His sheep.

The false teachers referred to earlier would never be willing to make such a sacrifice for their followers. Zechariah 11:17 refers to such leaders: "Woe to the idol shepherd that leaveth the flock! the sword shall be upon his arm, and upon his right eye: his arm shall be clean dried up, and his right eye shall be utterly darkened." The Hebrew word translated "idol" means "something worthless" or "good for nothing." Such a useless leader would suffer the destruction of his arm and eye, which could have provided protection for others but did not.

"When evening settled over the land of Palestine, danger lurked. In Bible times lions, wolves, jackals, panthers, leopards, bears, and hyenas were common in the countryside. The life of a shepherd could be dangerous as illustrated by David's fights with at least one lion and one bear (I Sam. 17:34-35, 37). Jacob also experienced the labor and toil of being a faithful shepherd (Gen. 31:38-40)" (Walvoord and Zuck, eds., *The Bible Knowledge Commentary,* Victor). Jesus, however, is the epitome of a good shepherd, willing to give His life in order to save His sheep.

Self-preservation (John 10:12-13). {The false teachers and selfish leaders of Israel were like hired servants instead of effective leaders. The *American Heritage Dictionary* defines a hireling as "one who works solely for compensation, esp. one who performs tasks considered menial or offensive." When it comes to assisting a shepherd, therefore, a hireling has no ownership of the flock; so the last thing he would do is give his life for the sheep under his care. When danger comes, he will flee for his own life.}[Q5]

Jesus said that since the hireling is nothing more than a wage earner, when he sees the wolf coming to attack, he will run in order to protect himself. This leaves the sheep unprotected, and the wolf runs in among them, killing some of them and scattering the rest. The panic that ensues will leave all the sheep vulnerable to any other predator that might be nearby. They will scatter in every direction and no longer even be in the protection of a group. The result could be total devastation.

This was an apt description of the attitudes and actions of the religious leaders in Jesus' day. They were so self-absorbed that they had little or no concern for the people. In fact, they did their best to lead the people astray when it came to their responses to Jesus.

They were more concerned to have people adhere to their traditions than to see them have a meaningful relationship with God. This became obvious in their repeated confrontations with Jesus. "In contrast with the Good Shepherd, who owns, cares, feeds, protects, and dies for His sheep, the one who works for wages—the hired hand—does not have the same commitment. . . . If a wolf attacks . . . he runs away and his selfishness causes the flock to be scattered. Obviously he cares nothing for the sheep. Israel had many false prophets, selfish kings, and imitation messiahs. The flock of God suffered constantly from their abuse" (Walvoord and Zuck).

Selflessness (John 10:14-15). {We noted earlier that the sheep can be called out of a fold where there are several flocks because they know the voice of their shepherd. He also knows each of his sheep, because as their owner he loves them and cares about them. Jesus assured His listeners that as the Good Shepherd, He knows each of His sheep and they know Him.}Q6 What an encouragement it is to know that we can have an intimate relationship with our Saviour! He knows us, and as we learn about Him, we can grow to know Him more deeply.

In this fast-paced world, it is easy to develop a feeling that we are all alone in the humdrum of life and that no one really knows about us or cares for us. This seems to be especially true of those who have lost their mates and find themselves very much alone in life. It is true that our sufficiency can be found in our relationship with God and His Son, but the reality is that it becomes a life of loneliness and frustration for many. We must know that our Shepherd is there and is always aware.

{The example Jesus gave to illustrate this closeness was His relationship with His Heavenly Father.}Q7 They know each other intimately and have for all eternity past! This is what made Jesus willing to lay down His life for the sheep. His love for those He created is so great He was willing to make this selfless sacrifice to provide for their redemption. For that reason He now stated plainly the fact that He was about to lay down His life for the sheep, making this a personal commitment.

THE WHOLE FLOCK

16 And other sheep I have, which are not of this fold: them also I must bring, and they shall hear my voice; and there shall be one fold, and one shepherd.

17 Therefore doth my Father love me, because I lay down my life, that I might take it again.

18 No man taketh it from me, but I lay it down of myself. I have power to lay it down, and I have power to take it again. This commandment have I received of my Father.

Other sheep (John 10:16). {The "other sheep" who are "not of this fold" is a reference to the Gentiles, among whom many in the succeeding years would come to know Jesus as their Shepherd and Saviour.}Q8 Jesus offered salvation to the Jews first, but His intention was to expand that offer to Gentiles as well. There would be many of them who would respond in faith, allowing Him to bring them into God's family along with believing Jews. This would result in a single flock under the one true Shepherd. Believers are united in Christ.

We read of the beginning of this movement in Acts 10, where Peter was summoned to the house of the Roman centurion Cornelius, a devout man who was searching for a relationship with God. God sent an angel who instructed him to send for Peter, who would come and teach him the things he wanted to understand.

The next day Peter received a vision from God in which he was told to eat unclean animals—something he had never done and had no intention of doing. After hearing the instruction three times and wondering what the vision meant, he was told by the Spirit that there were men at the door of his host's home searching for him. He was to go with them without doubting, because God had sent them.

When Peter entered Cornelius's house and found a ready audience, he realized God was doing something new, including the Gentiles in His offer of salvation. Some years later, the apostle Paul became a messenger to the Gentiles and won many of them to the Lord.

Resurrection power (John 10:17-18). {For the third and fourth times Jesus said in these verses He was laying down His life for the sheep (cf. vss. 11, 15). But He added an important note here—namely, that He was doing this voluntarily.}Q9 Because of Jesus' obedience unto death, the Father has a special love for Him. This loving relationship is a perfect example of the relationship we should have with God and with each other.

When the time came, the Jewish leaders were putting Jesus to death, and the Romans were the ones carrying it out. Satan surely thought he was gaining the ultimate victory in successfully killing the Son of God. Jesus made it very clear, however, that this was not true. {He voluntarily gave up His own life, and He had the power to take it back again. Since He is God, there is no human or spiritual power that can take His life from Him. He laid it down by His own choice because this was His Father's plan for the redemption of those He created.}Q9

When Jesus was in confrontation with the Pharisees earlier, John wrote that "no man laid hands on him; for his hour was not yet come" (8:20). Though they were standing around wanting in the worst way to take Him, they could not do it. The timing of His death was in accordance with His Father's will.

{Jesus claimed ultimate authority when He said He had the power to take His own life back again after having laid it down in death.}Q10 Once the work of redemption was completed through His death, He could take His life back through His resurrection. We see His deity here, for only God can give life and have the authority Jesus claimed here. He is God, just as His Father is God.

—Keith E. Eggert.

QUESTIONS

1. What factor made it possible for a shepherd to always lead his own sheep out every morning?
2. What did Jesus mean when He referred to Himself as the Door (John 10:7)?
3. Who were the "thieves" (vs. 8) of Jesus' day, and what were they doing to harm the people?
4. How does the sheepfold picture our salvation?
5. What was the difference between a shepherd and a hireling?
6. What do we know about Jesus as our personal Shepherd?
7. How did Jesus illustrate the relationship He has with His sheep?
8. Who are the "other sheep" (vs. 16)?
9. What important truth did Jesus communicate about His death?
10. What did Jesus do that no one else can ever do after death?

—Keith E. Eggert.

Preparing to Teach the Lesson

In our lesson this week we learn how Jesus is our Good Shepherd.

TODAY'S AIM

Facts: to explore Jesus' claim that He is the Good Shepherd.

Principle: to realize that as our Good Shepherd, Jesus cares for us.

Application: to understand that we can have an intimate relationship with Jesus when we know that He is indeed our Good Shepherd.

INTRODUCING THE LESSON

When we have needs, we want someone near us who will be able to meet those needs. The idea of Jesus as our Shepherd comes from the pastoral analogy of a shepherd taking care of his sheep. This means that Jesus takes care of our needs as a shepherd takes care of every need that a sheep has. The shepherd recognizes and does what is needed to meet the needs of all the sheep. When Jesus becomes our Shepherd, we must see Him as the One who loves us and meets all our needs.

DEVELOPING THE LESSON

1. Jesus is the Door of the sheep (John 10:7-10). In order to understand Jesus' analogy here, we must understand that the shepherd in ancient Israel did everything to protect his sheep. Often the shepherd counted his sheep as he herded them into the fold for the night. Then, for purposes of security, he lay across the entry to the fold. Sheep then could not leave the fold, and intruders could not enter it, without the shepherd knowing.

Help the students see that Jesus is that kind of Shepherd for us. He is the Door, the way to salvation. He pointed out to His hearers that those who came before Him were not true shepherds. They were thieves and robbers, who were there only for what they could get out of the sheep and not to care for them. This was a warning to His hearers that they must seek out what is genuine. Only Jesus is the true Shepherd.

The idea that Jesus is the Door or the Gate also indicates that there is no other way to get into the fold. The sheep can enter only through Him. He is that Gate to the fold, where the sheep are safe. If the sheep go through that Gate, the True Shepherd, they will find green pastures. The pastures are a picture of that which truly satisfies the sheep. Help the class see that we are the sheep in this lesson. We must go to Jesus, and through Him find that which ultimately satisfies. There is no other way.

Here Jesus tells us that the thief, or false shepherd, comes only with the purpose of stealing and destroying the sheep. Help the class to see that there are false shepherds around today and that we have to be careful, because they lure away unsuspecting sheep to their destruction. If we know the True Shepherd, we do not have to fear anything. Jesus came to give us abundant life, or life in all its fullness. This is the life God has prepared for us.

Help the class learn how they can differentiate between true and false shepherds today. Emphasize to them that only Jesus can give the fullness of life that God intended for us. The True Shepherd will meet all our needs.

2. Jesus lays down His life for the sheep (John 10:11-13). Here we see another trait of the Good Shepherd. He stops at nothing to protect His sheep, even if it means losing His own life. Jesus did this for the world. He died so that we might live. The one who is a mere hireling does not care for the sheep and will run for cover when danger threatens. He seeks to protect himself. The sheep are not his own, so he does not care. But Jesus owns us and will die to protect us. He truly cares for His own.

Get the class to see the contrast between the good shepherd who cares for the sheep and the hired hand who cares for himself. Show how Jesus will stop at nothing to protect and care for us.

3. The Good Shepherd knows His own sheep (John 10:14-16). I have often seen herds of sheep in India being cared for by various shepherds. When the shepherds make their own calls to their sheep, the herds sort themselves, with each shepherd's sheep following the voice they recognize. It is fascinating to watch how the sheep recognize the voices of their own shepherds.

Jesus compared His relationship with us, His sheep, to His relationship with His Heavenly Father. It is amazing that Jesus knows us in the same intimate way that He knows His Heavenly Father. Help the class grasp the gravity of what Jesus is saying about how much He loves us.

Jesus went on to say that there are other sheep that also must come into the fold. They also need to recognize His voice and become His sheep through faith in Him. Help your students to see that Jesus wants us to share in this task and bring those who do not know Him to recognize His voice and become part of His sheepfold, for there is only one flock and one Shepherd. He wants to be their Shepherd too. Ask the class members to discuss what specific steps they can take to be part of this effort to bring others into the fold.

4. Jesus, the Good Shepherd, came to die for us (John 10:17-18). The Good Shepherd is the special object of God the Father's love because He was willing to voluntarily sacrifice His life for the sheep. He also had the power to take back His life again when He wished. He would rise again for them. This authority came to Him from God the Father. This is the true authority of the Good Shepherd.

Jesus demonstrated that He has the authority to give His life for us and to take it back again. This authority came from God, to whom He was obedient. He was therefore legitimate in His calling, and we do not need to fear that we are following a false shepherd. Help the class see that when we trust Jesus, the Good Shepherd, we cannot go wrong.

ILLUSTRATING THE LESSON

There is only one fold, and only the sheep who enter it are saved. The Door to the sheepfold is the Good Shepherd Himself.

CONCLUDING THE LESSON

Challenge the class to trust the One who cares so much for us. We must train ourselves to know His voice from all the false voices around us. He protects us and cares for us.

ANTICIPATING THE NEXT LESSON

Next week we learn how Jesus is the Resurrection and the Life.

—A. Koshy Muthalaly.

PRACTICAL POINTS

1. The Holy Spirit is our source of discernment as to whether a voice belongs to Jesus (John 10:7-8).
2. Those who come to the Father through Jesus have ready access to all God's goodness (vs. 9).
3. Beware! Satan continually tries to sneak into the church to ruin it in any way he can (vs. 10).
4. In contrast to everyone else, only Jesus is willing to give all for His elect (vs. 11).
5. Hired workers will quit when the work costs them more than they value the pay (vss. 12-13).
6. Those who truly belong to Jesus will instinctively respond only to His leading (vss. 14-18).

—John Lody.

RESEARCH AND DISCUSSION

1. What does it mean to have spiritual discernment? How is it acquired? How is it developed?
2. Satan is our greatest enemy. Has he been prowling around your church?
3. How committed are you to the welfare of God's people? Could anything cause you to forsake your present church? What about the church in general? Meditate on the depth of your commitment.
4. If Christians have the mind of Christ (I Cor. 2:16) and the discernment of the indwelling Holy Spirit (I John 2:20, 27), why do so many Christians get confused about God's will for their lives and fall prey to false teachers (cf. vss. 19, 26)?

—John Lody.

ILLUSTRATED HIGH POINTS

Thieves and robbers (John 10:8)

Salem, Massachusetts, is known for its witch trials three hundred years ago. Recently, the Salem Religious Leaders Association officially welcomed the leader of a Wiccan coven into its ranks.

Jesus had zero tolerance for religious leaders who were intent on destroying His sheep. He called them thieves, robbers, and hirelings. We need to be discerning lest we be tricked by the enemy of our souls.

Know my sheep (vs. 14)

The missionary had shown many pictures of converts. I noticed that I had a hard time keeping track of their names since I had never met them.

I asked the missionary whether he could remember who they all were. He smiled and said that he could.

He could, of course, because he lived and worked with them. They were a part of his life.

Jesus said that just as a shepherd knows each sheep in his flock, so He knows His sheep, for He is the Good Shepherd.

I lay down my life (vs. 17)

Every day, firemen, policemen, soldiers, and others risk their lives to rescue comrades and even strangers. Some do it out of duty; others do it instinctively. Many are successful, but some end up losing their lives.

Jesus came into the world and voluntarily chose to suffer on the cross as our Substitute. This is far more than martyrdom, for Jesus satisfied God's justice and was able to take up His life again (John 10:17). His resurrection guarantees our salvation. Let us give Him thanks.

—David A. Hamburg.

Golden Text Illuminated

"I am the good shepherd: the good shepherd giveth his life for the sheep" (John 10:11).

Our golden text for this week is taken from the last of the seven discourses of Jesus in John's Gospel: the "Good Shepherd" discourse. Fittingly, the main focus of this final discourse before beginning the journey that would lead Him to the cross is that the Good Shepherd gives His life for His sheep.

Jesus was contrasting Himself with false messiahs who had been misleading God's people (cf. Acts 5:34-37). All their ministries had come to naught, and their followers had been scattered. This was because, unlike Jesus, their reason for shepherding people was for their own earthly gain. Their teachings and leadership brought their followers only spiritual ruin and death.

Besides our lesson text for this week, Psalm 23 is famous for giving us an accurate description of the Lord as our Good Shepherd. The Lord always leads His flock into situations where they will find abundant sustenance and resources to grow (vs. 2). By His all-sufficient sacrifice, He restores His people's lost souls, keeping their lives on righteous paths. He does this for the sake of the glory of His most holy name (vs. 3).

Even during the darkest times of their lives, the sheep need never succumb to fear, for the Lord is present with them to protect them and see them safely home. He is their hope and courage in the face of all opposition (vs. 4). Even in the face of great danger from their enemies, He abundantly provides for them because He has sovereignly marked them out as His own precious possessions (vs. 5).

The Lord's love and goodness surrounds His people throughout all the days of their lives, and afterward He welcomes them into eternal pastures where they will forever graze safely under His eternally watchful eyes (vs. 6).

As our Good Shepherd, Christ knows each and every person with all the profound knowledge of the Creator. But beyond this, He also knows those who belong to Him through faith in a special way, marked by His special covenant love of the Good Shepherd.

God's covenant love was extolled throughout the Old Testament, variously translated as His lovingkindness, His mercy, His goodness, or His steadfast love (cf. Ex. 34:6-7; Num. 14:18-19; Ps. 136:1-26; 118:1-4; Lam. 3:22-23). In Hebrew, the word is pronounced kheh-sed; in Greek, the parallel New Testament word is pronounced ah-gah-pay.

It was the Father's covenant love for us that led Him to send Jesus into the world to save us (cf. John 3:16-17). It was this same sovereign covenant love for us that led Jesus to offer Himself as the propitiation for our sins (cf. I John 2:2; 4:10). And crucially, it is this same covenant love of God that is imparted to us through the Holy Spirit, who dwells within us (cf. Rom. 5:5).

It is a special blessing of the new covenant that God's own covenant love is shed abroad in our hearts; for God's love is a transforming love. It is this love that sanctifies us, progressively conforming us to the image of Christ (Rom. 8:29; I Cor. 15:49; Phil. 3:21; I John 3:2) so that our hearts will one day be perfectly conformed to the heart of the Good Shepherd.

—*John Lody.*

Heart of the Lesson

During some evangelistic appeals to non-Christians, Jesus is often referred to as standing at the "door." The Lord knocks, and the sinner must open the door and invite Jesus into his life. Then he will receive eternal life and the forgiveness of sins. Revelation 3:20 is often quoted in this scenario: "Behold, I stand at the door, and knock: if any man hear my voice, and open the door, I will come in to him, and will sup with him, and he with me."

Using the text in this way is not true to its context. The book of Revelation was not written primarily for the purpose of evangelistic appeal. In fact, the opening section of Revelation says that it was written to the Lord's servants, that is, the church (1:1). In chapters 2 and 3, the Lord was addressing certain issues He saw within the church. So we should look at 3:20 as a call to His people for fellowship with Him.

If Jesus is to be referred to as the "door" in an evangelistic sense to non-Christians or in a comforting sense to Christians, John 10:7-18 is where we should look. Thus, as this section of Scripture is considered, three things will be briefly addressed: the way of eternal life, the means of eternal life, and your place in the story.

1. The way of eternal life (John 10:7-10). While many people question the exclusivity of Christianity, Jesus laid all of that to rest when He said, "Verily, verily, I say unto you, I am the door of the sheep. . . . if any man enter in, he shall be saved, and shall go in and out, and find pasture." Jesus Christ is the only way by which anyone can receive eternal life. He is "the" door, not merely "a" door, that people can walk through to "find pasture." All others who came before Jesus and will come after Him to present themselves as a "door" come only to "steal, and to kill, and to destroy."

2. The means of eternal life (John 10:11-15). In order for people from every tribe and nation to receive salvation (Rev. 5:9), Jesus needed to lay His life down for His sheep (John 10:11). He was crucified, He died, and He was buried. As the Apostles' Creed tells us, "The third day He rose again from the dead."

Moreover, by laying down His life for His sheep, He also protects them. "He that is an hireling, and not the shepherd, whose own the sheep are not, seeth the wolf coming, and leaveth the sheep, and fleeth: and the wolf catcheth them, and scattereth the sheep" (vs. 12). Since Jesus is the Good Shepherd, He does not allow the wolf to scatter His sheep. He is with them until the end (Matt. 28:20).

3. Your place in the story (John 10:16-18). Jesus addressed the issue of Gentile inclusion: "And other sheep I have, which are not of this fold." The fold to which Jesus referred are Gentiles. Foretold since the Old Testament, it is now a reality that there is neither Jew nor Gentile in God's sight. We all are one in Christ (Gal. 3:28). Having believed the good news of the gospel, you are a part of that fold, which Jesus said He would gather. He knows you personally, and you know Him (John 10:14). However, for those who have yet to come to faith in Christ, they must see Jesus as the "door" and enter by Him. If they do, they will find pasture just as you have.

—Leon Brown.

World Missions

One of the most touching narratives of foreign missionary work and its cost is found in a book by Robert Coventry Forsyth titled *The China Martyrs of 1900* (Revell). The Boxer Rebellion was an uprising mainly against foreign intervention in Chinese affairs. Gunboat diplomacy—first by Germany, then England, France, Russia, and Japan—had nibbled away at the rich eastern coastal territories of the kingdom. Missionaries and Christian converts were the easy victims of a national reign of terror.

Shansi Province was hardest hit, with 102 adults and 42 children murdered. The book provides 144 photos of the martyred missionaries and their children.

Western military forces restored order in the kingdom. China Inland Mission, which suffered the greatest losses in workers, along with other societies, resumed their labors among the millions of Chinese far from the more civilized eastern region (Forsyth).

The Chinese Communist scourge began to be felt in the back country in the 1930s. John and Betty Stam, Moody Bible Institute graduates and CIM missionaries, were slain as hated foreigners in December 1934.

Two large, indigenous churches began in China in the early 1920s. Interestingly, both groups were planted by missionary women! "The Little Flock" was the work of a native Christian, Watchman Nee, under an English missionary.

The second group, in Chinese *Ye-Su Chia-ting,* meaning Home of Jesus, was the work of Mr. Ching under the influence of Miss Dillenbeck, an American Methodist worker (Rees, *The "Jesus Family" in Communist China,* Christian Literature Crusade).

Dr. Rees, a physician of the China Inland Mission, first went to Mr. Ching's work in Machuang, Shantung Province, in 1921. After the Communist victory in China, Ching invited the doctor to the *Ye-Su Chia-ting* compound in 1948, where he stayed until his expulsion from the country the following year.

Rees found that Ching's great-great-grandfather had purchased the land more than a hundred years before. Trees were planted in a broad belt around the compound and were the sole protection from the outside. In true communal fashion, there were departments, from agriculture to spinning and weaving. Everyone involved was a born-again Christian. Communication was by birdcall. The Christians said even their dogs knew who was born again (Rees).

The center of life in the compound was the chapel. The Communists readily destroyed chapels and churches, but the "Home of Jesus" people used the chapel space for work, which the Communists must have recognized as truly progressive.

Ye-Su homes were self-sufficient, and labor was a trust. Members went from home to chapel at 4:00 A.M. and prayed until 8:00 A.M. Hymns were sung from memory, including Handel's *Messiah* in Chinese! They included birdcalls in their music (Rees).

The Communist regime was unable to find anything to complain about. In fact, some *Ye-Su* procedures were copied for use by government-led communal movements.

Making Christ known throughout northwest China was the primary work of the fellowship. Their missionaries were sent great distances. The *Ye-Su* lived out their Christian faith in every possible way (Rees). They knew and longed to please the Good Shepherd.

—Lyle P. Murphy.

The Jewish Aspect

The shepherd theme is important in the Old Testament as well as the New. That Jesus would describe His messianic purposes in the language of shepherding fits well with prophecies and teachings in the Old Testament, and it also fits well with the culture and people of Israel in His time.

The analogy between God and a shepherd and between the people of Israel and sheep is all over the Old Testament, most famously in Psalm 23. Yet there is a more specific theme of shepherding related directly to the mission of Messiah. This is evident both from reading the Old Testament and looking forward to Jesus and from reading the teachings of Jesus and looking back to the Old Testament.

The first place to look for the shepherd theme in relation to Messiah is in the person and prophetic statements about King David. David was, of course, a shepherd before he was a warrior and king (cf. I Sam. 16:19). God's language of shepherding was used in commissioning David as the king (II Sam. 5:2). David's role as king was a pattern that would be manifested in the Messiah, the ultimate King (7:14-16).

Prophecies of Messiah sometimes speak directly of the connection between Messiah and David. The Messiah is the Branch from David's line who will come (Jer. 23:5; 33:15).

In some prophecies of Ezekiel, it seems unclear at first whether David will be a king ruling with Messiah in the age to come or whether Messiah is called "David" in a symbolic sense. Thus, in Ezekiel 34:24 we read that David will be "a prince among them." Yet it is clear that "David" is symbolically the name of Messiah, since the previous verse also says, "I will set up one shepherd over them" (34:23; cf. 37:24). Messiah is so identified with David that before God revealed the Person and name of Messiah, it was proper to call Messiah "David."

Messiah will be a shepherd, and Israel and the nations will be His sheep. Ezekiel described the people of Israel during the Exile as "scattered, because there is no shepherd" (Ezek. 34:5). The shepherds, or leaders of Israel, in Ezekiel's generation did not search for the flock. They let the flock be eaten by predators. The shepherds fed themselves instead of feeding the sheep (vs. 8). These descriptions are nearly identical to Jesus' description of the hireling in John 10:12: "He that is an hireling, and not the shepherd, whose own the sheep are not, seeth the wolf coming, and leaveth the sheep, and fleeth."

In contrast to these selfish shepherds who do not care for the flock is Messiah. After denouncing the shepherds who let his generation fall into disfavor with God and suffer the judgment of exile, Ezekiel foretold the days of a Good Shepherd, the Messiah: "I will set up one shepherd over them, and he shall feed them" (Ezek. 34:23).

Jesus spoke about His role as a shepherd in other places besides John 10. Jesus came for the "lost sheep of the house of Israel" (Matt. 15:24). A shepherd rejoices more over finding one lost sheep than about ninety-nine that were not lost (18:12-13). At the end of the age, the Son of Man will return and separate the sheep from the goats (25:32). Jesus saw His death as reflected in the prophecy in Zechariah 13:7. Jesus would be stricken down (Matt. 26:31).

Jesus' teaching about His identity and purpose is steeped in Old Testament teachings about the Messiah. Jesus is the Shepherd of Israel and the nations.

—Derek Leman.

Guiding the Superintendent

The two main points we focus on in this week's lesson are the safety and protection Jesus provides for His own and the sacrificial love He has for them as well. The text before us is one of the most beautiful and promising of the entire Gospel of John.

DEVOTIONAL OUTLINE

1. The symbol of a door (John 10:7-10). Here is another instance of "Verily, verily" in John's Gospel, where it is found roughly two dozen times. All of Jesus' words are true, as is all of Scripture, but "Verily, verily" draws attention to what is about to be said: that Jesus is the Door to the fold of His sheep.

Sheepfolds were enclosed with stone walls with an open space as a door. Once the sheep were inside for the night or when a predator was around, the shepherd would stand or lie in the doorway, thus becoming a "door" that protected the sheep. The spiritual lesson behind the words of Jesus and the picture they painted is that believers in Christ, His sheep, would be His charge to provide for and to protect.

The abundant life is one that many people want and search for in many different directions. Some climb over others, some get ulcers, and some do almost anything to get what they think constitutes this good and abundant life. The true abundant life, however, is available only in Jesus and to those who come to Him in repentant faith.

2. The symbol of a shepherd (John 10:11-18). Jesus is not just the Door through which safety and the abundant life are obtained; He is also the Good Shepherd. There are shepherds, and then there are shepherds. Not all of them are good. Some are more concerned about themselves than their sheep and flee at the first sign of danger. Not so with a good shepherd.

Jesus is a shepherd who not only cares for His sheep but also knows and loves them. He knows them, and they know Him. They recognize His voice, and they follow Him. The ultimate act of this Good Shepherd is that He lays down His own life so that His sheep might live.

In verse 16, the other sheep not of "this fold" (Israel) is a reference to the Gentiles who would believe in Him through the preaching of the gospel. Salvation begins with the Jews, but it extends far beyond that tiny plot of ground in the Middle East and far beyond that tiny group of people who are Jews by birth.

The one "fold" of John 10:16 actually references the one "flock" believers become when there is faith in the Good Shepherd, Jesus. The mystery of the church is that Jew and Gentile will be in one body with one Lord (cf. Eph. 3:1-6).

Jesus voluntarily laid down His life for all who will believe—an act that pleased His Father and that the saints of all time remember with great appreciation and devotion. Each Lord's Day the saints gather together to celebrate the Good Shepherd's sacrifice, as well as His resurrection.

CHILDREN'S CORNER

Help children visualize a sheepfold with an open door where Jesus stands. Emphasize His care and protection. Children should learn that sheep follow their shepherd wherever he goes because they trust him to lead them and keep them safe. In the same way, the children can safely trust Jesus and follow Him wherever He leads them.

—*Darrell W. McKay.*

LESSON 11   MAY 14, 2023

Scripture Lesson Text

JOHN 11:17 Then when Jesus came, he found that he had *lain* in the grave four days already.

18 Now Bethany was nigh unto Jerusalem, about fifteen furlongs off:

19 And many of the Jews came to Martha and Mary, to comfort them concerning their brother.

20 Then Martha, as soon as she heard that Jesus was coming, went and met him: but Mary sat *still* in the house.

21 Then said Martha unto Jesus, Lord, if thou hadst been here, my brother had not died.

22 But I know, that even now, whatsoever thou wilt ask of God, God will give *it* thee.

23 Jesus saith unto her, Thy brother shall rise again.

24 Martha saith unto him, I know that he shall rise again in the resurrection at the last day.

25 Jesus said unto her, I am the resurrection, and the life: he that believeth in me, though he were dead, yet shall he live:

26 And whosoever liveth and believeth in me shall never die. Believest thou this?

27 She saith unto him, Yea, Lord: I believe that thou art the Christ, the Son of God, which should come into the world.

NOTES

The Resurrection and the Life

Lesson Text: John 11:17-27

Related Scriptures: Daniel 12:1-3; John 11:1-16, 28-45;
I Corinthians 15:20-26; Philippians 3:7-14

TIME: A.D. 30   PLACE: Bethany

GOLDEN TEXT—"I am the resurrection, and the life: he that believeth in me, though he were dead, yet shall he live" (John 11:25).

Introduction

John 11 records an incident that is perhaps Jesus' greatest miracle, the raising of Lazarus from death.

Jesus could have reached Lazarus sooner after receiving word of his sickness, but He purposely delayed two days (John 11:6). This was going to be quite a lesson for the disciples. He told them this sickness was not unto death but so that the glory of God might be manifested (vs. 4). Finally, two days later, he suggested they all go back to Judea. This instantly caused fear in the hearts of the disciples. The last time He had been there an attempt had been made on His life (10:31-40); surely it was not safe to go back!

Jesus told the disciples that Lazarus was asleep; but after they argued again about going back, He told them plainly that he was dead. He was about to perform a big and impressive miracle to reveal His deity.

LESSON OUTLINE

I. THE TOMB—John 11:17-19

II. THE HOPE—John 11:20-23

III. THE REASSURANCE—John 11:24-27

Exposition: Verse by Verse

THE TOMB

JOHN 11:17 Then when Jesus came, he found that he had lain in the grave four days already.

18 Now Bethany was nigh unto Jerusalem, about fifteen furlongs off:

19 And many of the Jews came to Martha and Mary, to comfort them concerning their brother.

Death and burial (John 11:17). {By the time Jesus arrived in Bethany, Lazarus had already been in his tomb four days. Since it would have taken at least one day to travel there after He waited two extra days before leaving, Lazarus probably was dead by the time Jesus received word of his illness.}^Q1 It is clear that He knew all about what was happening and what He was going to do about it; so He sensed no need to hurry. This was going to give Him an opportunity to reveal Himself in His divine glory.

{It seems that Jesus' primary purpose in not heading immediately to Bethany was for the sake of His disciples. From the concern they expressed and the comments they made, it seems quite certain that they had more to learn before they would be ready to assume their ministries after Jesus was gone.}^Q2 He gradually taught them about Himself so that they would be ready for the days to come.

Maybe some reflection on this scene would be helpful to us. Jesus and His Father are never caught off guard when unexpected things happen in our lives. God never experiences a sense of surprise or panic, because He is always in complete control. We often need to be reminded of this, for when we get hit with unexpected news or suddenly face an unexpected situation, our human nature tends to panic and fear. We need to develop greater trust in God and then focus on Him instead of on our circumstances.

"Some little time before, Jesus . . . had gone into Perea on the east side of the Jordan. . . . At this time a tragedy fell on a Bethany household. . . . Lazarus, the brother of Mary and Martha, became seriously ill, and in their need the sisters turned to the Lord for help. We see their implicit faith in Him in that they told Him, 'The one you love is sick' (John 11:3). They made no specific request. They trusted the Lord to meet the need in response to the message" (Pentecost, *The Words and Works of Jesus Christ*, Zondervan).

That is the kind of trust we need when difficult things unfold. We can pray, thus giving Him the message, and then trust that He will meet the need in response to our prayers. He is a personal, caring Saviour upon whom we can cast our every concern.

Comforting friends (John 11:18-19). The town of Bethany was about two miles east of Jerusalem on the southeast slope of the Mount of Olives and on the road leading to Jericho. {The mention of "many of the Jews" indicates there were people there from Jerusalem as well as Bethany. The close location explains why many friends had traveled there to comfort Lazarus's sisters, Mary and Martha. Such a large number of friends also indicates that this was a rather prominent family in the town. Many were drawn there in this time of need.}^Q3

It was customary for the Jewish people to have lengthy times of mourning following a death, often at least a week. By the time Jesus and His disciples arrived, the mourning had begun. Many people were there to comfort Mary and Martha. The Greek verb means "to come with soothing words," particularly for the purpose of consoling or encouraging. In the minds of everyone present, the death of Lazarus had left his sisters with no hope of ever seeing him alive again. So they were there to provide whatever comfort they could.

One of the greatest joys of being believers in Christ is knowing the comfort we can give one another in times of sorrow. Several years ago a young boy died tragically in a freak accident in North Carolina. The family was fairly new in a community where new families were most often viewed as outsiders because they did not have longterm roots in the area. In an amazing display of Christian love, friends and neighbors came one after another to the home for two days, expressing words of comfort.

How different it is for believers from those without Christ! We have a hope they do not have, the hope of seeing our loved ones again. This is what the apostle Paul meant when he wrote to the Thessalonian believers about the comfort they had concerning loved ones who had died, so that they would "sorrow not, even as others which have no hope" (I Thess. 4:13). What Mary and Martha did not know at the time was that Jesus was coming to give them more than a hope for the future.

THE HOPE

20 Then Martha, as soon as she heard that Jesus was coming, went and met him: but Mary sat still in the house.

21 Then said Martha unto Jesus, Lord, if thou hadst been here, my brother had not died.

22 But I know, that even now, whatsoever thou wilt ask of God, God will give it thee.

23 Jesus saith unto her, Thy brother shall rise again.

A disappointment (John 11:20-21). {As soon as Martha heard that Jesus was coming, she left the house to go meet Him. Mary stayed behind and sat in the house.}[Q4] It was customary for those who were bereaved to remain seated in the house while comforting friends came by to sit with them. No doubt there were tears and sobs and sometimes open wailing (Mark 5:38), but it was a time in which family members were comforted.

This scene fits what we already know about Mary and Martha based on an earlier incident in their lives. Luke 10:38-42 tells of a visit Jesus made to their home. Martha immediately became busy preparing to entertain Him, while Mary quietly sat at His feet and listened to Him teach. When Martha complained that Mary was not helping her, Mary received commendation from the Lord for what she was doing. It seems Mary was a contemplative person, while Martha was an activist. So it was now that the activist immediately left to greet Jesus when she heard He was coming; the contemplative one stayed behind and continued receiving the comforters.

{Martha's first words to Jesus were an expression of regret. She probably knew that Lazarus was dead before Jesus received word of his illness, so this was not a complaint against Him. It was, rather, an expression of confidence.}[Q4] She knew that if Jesus had been there, Lazarus would not have died. Jesus had been known to heal others, so she was confident He also would have healed her brother. Mary later made the same comment (John 11:32). They had strong faith in Jesus in spite of the presence of their own pain.

There are times in our lives when the pain is great and we would like to live in the thought of "if": "If only" we had done something different from what we did; "if only" we had paid better attention to what was going on; "if only" we had been sensible enough to stay away from that dangerous situation that resulted in a tragic consequence. But as it is when we confess our sins and He forgives us and allows us to go on living without guilt, so it is in situations that might have been completely different "if only."

We can go on with life, knowing that our compassionate God is still in control. Martha knew that if Jesus had just been there in time, the circumstances would have been different. Yet she also knew that He was still under the guiding hand of His Father in heaven. We must never lose our faith in God's guidance.

A promise (John 11:22-23). We are unable to tell whether Martha's words in this statement were a request or an expression of faith. Because of what follows, it seems she was not directly asking the Lord to raise Lazarus but rather was expressing her confidence that Jesus' Father was always pleased with Him. If Jesus had been there and asked His Father to spare Lazarus's life, He would have done so. Perhaps in her mind, death was so final she did not consider the possibility of Jesus reversing it, especially after several days.

{Jesus assured Martha that her brother would rise again.}Q5 How different it is for those of us who believe in resurrection than for those who believe death ends everything! {Death is separation. Physical death is the separation of the immaterial part of us from the material. Spiritual death is being separated from God and having no relationship with Him. Eternal death is permanent separation from the presence of God and an eternity spent in hell instead.}Q6 For those without Christ in their lives, death is indeed a frightening thing.

An incident recorded by Kenneth O. Gangel in the *Holman New Testament Commentary: John* (Broadman & Holman) is worth repeating. "On a difficult Sunday evening some twenty years ago I found myself locked in bitter public debate with Madeline Murray O'Hare on a live television broadcast in Miami, Florida. The debate lasted for ninety minutes and was played by no rules other than those the two hostesses made up as we went along. . . .

"One caller asked Mrs. O'Hare, 'In the view of atheism, what happens when I die?' You can imagine the response. Though I do not recall the exact words, Mrs. O'Hare indicated that death presented the absolute end of any existence and the caller need not pay any attention to Christian nonsense about life after death." This unbiblical view cannot stand in light of Jesus' conversation with Martha that day!

THE REASSURANCE

24 Martha saith unto him, I know that he shall rise again in the resurrection at the last day.

25 Jesus said unto her, I am the resurrection, and the life: he that believeth in me, though he were dead, yet shall he live:

26 And whosoever liveth and believeth in me shall never die. Believest thou this?

27 She saith unto him, Yea, Lord: I believe that thou art the Christ, the Son of God, which should come into the world.

Resurrection promised (John 11:24-25). Jesus' statement to Martha did not provide her with any immediate comfort, for she was thinking of resurrection the way the Old Testament refers to it. We would think that she would have heard about the other two times Jesus raised someone from death and realized it could occur again, but of that we cannot be certain. She was no more made hopeful by Jesus' presence than she had been in His absence. Martha was thinking only in terms of the end times, not of something immediate.

{Jesus then made another "I am" statement, the fifth one recorded by John. He stated that He is the Resurrection and the Life. In the face of death, Jesus claimed that He offered everything that could overcome death.}Q7 He Himself would rise from death, but He would also be the source of resurrection for all who die. {Resurrection power is part of who Jesus is, so He could confidently say that even if those who believe in Him die, they will live again. Physical death may come, but eternal death never will.}Q8

Later the apostle Paul said it this way to the Thessalonian believers: "But

I would not have you to be ignorant, brethren, concerning them which are asleep, that ye sorrow not, even as others which have no hope. . . . For the Lord himself shall descend from heaven with a shout, with the voice of the archangel, and with the trump of God: and the dead in Christ shall rise first: then we which are alive and remain shall be caught up together with them in the clouds, to meet the Lord in the air" (I Thess. 4:13, 16-17).

Eternal life promised (John 11:26-27). It would be very difficult for those outside of God's family to understand what Jesus meant when He said, "Whosoever liveth and believeth in me shall never die." Reality reveals to us that everyone who lives on earth dies, without any exceptions. That includes believers as well as unbelievers. So what did Jesus mean?

A. T. Robertson, in *Word Pictures in the New Testament* (Broadman), explained that "shall never die (ou mēapothanē eis ton aiona)" is a "strong double negative" with the word apothnēskō here meaning "spiritual death." Thus, it says quite literally "'shall not die for ever' (eternal death)." In other words, this is in reference to spiritual death instead of physical death, and it is a strong statement that all believers in Jesus Christ will never, ever experience separation from God.

{Once we have become part of God's family through faith in Jesus Christ as our personal Saviour, we will never lose that family relationship. From that moment on, we possess eternal life (cf. John 3:16; 5:24; 10:28).}Q9 Jesus said this: "And I give unto them eternal life; and they shall never perish, neither shall any man pluck them out of my hand. My Father, which gave them me, is greater than all; and no man is able to pluck them out of my Father's hand" (10:28-29).

{Jesus wanted to know whether Martha believed this. Her response was that she did. She revealed a deep, genuine faith in Him when she called Him the Christ and the Son of God who was to come into the world.}Q10 She understood that He was the promised Messiah and that everything was going to be all right with Him in control. Her heart was again at ease, and her faith in Jesus as the Messiah was powerfully vindicated when Jesus miraculously raised Lazarus from the dead.

What about you? Is your heart at ease, knowing that you have eternal life? We will all exist forever, but unbelievers are not going to be with God. They will experience eternal death.

—Keith E. Eggert.

QUESTIONS

1. How long had Lazarus been buried when Jesus got to Bethany, and when had he probably died?
2. Why did Jesus delay His return to Bethany?
3. Why were there so many people at the home, and what does this indicate?
4. Which sister went to Jesus right away, and what did she say to Him?
5. What did Jesus promise Martha?
6. What kinds of death are referred to in Scripture?
7. What "I am" statement did Jesus make at this time, and what was He claiming by it?
8. What did Jesus say about believers dying physically?
9. What did Jesus mean by saying that believers will never die?
10. How did Martha respond to Jesus' question about whether she believed this?

—Keith E. Eggert.

Preparing to Teach the Lesson

For many people, death brings a sense of hopelessness. In this lesson, Jesus offers us Himself as the Resurrection and the Life, the One who has power even over death.

TODAY'S AIM

Facts: to relate the events leading up to the raising of Lazarus from the dead.

Principle: to present Jesus as our Resurrection and Life.

Application: to teach that if we believe in Jesus, we will experience the resurrection and the life to come with Him.

INTRODUCING THE LESSON

Someone rising from the dead is not an everyday event. Even though it happened several times in the Bible, it was still rare and always caught people by surprise. Jesus, however, shows us through the raising of Lazarus from the dead that new life comes from believing in our Lord Jesus, for He is the Resurrection and the Life for us. New life comes from God alone. He is the Author and Giver of life. In this week's lesson, we learn that where Jesus is, there is always the hope of new life.

DEVELOPING THE LESSON

1. Lazarus was already dead (John 11:17-22). The situation in Bethany was far beyond any repair from a human perspective. Lazarus had been dead for four days already, and the corpse was decomposing. Bethany was close to Jerusalem, and so many friends from there had already come to pay their respects to Lazarus and to comfort his sisters, Mary and Martha. But Jesus was not there yet. In fact, He had been in no hurry to get there (vss. 1-15). The time came, though, that Martha heard that Jesus was coming.

While this bit of good news was comforting to the sisters, it seemed to them that Jesus had come too late. Mary waited eagerly at their home for Jesus. Martha went out to meet Him. She seemed upset that He had not shown up earlier, before Lazarus had died. Maybe then something could have been done to keep him from dying. Where was Jesus when they needed Him so badly? Now it seemed He was four days too late!

Help the class see that we all probably have thought that way at some time in the past. In the midst of our crises, God seems to be absent. Ask your students how they would have reacted if they had been in Martha's place. Remember that it was Martha who said to Jesus, "If thou hadst been here, my brother had not died" (John 11:21). Show the class that our God is never late. He is always on time, and as we trust in Him, He is still able to change our situations for the better.

Martha did show some faith and admitted that even though it seemed too late, Jesus could still change things. Read John 11:22 out loud: "But I know, that even now, whatsoever thou wilt ask of God, God will give it thee." Do we believe this? Do our words and actions show that we trust God in our worst situations? Show the class that if ever there was a test of faith, it was here. Jesus was about to teach Martha something vitally important.

2. There is a day of resurrection for all (John 11:23-24). Jesus assured Martha that her brother would rise again. Martha brushed that off with the comment, "I know that he shall rise again in the resurrection at the last day." Her response here may not really be one of deep faith. It was more of a head affirmation of the fact that all people will rise again at the final resurrection. She knew that from going to the synagogue and from her reading of the Prophets.

Many of us are like Martha. Though she believed in the future resurrection, she did not believe that was a possibility for Lazarus in that present moment with Jesus. We have a head affirmation of the truth, but our hearts are sometimes far from believing God's word to us. Help the class see that unlike Martha here, we must trust that He can change our worst predicaments. That is where God glorifies Himself by showing us what He can do. Encourage the students to trust God to do His best work in their lives.

Show the class that our God is a very practical God. Unlike the dead deities of the pagans, the God of the Bible excels in interrupting our lives and surprising us with His goodness because He loves us so much. He does the impossible for us. Challenge the class with this question: How much are you willing to stretch your faith to believe that God can change your situation? Jesus was about to show Martha and Mary that He is indeed the Resurrection and the Life.

3. Jesus is the Resurrection and the Life (John 11:25-27). Jesus' response to Martha's feeble faith was to affirm that He is truly the Resurrection and the Life. He is the source of all life. It did not really matter how long Lazarus had been dead. Jesus could still give life. In fact, all who believe in Jesus will live again forever. Death cannot stop that. Eternal life is given to those who believe in Jesus, who is the only one who can give us life.

Challenge the class to see this simple but very important truth. Jesus asked Martha whether she believed that He is the Giver of life. We need to answer the same question for ourselves. When we believe in Jesus, we too receive eternal life. Help the class to see that death cannot stand in the way of eternal life if we choose to believe in the Author and Giver of life. Jesus is our Resurrection. When we trust Him, He gives us new life inside, a new life that transforms us and endures forever.

ILLUSTRATING THE LESSON

Jesus is the Resurrection and the Life. In Him we can not only look forward to a future resurrection but also have new and eternal life right now.

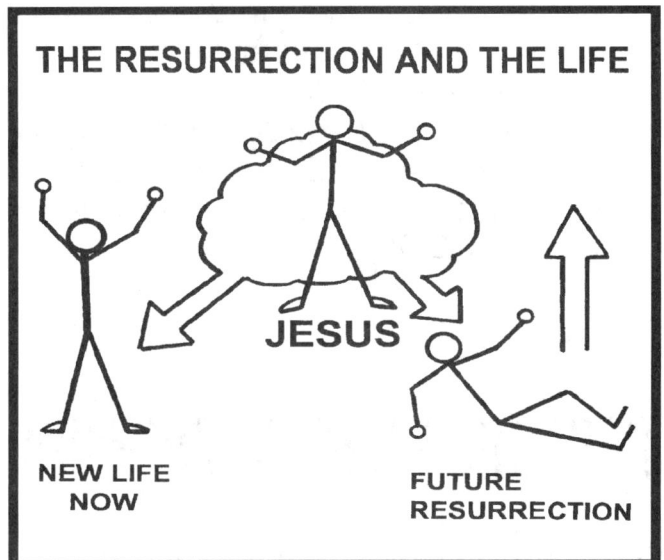

CONCLUDING THE LESSON

Leave the class with the challenge to be certain they have believed in Jesus, the Resurrection and the Giver of life. Without Him, we are spiritually dead and are bound for hell. With Him, we have assurance of future resurrection as well as new life now. He gives us all the resources we need to live a new life in tune with His will. New life comes through believing in Jesus.

ANTICIPATING THE NEXT LESSON

In our lesson next week, we learn how Jesus is the True Vine that gives life to the branches. We must remain in Him if our lives are to have any lasting value.

—A. Koshy Muthalaly.

PRACTICAL POINTS

1. Even in our deaths we can fulfill God's sovereign plan and glorify Him (John 11:17-18).
2. Only Christians have a true hope that comforts and consoles those who mourn (vs. 19).
3. Christians vary in their reactions to the death of a loved one (vs. 20).
4. Jesus is with us, even when we think He is absent (vs. 21).
5. Faith that believes in the power of Christ to right all wrongs is never in vain (vss. 22-24).
6. True faith in Jesus Christ is never a mere mental or academic exercise; it is a matter of life and death (vss. 25-27)!

—John Lody.

RESEARCH AND DISCUSSION

1. Lazarus's death was allowed in order to bear witness to Jesus' power. How does this violate most people's expectation of what God is like?
2. How are Christians uniquely equipped to deal with the most profound tragedies of life?
3. Do all Christians react to death the same way? Should they, given the content of our faith?
4. During times when we feel God is far away from us, is He really? What does it mean to feel God's presence? Discuss the validity of feeling close to or far from God's presence.
5. What is the relationship between doctrines of faith and the practices of daily Christian living?

—John Lody.

ILLUSTRATED HIGH POINTS

Four days already (John 11:17)

Many have said, "God's delays are not denials." God always has a perfect plan, and He reveals it step-by-step in order to show us who Jesus is.

We tend to be impatient. We want God to do the things we think are best right now! But look back on your life and review times when you were disappointed but later God provided something or someone far better.

If thou hadst been here (vs. 21)

Needlepoint and weaving help us understand God's perspective on our trials. He is omniscient; so He knows what He is doing as He gives us His best. An anonymous poem, "My Life Is but a Weaving" brings out these thoughts.

> My life is but a weaving
>   Between my Lord and me.
> I cannot choose the colors.
>   He worketh steadily.
> Oft times He weaveth sorrow.
>   And I in foolish pride
> Forget He sees the upper,
>   And I, the underside.
> Not till the loom is silent
>   And the shuttles cease to fly
> Shall God unroll the canvas
>   And explain the reason why.
> The dark threads are as needful
>   In the Weaver's skillful hand
> As the threads of gold and silver
>   In the pattern He has planned.

Thy brother shall rise again (vs. 23)

If Jesus were to bring Lazarus back to life today, surely someone would record a video and post it on social media.

Would people believe? Some would, but there would always be some like the first-century religious leaders. Although they could not deny the reality of the miracle, they chose to reject the Saviour (cf. John 11:47-53) and tried to eliminate Lazarus (12:9-11).

—David A. Hamburg.

Golden Text Illuminated

"I am the resurrection, and the life: he that believeth in me, though he were dead, yet shall he live" (John 11:25).

Where is Jesus when you need Him? Have you ever felt that way? He can supply all your need. That is what Philippians 4:19 says. But where was He when your bills came due this month? What part of the verse did you misunderstand? He will never leave you or forsake you. That promise is still in Hebrews 13:6. So why is it that your prayers seem to bounce off the ceiling? Why do you feel so lonely? Where is Jesus when you need Him?

Mary and Martha must have felt that way when Lazarus died. They were close friends with Jesus. They thought He cared about them, but His actions did not seem to indicate it. He did not arrive until four days after Lazarus's death. What is worse is that He had delayed His trip to Bethany, where Lazarus lived with his sisters. The passage makes that clear. "When he had heard therefore that [Lazarus] was sick, he abode two days still in the same place where he was. Then after that saith he to his disciples, Let us go into Judaea again" (John 11:6-7). It looked like pretty bad timing.

Understand this about God's timing, though. It is always perfect, but it does not always align with our schedules. God does not always show up when we think He must. Take a look at Habakkuk 2:3: "For the vision is yet for an appointed time, but at the end it shall speak, and not lie: though it tarry, wait for it; because it will surely come, it will not tarry." If ever there were a verse that seemed to contradict itself, this is it. Notice the words "though it tarry . . . it will not tarry." You cannot have it both ways. Either it will tarry, or it will not. How do we explain the apparent conflict?

There is a difference between God's outlook on time and our own. He is an eternal Being, without beginning or end. He is not just Someone out there with a lot of time on His hands. He is actually outside of time and space. Time does not affect Him. That is why He could tell Habakkuk that the fulfillment of the vision would not tarry. There is no "slow" to God, for He is not affected by time.

The apostle Peter described it this way: "But, beloved, be not ignorant of this one thing, that one day is with the Lord as a thousand years, and a thousand years as one day. The Lord is not slack concerning his promise, as some men count slackness; but is longsuffering to us-ward, not willing that any should perish, but that all should come to repentance" (II Pet. 3:8-9).

God is not subject to time. However, Habakkuk was. That is why God said, "Though it tarry (from your perspective, Habakkuk) . . . it will not tarry (from My divine perspective)."

There are two things we need to remember when life bombards us with questions. First, we are no longer in Eden. The garden is gone. The sweet smell of flowers has been overwhelmed by the smell of brimstone. We now live in a cursed world. Believers and unbelievers alike suffer the effects on our world.

Second, we are not yet in eternity. While we may know the One who is the "resurrection, and the life," we have not yet experienced resurrection. We are not home yet, and we "groan, earnestly desiring to be clothed upon with our house which is from heaven" (II Cor. 5:2).

—*Joseph E. Falkner.*

Heart of the Lesson

Although over 150,000 people die every day, death is an unnatural phenomenon. Humans were not created to die. In the garden, Adam was made perfect, without sin or death. After his fall into sin, physical and spiritual death was the result. For thousands of years to come, men, women, and children would die, some violently, others peacefully. But death is always a painful event, especially when someone who is close to you dies.

Martha the sister of Mary had firsthand experience with death, namely, the death of her brother. "Then said Martha unto Jesus, Lord, if thou hadst been here, my brother had not died" (John 11:21). This event was painful not only for Martha but also for Jesus (vs. 35); but death is not the end of the story.

1. Martha's initial response (John 11:17-22). Martha and her sister Mary were offered comfort by the Jews over the death of their brother. While this may have provided a temporary comfort, once Martha heard that Jesus was coming, she sought ultimate comfort in her Lord. Martha believed that if Jesus had been there, her brother would not have died. Where was her trust? It was in Christ, for she knew that whatever He asked of God, He would receive. And that included the resurrection of her brother.

2. Jesus' response and Martha's final response (John 11:23-27). The Lord was confident that Martha's brother would rise again. In fact, He further emphasized this as He said, "I am the resurrection, and the life: he that believeth in me, though he were dead, yet shall he live. And whosoever liveth and believeth in me shall never die." Jesus Christ is the Resurrection and the Life. Not only would Christ rise from the dead, but He would also make a provision through His sacrifice to ensure that all those who believe in Him would also be raised.

Martha's initial concern was for her brother. Her final concern demonstrated her confession of faith, which encompassed her initial concern, for to believe in Christ is to realize that He is sovereign over all things and will accomplish what He wills for His good pleasure and purpose.

Jesus asked her, "Believest thou this?" (vs. 26). "She saith unto him, Yea, Lord: I believe that thou art the Christ, the Son of God, which should come into the world" (vs. 27). She believed that Jesus was the Son of God who came into the world to save His people from their sins. She believed this for her brother as well. It was just that in the midst of her pain over the death of her brother, she believed that it was not quite his time to die. Indeed, it was not (cf. vss. 28-44). Jesus would raise Lazarus from the dead, and the glory of God would be displayed.

In Christ, you have been spiritually raised from the dead. At one point you were dead in your trespasses and sins, and now you have been made alive in Christ. What a privilege it is to know that the Lord, who is the Resurrection and the Life, loved you enough to die and rise for you! Now you, along with the universal church, await the physical resurrection from the dead. When that day comes, there will no longer be any pain, suffering, trials, or discomfort, for all that the Scriptures speak of, from Genesis to Revelation, will be fully realized in heaven. Are you excited? Do you anticipate that day?

—Leon Brown.

World Missions

Some years ago, we sketched the life of Dr. Andrew P. Stirrett of the Sudan Interior Mission. An outstanding man of God, Dr. Stirrett was in active professional service and worked as a pharmacist with two shops. But early in life, he had felt the stirrings of missionary service. He read of the great need in the Sudan. In this forbidding region, six hundred miles wide and stretching over thirteen hundred miles north to south, some forty million people lived (Percy, *Stirrett of the Sudan*, Sudan Interior Mission).

Our earlier study of the doctor largely dealt with his tremendous medical work in Nigeria. He practiced and taught missionary medicine, including case studies of the vast number of deadly tropical diseases that afflicted the native population. His studies provided missionary medical personnel an invaluable reference source.

Stirrett was rather short and walked with a stiff-kneed gait, compounded by heavy boots he wore for his forty-six years on the field. He dressed in shirt, tie, and coat and once was known to wear full-length underwear! From his earliest days in the Sudan, he wore a large, felt-lined hat and carried a parasol.

Stirrett was an action-filled personality. He walked great distances, often leaving younger missionaries panting for breath. His diet was designed for the most healthful value. Guinea corn porridge was a daily habit through all his years on the field. He often added spinach and carrots. In later years, he added two Spanish onions a day.

He spent morning after morning on his knees in prayer. This routinely began at 3:45 A.M. He rushed off to a prayer meeting with Africans at 8:00 A.M. His prayer was mainly for the Hausa people, but he did not neglect prayer for special needs and for other missionaries. The Mission reported that Stirrett preached twenty thousand messages to an estimated 1,500,000 people. Yet, he continued ministering physically to three hundred each day.

Dr. Stirrett was a Hausa language scholar. He knew its grammar and intonation and spoke the tongue fluently. In 1910, he was added to the standing literature commission and later was one of the most faithful members of the translation committee. It must have been difficult to wait until November 1932, when the British and Foreign Bible Society sent the first shipment of Hausa Bibles. Percy wrote, "He held one copy lovingly in his hands, seeing a new day dawn for the furtherance of the gospel in Nigeria."

In addition to his work on the Bible, Stirrett produced a cross-reference volume and a chapter-by-chapter exposition. In the host of Christian schools throughout the land, Bible teaching was done in the Old Testament in the morning and the New Testament in the afternoon.

Stirrett was especially noted for his work in the market of the central city of Jos, Nigeria. He preached there every day, rain or shine, standing on a rock that elevated him above his listeners. He preached on sin and righteousness and judgment to come. Jesus was proclaimed as the "resurrection, and the life" (John 11:25).

On one occasion, a Muslim hurled a rock at the doctor. It took his helmet off, but he was uninjured. Other lost men went for the assailant. "Do not go after him; come and speak to the Lord of life," cried Stirrett. Dr. Stirrett gave his life for the salvation of the souls of Africa.

—*Lyle P. Murphy.*

The Jewish Aspect

The discussion between Jesus and Martha in John 11 is filled with Jewish ideas about the afterlife and the future hopes of Israel. It is not just a Christian idea that God will raise His people from the grave and that there will be a life to come. The Christian truth in Jesus' words is that He and He alone is the Resurrection. Yet the discussion between Martha and Jesus occurred before the New Testament was written, and it reflects Jewish concepts derived from the Old Testament and discussed further in other Jewish writings.

Jesus offered Martha comfort, saying her brother would rise again (John 11:23). This hope of the body being raised to a full existence, body and soul—not just a disembodied spirit in the underworld as in pagan thought—is the subject of several prophecies in the Old Testament. Isaiah spoke of bodies in the dust waking and singing (Isa. 26:19). And Daniel spoke of those sleeping in the dust waking to everlasting life and shining like stars (Dan. 12:2-3).

One of the later Jewish writings, II Maccabees, from about 124 B.C., states the hope of bodily resurrection very clearly in more than one place. For example, there is a story of a mother and her seven sons being executed for refusing to disobey God's laws and eat unclean meat. One of the sons says to his executioner, "You dismiss us from this present life, but the King of the universe will raise us up to an everlasting renewal of life, because we have died for His laws" (7:9) (Wright, *Resurrection of the Son of God,* Fortress).

Jewish writings from slightly before and during the New Testament era are filled with talk about bodily resurrection. One text even mentions the timing of the resurrection as "on the last day," much as Martha spoke of her belief that Lazarus would be raised "at the last day" (John 11:24). In the Apocalypse of Moses, a writing whose exact date is uncertain, the writer imagined God speaking to the dead body of Adam, saying, "I shall raise you on the last day in the resurrection with every man of your seed" (Wright).

Martha thought that this kind of comfort was what Jesus was offering her. When Jesus clarified that He was the source of resurrection, Martha began to understand. Her reply (John 11:27) makes perfect sense in Jewish thinking. She believed Jesus because she was convinced that He was the Messiah. What does Jesus' identity as the Messiah have to do with the future resurrection?

The coming of Messiah is part of the future hope of Israel, along with the resurrection of the dead. The idea that Messiah would come, that the dead would be raised, and that there would be a renewed world (a new heavens and earth) is the basic outline of that hope (cf. Isa. 65:17).

Pagan cultures surrounding Israel believed in a dark underworld where people live on as shades or ghosts, with only parts of their minds and souls. Some Greeks developed a belief in reincarnation, or the recycling of souls into new people. Some developed a belief in a place of blessing and a corresponding place of torment for the souls of people after death. Only the Old Testament, Judaism, and then Christianity developed a belief in a physical afterlife.

To Martha, if Jesus was the Messiah, then the time of resurrection could be near. Martha knew that in the days of Messiah, God "will swallow up death in victory" and "wipe away tears from off all faces" (Isa. 25:8).

—Derek Leman.

Guiding the Superintendent

Death is a fact of life that intrudes into every family at one time or another. When death touches a family, various reactions arise, depending on numerous factors, such as the closeness of the relationship, the age and previous health of the deceased, and the presence or absence of faith. Typically speaking, where there is a strong Christian faith, a sense of celebration is as much present as that of sorrow. Jesus makes all the difference.

DEVOTIONAL OUTLINE

1. Faith in a time of sorrow (John 11:17-22). Jesus had been notified of Lazarus's condition while at a place some distance from Lazarus's hometown of Bethany. He did not hasten back to intervene in this crisis, for as with the man born blind (cf. chap. 9), what had happened to Lazarus had happened for the glory of God. Jesus and His disciples did go to Bethany, but they arrived four days after Lazarus's death.

Before Jesus arrived at the house where Lazarus's sisters Mary and Martha were, along with many friends and mourners, word of His coming preceded Him, and Martha hastened out to meet Him. As deep as her hurt was when Jesus had not hurried back to be with Lazarus, and as deep as her sorrow was in her brother's death, she still had faith that Jesus could perform a miracle.

Here is the beauty of faith in Christ. It survives the rough spots in life, even the taking of a loved one in death.

2. Promise in the place of sympathy (John 11:23-24). Instead of apologizing and telling Martha He was sorry for His tardy appearance and for what had happened to Lazarus, Jesus gave her a promise: "Thy brother shall rise again."

When we have an opportunity to visit believers who have lost loved ones to death, the reminder of the promise of Scripture that death for a believer is not permanent can bring a great sense of comfort, encouragement, and hope to those who remain behind. There is nothing wrong in weeping with those who weep, but we also need to point to the great and sure hope we have in Christ.

3. Affirmation in the Person of God's Son (John 11:25-27). The well-known pronouncement of Jesus that He is "the resurrection, and the life" and that those who believe in Him will live even though they die has brought comfort to millions as they faced their own demise and to their survivors as well.

Jesus questioned Martha as to the extent of her faith in Him, and she responded with a strong and firm affirmation of the Person and deity of Christ. This was not some quickly contrived response to being put on the spot by a straightforward question; it came from the very depths of her soul.

As others have pointedly said, either Jesus is who He said He was—the Son of God—or He was a liar and a fraud. We know He was not a liar or a fraud.

CHILDREN'S CORNER

Lead children to know that Jesus can help them deal with the mystery of death. First, they can know that if their loved one was a believer, he or she is now safely with Jesus. Second, they can know that even though they miss that person terribly, Jesus is with them and they can turn to Him for help and comfort. He will not fail them.

—Darrell W. McKay

LESSON 12   MAY 21, 2023

Scripture Lesson Text

JOHN 15:1 I am the true vine, and my Father is the husbandman.

2 Every branch in me that beareth not fruit he taketh away: and every *branch* **that beareth fruit, he purgeth it, that it may bring forth more fruit.**

3 Now ye are clean through the word which I have spoken unto you.

4 Abide in me, and I in you. As the branch cannot bear fruit of itself, except it abide in the vine; no more can ye, except ye abide in me.

5 I am the vine, ye *are* the branches: He that abideth in me, and I in him, the same bringeth forth much fruit: for without me ye can do nothing.

6 If a man abide not in me, he is cast forth as a branch, and is withered; and men gather them, and cast *them* **into the fire, and they are burned.**

7 If ye abide in me, and my words abide in you, ye shall ask what ye will, and it shall be done unto you.

8 Herein is my Father glorified, that ye bear much fruit; so shall ye be my disciples.

9 As the Father hath loved me, so have I loved you: continue ye in my love.

10 If ye keep my commandments, ye shall abide in my love; even as I have kept my Father's commandments, and abide in his love.

11 These things have I spoken unto you, that my joy might remain in you, and *that* your joy might be full.

12 This is my commandment, That ye love one another, as I have loved you.

13 Greater love hath no man than this, that a man lay down his life for his friends.

14 Ye are my friends, if ye do whatsoever I command you.

15 Henceforth I call you not servants; for the servant knoweth not what his lord doeth: but I have called you friends; for all things that I have heard of my Father I have made known unto you.

16 Ye have not chosen me, but I have chosen you, and ordained you, that ye should go and bring forth fruit, and *that* **your fruit should remain: that whatsoever ye shall ask of the Father in my name, he may give it you.**

17 These things I command you, that ye love one another.

NOTES

The True Vine

Lesson Text: John 15:1-17

Related Scriptures: Isaiah 5:1-7; 27:2-6; Colossians 2:6-10; I John 2:24-29

TIME: A.D. 30　　　　　　　　　　　　　　　　　　　PLACE: Jerusalem

GOLDEN TEXT—"I am the vine, ye are the branches: He that abideth in me, and I in him, the same bringeth forth much fruit: for without me ye can do nothing" (John 15:5).

Introduction

The time for Jesus' crucifixion was rapidly drawing near. He had just celebrated the Passover with His disciples in the upper room (John 13:1). Judas had been identified as the traitor of the Lord and had left the group. After the instructions in chapter 14, Jesus said, "Arise, let us go hence" (vs. 31), indicating that it was time to leave.

The teachings in chapters 13 through 17 are often referred to as the Upper Room Discourse. There is a disagreement among Bible scholars concerning when the Lord Jesus and the disciples actually left the upper room. Some think they left as soon as Jesus said they should go.

If Jesus was going to leave, how could the disciples be certain they would stay true to Him in the future, when He was no longer there to give immediate guidance? The remainder of this discourse seems to address this concern in great detail.

LESSON OUTLINE

I. A COMMAND TO ABIDE—
John 15:1-8

II. A COMMAND TO LOVE—
John 15:9-17

Exposition: Verse by Verse

A COMMAND TO ABIDE

JOHN 15:1　I am the true vine, and my Father is the husbandman.

2　Every branch in me that beareth not fruit he taketh away: and every branch that beareth fruit, he purgeth it, that it may bring forth more fruit.

3　Now ye are clean through the word which I have spoken unto you.

4　Abide in me, and I in you. As the branch cannot bear fruit of itself, except it abide in the vine; no more can ye, except ye abide in me.

5　I am the vine, ye are the branches: He that abideth in me, and I in him, the same bringeth forth much fruit: for without me ye can do nothing.

6　If a man abide not in me, he is

cast forth as a branch, and is withered; and men gather them, and cast them into the fire, and they are burned.

7 If ye abide in me, and my words abide in you, ye shall ask what ye will, and it shall be done unto you.

8 Herein is my Father glorified, that ye bear much fruit; so shall ye be my disciples.

Bearing more fruit (John 15:1-2). Psalm 80:8-16 gives a clear analogy of Israel as God's vine. God had removed other nations, planted Israel there instead, watched her grow and spread throughout the land, and then destroyed her. This psalm is a prayer for her restoration. Isaiah 5:1-7 describes Israel as a vineyard that was planted and nurtured by God, only to bring forth wild grapes. The lack of production by His vineyard caused God great disappointment. He said He would punish her, laying her waste and letting weeds grow within her.

{With the proliferation of grapevines in Israel, the disciples could easily understand Jesus' message. He is the True Vine, producing for His Father what the nation had not. His Father is the farmer caring for his vineyard. Believers in Jesus are the branches He said are "in me" (John 15:2).}Q1 Israel had been God's choice vine, upon which He had lavished a great deal of care. Since the Jews had not produced righteousness, God sent the "true vine" (vs. 1) to accomplish His work. Jesus was going to show the world for Him what the nation had failed to show.

The farmer (God) takes special interest in the branches. {Those that do not produce he "taketh away" (vs. 2). The Greek word here can mean "to lift," and since the branches are said to be in Christ, some take the interpretation that it refers to true believers. It might picture the farmer seeing a branch hanging close to the ground, unable to produce and needing to be lifted up so that it can.}Q2 Those already bearing fruit, however, are pruned so that they will bear even more. It is clear that God works with His own in ways that make them more righteous.

Abiding in the Vine (John 15:3-4). When Jesus said to His disciples, "Now ye are clean through the word which I have spoken unto you," He was adding to the thought of pruning. {He indicated that they had already been cleansed by the pruning process. "Pruning" refers to cutting a plant back in order to give the opportunity for new and fresh growth.}Q3 The process God uses in pruning His children is at times very painful. It is through suffering and pain that we often grow the most and become more godly and productive.

{The disciples had been through a lot with Jesus and had learned a great deal by listening to Him. If they wanted to continue to be spiritually fruitful, they needed to continue to be godly and obedient to His instruction.}Q4 To abide in Him refers to a constant and continuous effort to be in right relationship with Him. God does not want a person to be godly one day and sinful the next. The Christian life must be consistent if the believer is going to be fruitful. This is not a passive, do-nothing approach to life, but an active and diligent walk with Jesus.

Jesus then went back to His analogy of the vine. On a grapevine, or any other greenery, a branch cannot bear fruit if it does not stay anchored in the vine or trunk. This is just as true of an apple tree, for example. If a branch becomes severed from the trunk in any way, it will no longer produce apples. Nor can a Christian be righteous without staying connected to Jesus Christ. Each one of us must live in the light of our understanding of what He expects of us as His children. In that way we will live godly, fruitful lives.

Chastening for disobedience (John 15:5-6). There is a progression of thought in Jesus' words. He spoke first of no fruit, then of "fruit" and "more fruit" (vs. 2), and now of "much fruit" (vs. 5). Once again He clarified, "I am the vine, ye are the branches." It is only the person who abides in Him who will be able to bear "much fruit." The reason is that apart from Him, His followers can do nothing spiritually. The gradation of production should encourage us to want to be just as close to Him as we possibly can be.

Does all this not cause us to wonder how effective we could be in our Christian lives if we consistently lived in an intimate relationship with Jesus? It would be good for us to ask honestly, "How fruitful am I in God's eyes?" Far too many believers attempt to be right with God while at the same time staying close to the world and its lack of spiritual standards.

{Verse 6 has been interpreted in a number of ways. Since the context is about branches in the vine, it seems to refer to those who do know the Lord. Perhaps the casting out speaks of a loss of fellowship, the withering to a loss of spiritual vitality, the vitality that is part of being in a right relationship with Christ, and the burning to the loss of reward at the time of judgment. Some think a better interpretation is to view this as referring to professing believers who are not truly saved and are judged accordingly.}Q5

Receiving what is requested (John 15:7-8). "How do we let Jesus' words abide in us? The word abide implies intimate knowledge of what a person has said. But it also implies that the words become a vital part of the way a believer lives. So Jesus' words abide in us when we know what he said and did, and when we allow those words and actions to affect the way we live. By reading and memorizing we take in God's Word; by obeying we indicate that the words abide in us" (Osborne, ed., *Life Application Bible Commentary,* Tyndale).

{One of the most encouraging aspects of abiding in Christ is the reality of answered prayer.}Q6 Often we hear complaints about God not really caring and not answering prayer, but such complaints perhaps indicate a lack of abiding on the part of the complainer. The person who abides in Christ knows the mind of Christ and as a result has a more effective prayer life. This leads to a display of the working of God that results in Him receiving glory. As others see our walk with Him and witness answered prayer, God is honored.

The concept of bearing fruit must include two ideas, one of which is the leading of others to saving faith in Jesus Christ. The other is found in Galatians 5:22-23, which says, "But the fruit of the Spirit is love, joy, peace, longsuffering, gentleness, goodness, faith, meekness, temperance: against such there is no law." Jesus wants His followers to show others the way of salvation, but He also wants to see godliness displayed in their lives.

A COMMAND TO LOVE

9 As the Father hath loved me, so have I loved you: continue ye in my love.

10 If ye keep my commandments, ye shall abide in my love; even as I have kept my Father's commandments, and abide in his love.

11 These things have I spoken unto you, that my joy might remain in you, and that your joy might be full.

12 This is my commandment, That ye love one another, as I have loved you.

13 Greater love hath no man than this, that a man lay down his life for his friends.

14 Ye are my friends, if ye do whatsoever I command you.

15 Henceforth I call you not servants; for the servant knoweth not what his lord doeth: but I have called you friends; for all things that I have heard of my Father I have made known unto you.

16 Ye have not chosen me, but I have chosen you, and ordained you, that ye should go and bring forth fruit, and that your fruit should remain: that whatsoever ye shall ask of the Father in my name, he may give it you.

17 These things I command you, that ye love one another.

Abiding in Jesus' love (John 15:9-10). Can we possibly comprehend the truth that the way God the Father loves His Son is the way Jesus loves us? The depth of that love is far beyond our understanding and ability to grasp. We are loved by Jesus in the same way Jesus is loved by God! In a few verses we will get a glimpse of how great that love is. The thought of such great love for us should cause a response of deep love for our Saviour. We should be totally dedicated and committed to loving and serving Him.

If we fully comprehended the love of which we speak, we would indeed abide in that love. At this point Jesus explained succinctly exactly what that abiding entails: "If ye keep my commandments, ye shall abide in my love; even as I have kept my Father's commandments, and abide in his love" (vs. 10). The emphasis is on obedience to Jesus' commands. There is no mystical secret to abiding in the love of Jesus; it is simply a matter of listening to Him, learning what He wants us to be and do.

What is the example Jesus gave? It is His own obedience to His Father. The very fact that He came to earth knowing it was for the purpose of dying for our sins gives evidence of His willing obedience. The price Jesus paid for our redemption, in obedience to His Father's will, should never cease to be an incentive for our obedience to Him.

Loving as Jesus loves (John 15:11-13). {Here is another blessing that is a result of abiding in Jesus: it yields the presence of joy in our lives.}Q7 Jesus does not expect His followers to grudgingly and dutifully carry out His wishes while longing for life to end so that we can be delivered! He wants His children to have His joy within themselves, resulting in what He called a "full" joy.

The word "full" is a translation of the Greek word *plēroō,* which means "to cause to abound" or "to fill to the top." The joy Jesus wants His followers to have is a joy that fills their lives completely, to the point where it is ready to spill over. Why should we ever resent being told we must be obedient to Christ? Our obedience will result in a greater joy than anything else in life can give.

{The real test is now given: not only are we to respond by loving Jesus, but we are also to love one another in the same way Jesus loves us.}Q8 What a difference it would make in our churches if we fulfilled this command of Christ! If we loved and forgave as He loves and forgives, the petty bickerings that cause dissension and hurt feelings among believers would disappear. {Jesus set the standard as high as it could go by saying that there is no greater love possible than that which is shown when a person gives his life for his friends (vs. 13).}Q9

We sometimes hear of people giving their lives so that someone else can live. Is this our attitude toward fellow believers, or are we at times glad they are gone? Jesus is the greatest example of all, for He willingly laid down His life on the cross for every one of us.

Learning from Jesus' love (John 15:14-15). In the opening statement in his letter to the Romans, Paul called himself "a servant of Jesus Christ, called to be an apostle, separated unto the gospel of God" (1:1). The word for "servant" is a word that means slave.

{Paul was a voluntary slave for Jesus, as we should be. While we are in one sense slaves of Christ, we are also His friends as we live in obedience to Him. He could say this to His disciples because He had told them everything God had revealed to Him.}Q10

One Old Testament personality was called a friend of God. "And the scripture was fulfilled which saith, Abraham believed God, and it was imputed unto him for righteousness: and he was called the Friend of God" (Jas. 2:23). King Jehoshaphat knew this, as revealed in one of his prayers: "Art not thou our God, who didst drive out the inhabitants of this land before thy people Israel, and gavest it to the seed of Abraham thy friend for ever?" (II Chr. 20:7).

The thing that showed Abraham to be a friend of God was God's sharing of intimate matters with him. Friends are those who reveal their hearts and innermost thoughts to one another. God has revealed His mind and desires to His children. While the thoughts expressed here were given first to His disciples, it is accurate to apply the same truths to ourselves. We have become His followers and desire to learn from Him just as His disciples did. The universal principles He was teaching them will also make us what God wants us to be.

Blessings through Jesus' love (John 15:16-17). Although it was common for followers to choose which teacher they wanted to learn from, Jesus reminded His disciples that in His case He had done the choosing, personally calling each of them to follow Him. Later in his life the apostle John wrote, "Herein is love, not that we loved God, but that he loved us, and sent his Son to be the propitiation for our sins" (I John 4:10). We also have a relationship with God because He initiated it. In each case, however, the choosing was just the beginning. He wants fruit from us.

The disciples were chosen and appointed to spread the gospel, bearing fruit for God's kingdom. We have been chosen and placed as branches in the Vine, Jesus, with the expectation that there will be fruit for Him. In the process of bearing fruit, we have the promise that we can ask for what we need and receive it. God will respond to the needs we present that are relative to getting His message out to those who do not know Him.

Jesus always remains central, for even our prayers should be presented to the Father in His name. Above all, we must remember His pressing command: we who are His children should love each other, even sacrificially.

—Keith E. Eggert.

QUESTIONS

1. Who was Jesus referring to when He spoke of the vine, the husbandman, and the branches?
2. What might it mean that God takes away unfruitful branches?
3. What does God do to give His children further opportunity for spiritual growth?
4. What is necessary if a Christian is going to produce spiritual fruit for the Lord?
5. What does it mean for God to take the unfruitful branches and cast them into the fire?
6. What is one rewarding result that comes from abiding in Christ?
7. What is a second rewarding result?
8. In what way did Jesus say that believers should love one another?
9. What is the highest standard of love that can be shown to anyone?
10. How can we be both a slave and a friend of our Lord?

—Keith E. Eggert.

Preparing to Teach the Lesson

Jesus described Himself through various analogies. In this lesson, we examine the passage in John in which Jesus declared Himself to be the True Vine and His followers to be the branches.

TODAY'S AIM

Facts: to explore John 15:1-17, a passage that deals with Jesus' productive relationship with His followers and His followers' loving relationship with each other.

Principle: to emphasize the need for Christians to maintain an intimate and meaningful relationship with Christ.

Application: to exhort Christians to cultivate the kind of relationship with Christ that bears fruit in their lives.

INTRODUCING THE LESSON

Rose loves to grow tomatoes. In the fall she harvests and dries her seeds. In the early spring she carefully plants the precious seeds in disposable cups, which she sets along her window ledge. When the snow has melted and the soil in the garden has warmed, Rose transplants her healthy little tomato plants to their new outdoor home.

As the growing season progresses, Rose keeps a watchful eye over her garden. She pulls weeds, loosens soil, and adds fertilizer and water as necessary. As the vines grow, she fastens them to trellises. She prunes them frequently, cutting off the tops of the plants and the little branches at the base of the leaves so that the ripening fruit can get all the necessary nutrients. In the late summer, Rose begins to enjoy the results of her close and careful relationship to her plants.

Jesus called Himself the True Vine, with His followers being the branches. The relationship of vine to branches teaches us much about our relationship to Christ and to each other.

DEVELOPING THE LESSON

1. The branch-to-Vine relationship (John 15:1-11). "I am the true vine" is the last of Jesus' seven "I am" statements in John. Let the class know that Isaiah, Jeremiah, Ezekiel, and Hosea had referred to Israel as God's vine. That vine had produced bad fruit. This background adds meaning to Jesus' statement "I am the true vine."

Jesus said, "Every branch in me that beareth not fruit he taketh away" (vs. 2). One view is that this refers to those who followed Jesus superficially and were not truly His disciples. Fruit-bearing indicates life. Those who did not bear fruit were dead branches and not truly Jesus' disciples. Many today profess Christ, but their lives do not bear fruit (cf. Matt. 7:21).

Describe what it means to "purge" the vine (John 15:2) and how this removal of extra material allows more and better fruit to be produced. Discuss how this purging occurs in our lives as Christians. God takes away those things that hinder our productivity for Him.

The disciples had been cleansed by Jesus' words. God's Word has a cleansing effect on lives. Refer to Psalm 119:9, 11. Are you allowing God's Word to cleanse your life?

Discuss what it means to "abide" in the vine (John 15:4). Fruit-bearing branches need to stay vitally connected to the vine. The sap needs to flow unhindered from the vine to the branches. How do we maintain a vital relationship with Christ? Note that the kind of fruit the Lord desires can be produced only in branches vitally connected to the vine. Discuss "without me ye can do nothing" (vs. 5).

John 15:6 has been interpreted in several ways. What problem is there with the interpretation that assumes that real, nonabiding Christians can be lost? How else might this verse be interpreted?

Discuss the promise in John 15:7. What does having Jesus' words inside one have to do with getting prayers answered? Those who are saturated with God's Word are in a better position to ask according to God's will (cf. I John 5:14) and unselfishly (cf. Jas. 4:3).

Work through the following questions regarding John 15:8-11. How does a productive (fruitful) life bring glory to God (vs. 8)? What does it mean to "continue ye in my love" (vs. 9)? "This means we should continue to realize His love and to enjoy it in our lives" (MacDonald, *Believer's Bible Commentary,* Nelson). If we must keep His commandments to abide in His love, does this mean that His love is conditional?

How is fullness of joy related to what Jesus disclosed in this passage? Those who live in vital relationship with Christ and do what He says and produce fruit have great joy in living.

2. The branch-to-branch relationship (John 15:12-17). Jesus commanded His disciples, "Love one another, as I have loved you." Explain the nature of Jesus' love, based upon verse 13. True love is self-sacrifice. Discuss how this loving self-sacrifice can be manifest in many areas of life.

It is heartwarming to be thought of as Jesus' friends. What qualifies one to be Jesus' friend (vs. 14)? Discuss the difference between "friends" and "servants" (vs. 15).

Notice that Christ has initiated the Vine-branch, friend-friend relationship. Notice also His purpose in initiating this relationship. He wants us to bear lasting fruit. What is this fruit that Jesus wants us to bear? John 15:17 repeats Jesus' command of verse 12. Why the repetition? In Scripture, repetition is often for emphasis. It is really important that we love one another.

ILLUSTRATING THE LESSON

What better way to illustrate the lesson than with branches productively connected to a vine?

CONCLUDING THE LESSON

Jesus is the True Vine. His true disciples are those who abide in Him, obey Him, produce fruit for Him, and love one another. Some may view the Christian life as static and passive. In this lesson it has been presented as dynamic and active. It is a life that results from a vital, intimate relationship with our Lord Jesus Christ. We need to abide in the true Vine and allow His true fruit to be produced in our lives. Encourage each student to examine his Vine-branch, branch-branch relationships.

ANTICIPATING THE NEXT LESSON

In the final lesson this quarter, we are invited into Jesus' prayer closet as He prays to the Father for His followers.

—*Bruce A. Tanner.*

PRACTICAL POINTS

1. Following Jesus is not an easy task, but through all the hardships, we can be certain that God's desire is to make us more fruitful (John 15:1-3).
2. The believer's fruitfulness is wholly dependent on his relationship with Christ (vss. 4-5).
3. Spiritual fruit is the mark of a true Christian (vss. 6-8).
4. Jesus' relationship to the Father is the model for our relationship to Christ (vss. 9-10).
5. The fruitful life is a joyful life (vs. 11).
6. True love is at the core of our relationship with God and with other Christians (vss. 12-17).

—Ralph Woodworth.

RESEARCH AND DISCUSSION

1. The stress on "the true vine" in John 15:1 suggests the possibility of a false vine. What might that false vine be?
2. In what ways does God purge, or prune, us to make us more fruitful (vs. 2)?
3. What is the "fruit" that Christ expects from every believer (John 15:2; cf. Rom. 1:13; 6:22; Gal. 5:22-23)?
4. What is the relationship between bearing fruit and being a disciple of Christ (John 15:8; cf. Matt. 3:8; Rom. 7:4; Col. 1:10)?
5. How is it possible for us to love one another as Christ loves us (John 15:12; cf. Rom. 12:9; I Thess. 3:12; I Pet. 1:22)?

—Ralph Woodworth.

ILLUSTRATED HIGH POINTS

Bear much fruit (John 15:8)

The Bible teaches that in Old Testament times the faithful gave a tenth for the support of the priests and the tabernacle. Actually, they gave more than that. A second tithe, called the festival tithe, was to be used for religious celebrations.

There was still another tithe called the poor tithe. This tithe was instituted for the aid of aliens, the fatherless, and widows. It amounted to 10 percent over three years. That was not all. The Israelites were told not to harvest their fields to the very edges so that the poor and aliens could glean something at harvest.

Why all this generosity? It was because the Israelites knew they worshiped a God who loved giving. Cheerful givers would become even more fruitful.

Spoken unto you (vs. 11)

Before the invention of refrigerators, people preserved food in icehouses. In winter, when lakes and rivers were frozen, large blocks of ice were cut and stored under sawdust.

One man lost a valuable watch while working in an icehouse. He carefully raked the sawdust in his search but without success. He sadly figured his watch was gone for good.

A small boy who heard about the man's problem slipped into the icehouse during lunch and soon emerged with the watch.

"I went in and lay down in the sawdust," the boy explained. "Soon I could hear it ticking."

Often the question is not whether God is speaking but whether we are still enough to listen.

—Ted Simonson.

Golden Text Illuminated

"I am the vine, ye are the branches: He that abideth in me, and I in him, the same bringeth forth much fruit: for without me ye can do nothing" (John 15:5).

Our golden text marks the last occurrence in John's Gospel of Jesus' use of the phrase "I am" to claim equal divinity with the Father by alluding to God's name as revealed to Moses (cf. Ex. 3:14).

Up to this point, Jesus and His disciples had been celebrating the Passover in the upper room. Before the supper, Jesus had washed His disciples' feet, setting the example for us of true Christian humility (John 13:1-16). From the other Gospels, we know that after the Passover meal, Jesus had instituted the Lord's Supper (Matt. 26:26-29; Mark 14:22-24; Luke 22:14-20).

Jesus and His disciples had just left the upper room and were on their way to the Garden of Gethsemane when our lesson text for this week begins. Perhaps they had passed by a vineyard on their way, and Jesus took it as an opportunity to begin teaching about Himself as the True Vine.

In claiming to be the vine, Jesus was claiming to be Israel. He was alluding to the many prophecies in the Old Testament about Israel as the Lord's choicely planted and nurtured vine (cf. Ps. 80:8-16; Isa. 5:1-7; Jer. 2:21; 5:10-11; Ezek. 15:1-8; 17:5-10; 19:10-14; Hos. 10:1). But the nation of Israel never bore the spiritual fruit for God that He had called for (cf. Jer. 5:11). They were continually unfaithful to Him, worshipping foreign gods and neglecting their proper worship of the Lord.

God judged Israel and Judah for their idolatry, sending them into captivity (cf. Jer. 15:1-2). Thereafter, they were conspicuous about avoiding any hint of literal idolatry (cf. Zech. 13:2), but their faithfulness to God in many other areas was greatly deficient (cf. Mal. 1:6-10; 2:1-4, 8-9, 13-17; 3:8-9, 13-15).

Jesus therefore was now rightfully claiming to be the fulfillment of all that God had intended His covenant people to be. He is the true seed of Abraham, in whom all the nations of the world have been blessed (cf. Gen. 12:3; 18:18; 22:18; 26:4; 28:14). Through Jesus Christ, salvation and the righteousness of God through faith has been spread throughout the world (cf. Rom. 3:21-22; Phil. 3:9).

But what exactly did Jesus mean when He spoke of "abiding?" The Lord provides additional clues in verses 7 and 10, adding that abiding in Him has to do with keeping His word and His commands. So a person who keeps Christ's word in his heart and obeys Him is abiding in Him.

To state the issue as simply as possible, we can say that abiding in Christ equates to remaining His disciples; that is, testifying by our words and actions that we belong to Him. This has everything to do with our faith, which is a gift from God (cf. Eph. 2:8).

Although genuine saving faith in Christ perseveres, those without genuine saving faith will fall away from Christ. In fact, the sign that they were never truly connected to Christ is their fruitlessness and eventual falling away (cf. John 15:6; I John 2:19).

Without Christ we can do nothing of spiritual benefit. Abide in the true Vine, the Lord Jesus.

—*John Lody.*

Heart of the Lesson

It appears that Jesus was giving final instructions to the apostles before His death. His time with them on earth was about to end. How magnificent it must have been to sit and listen to Jesus, the Master Teacher!

Jesus used an example of a vine to get His point across to His disciples. The vine was very familiar to the Jews. Israel had been referred to as God's vine (Ps. 80:8). What is known to some as the Song of the Lord's Vineyard is found in Isaiah 5:1-7.

A vine requires support and climbs by tendrils. Branches on the vine will produce either good fruit or bad fruit. Cultivation of the vine is needed to produce good fruit. Periodically, the vine must be pruned to produce more fruit. Pruning is cutting away dead portions and sometimes living portions of the branch to promote growth. Pruning also serves as a means to cleanse. Otherwise the branches may wither and become unfruitful. Unfruitful and withered branches do not serve their purpose. Therefore, they are gathered together and burned.

1. A command to remain in Jesus (John 15:1-4). There are many leaders in the world today, and there have been throughout the ages. Not all leaders are righteous. They are called false leaders because they do not always speak the truth. False leaders do not have the best interests of their followers at heart. However, Jesus is a true and righteous Leader. He called Himself the True Vine. His Father is the husbandman, also known as a vinedresser. Believers are the branches of the True Vine.

Jesus commanded His disciples to remain connected to Him, the True Vine. Believers today are also commanded to remain in Jesus Christ. We must also be fruitful. This is accomplished through the Holy Spirit. As long as the branch stays connected to the Vine, it remains healthy and produces fruit. This is the power of Christ at work in our lives.

Unfruitful believers do not serve a meaningful purpose for the Vine. There are (at least) two ways to become unfruitful in God's kingdom: not living a godly life and not sharing the gospel of Jesus.

2. A command to abide in Jesus' love (John 15:5-12). There is no greater love than the love of Jesus Christ. Jesus loved us so much that He sacrificed His life for us. Believers are encouraged to abide in Jesus' love. Jesus' love for us is the same love His Father has for Him. That is great love!

Believers are commanded to love one another. This was a new commandment given to the apostles by Jesus (John 13:34). It still applies to us.

There are benefits for the believers who obey the commandments of Jesus. We will experience full joy. Jesus said His joy will remain in us. Full joy has lasting effects. It is not like joy from the world, which is only temporary. Full, or complete, joy comes from God. The joy of the Lord is your strength (Neh. 8:10). Joy is a fruit of the Spirit (Gal. 5:22). The fruit of the Spirit should be evidenced in all believers.

3. Friends of the Lord (John 15:13-17). Jesus called the apostles His friends. One mark of their friendship would be obedience to Him. Friends know all about one another. Jesus had shared with them all the things His Father had given Him. Therefore, He no longer called them servants. The servant does not know all that his master does. Are you a friend of the Lord? Live a life of fruitful abiding in Him.

—Arletta Merritts.

World Missions

Missionaries often go to parts of the world where people grow their own food. They have to toil in the fields, tilling, planting, weeding, and harvesting food of one kind or another. Some places grow peanuts. Other places grow manioc. If the people do not tend their fields, they go hungry. The illustration of the vine is more understandable to these people than it is to some of us whose only experience with plants is to mow grass.

To them the branch analogy is apt. As they care for their gardens, they think of Christ and their relationship to Him. It is a personal relationship with no middleman. The missionary evangelist may preach salvation, but he does not come between Jesus and the new Christian. The missionary is not a priest to whom the convert has to come for contact with God. The new believer has direct access to God just as the missionary does, and just as the branch is connected directly to the vine.

Some tribes deep in the jungle are hunters and gatherers, but even they understand that the various plants on which they depend bear fruit at certain times. They go to those trees, bushes, or vines and seek the fruit in season. If they find it, they are happy. If not, they are not pleased. God is like that. He seeks fruit from us.

We in the West live in a highly technical society, but people throughout much of the world have much closer contact with nature. They live closer to the ground or perhaps right on it. Their food comes from hands-on labor. They are surrounded by the fruits of their toil. Dried gourds and peppers hang here and there. Jars of corn or flour sit on counters or shelves. The hoe and shovel are close at hand. In some places the houses are on stilts, and pigs roam right below the floor slats. Goats and sheep are corralled within sight and hearing. The smells of animals, plants, people, and cooking waft in and out as the breeze shifts.

For such people, the figure of a plant growing is more meaningful. Jesus used it to draw attention to His words because people live on words. They are more than animals. They seek meaning in life, and Jesus offers the ultimate meaning.

It is fascinating to see pictures of people living right on the ground and blending in with their surroundings. They seem to be so very different from us. We live in a sterile environment. Our feet hardly ever touch the dirt as we scurry from air-conditioned car to air-conditioned and carpeted home. We seem so different. Yet, as we observe the missionary's presentation, their hearers read the Bible, sing, and give evidence of being people just like us. They are part of the same Vine as we are. There is so very little that is different other than the surroundings.

They have eternal souls as we do. They have feelings and can understand philosophical discussions. They are capable of learning and going to college to become doctors and professors. They are one with us in the human race. They have the same needs. They can be saved by grace through faith just as we can, which is why the missionary goes to them. They are people for whom Christ died.

There is only one Vine. All Christians are branches in it. Perhaps it will be, or has been, your privilege to meet a Christian from one of these far-off places who was saved out of physical and spiritual darkness. You will find that he or she is a precious brother or sister.

—Philip J. Lesko.

The Jewish Aspect

When Jesus called Himself the Vine, He invoked a rich heritage of Jewish prophetic writings about Israel as the vine. At a time when the Jewish people were wondering about Israel's purpose and destiny, Jesus was, in effect, declaring Himself to be the purpose.

One prophet who described Israel as a vine was Isaiah: "My wellbeloved hath a vineyard in a very fruitful hill: and he fenced it, and gathered out the stones thereof, and planted it with the choicest vine" (Isa. 5:1-2). In the Isaiah parable, the "wellbeloved" is God the Father and the vine is Israel.

God planted a choice vine, highly cultivated to produce sweet grapes, but got sour grapes instead (cf. vs. 4). In other words, God gave Israel all they needed to obey and thrive. God gave them a good land and good laws, but the people turned aside and did not obey. God planted well, but Israel failed to thrive because of their unbelief.

Ezekiel also spoke of Israel as a vine: "As the vine tree among the trees of the forest, which I have given to the fire for fuel, so will I give the inhabitants of Jerusalem" (Ezek. 15:6). The similarity of Jesus' saying in John 15:6 is striking: "If a man abide not in me, he is cast forth as a branch, and is withered; and men gather them, and cast them into the fire, and they are burned."

Hosea lamented that "Israel is an empty vine, he bringeth forth fruit unto himself" (Hos. 10:1). Israel should have been a vine bringing forth fruit for God, but instead they brought fruit only for themselves and their idols. The people sought their own wealth and pleasure instead of looking to God, who had promised them wealth and pleasure in the land as they trusted and obeyed Him. Hosea's lament is somewhat similar to Paul's, who described the Jewish people in his day as "being ignorant of God's righteousness, and going about to establish their own righteousness" (Rom. 10:3).

Jesus' disciples were to understand that the true Vine is Jesus. Israel had not been following God, and the righteousness God desired had not been produced; in Jesus that righteousness was seen.

Jesus was what Israel was supposed to be. God called Israel to be priests to the world (cf. Ex. 19:6). It was Jesus who drew men to God and became a light to the nations (Isa. 42:6). Jesus lived the Law of Moses according to its true interpretation (cf. Matt. 5:17).

God was grieved over His ruined vine, Israel, and said, "What could have been done more to my vineyard, that I have not done in it?" (Isa. 5:4). What a contrast to the nation of Israel Jesus provided! He was he True Vine and the one who truly lived out Israel's purpose.

When Jesus told His disciples that they had to remain in Him, He was telling them that continuing to believe and follow His teachings was the way for them to be the true Israel.

This is the same thing that Paul taught in Romans 9:6: "For they are not all Israel, which are of Israel." God's promised line has always been based on faith. The promise through Abraham did not go through Ishmael but through Isaac, and then Jacob, not Esau. In the same way, the way for a believer to be a part of the true Israel is to follow the Messiah.

Many Jewish believers in Jesus do not have a full understanding of their relationship to the Israel of God. But according to Jesus, having faith in Him is the only way to be truly connected to the true Israel.

—*Derek Leman.*

Guiding the Superintendent

Wherever a person traveled in ancient Israel, he could see grape vineyards. Grapes were an important product for the people. It is fitting that Jesus would use a grapevine to illustrate His relationship with His followers. He pictured Himself as the True Vine, and His followers are the branches.

Our last few lessons have focused on Jesus as the Bread of Life, the Light of the World, and the Good Shepherd. What does the imagery of a vine add to our understanding of our relationship with Him? More specifically, what is the fruit that He desires to produce through us?

DEVOTIONAL OUTLINE

1. Maintain close fellowship with Christ (John 15:1-8). Jesus' command is quite simple: "Abide in me." Fruit is only possible for those who abide in, remain in, or maintain close fellowship with Jesus.

Fruit bearing is very dependent on close fellowship in Christ (vss. 5-8). If one abides in Christ, he will produce fruit. Two things will happen: prayers will be answered, and the Father will be glorified.

The order is very specific: the believer abides, bears fruit, and has his prayers answered, and the Father is glorified.

2. Maintain close fellowship with other believers (John 15:9-17). To accomplish this close fellowship, two things are required.

First, the believer must remain (abide) in Christ's love. This is accomplished by obeying Jesus' commandments. In the end, it will produce great joy in the person's life.

Second, believers are to love each other, following the example of Jesus. They must have self-sacrificing love. When these things happen, we see our prayers answered. The main reason is that our focus is no longer on ourselves but on others. Since they are also the focus of God, our prayers will naturally be answered.

Notice how similar the order of the commands is to the first part of the lesson. Believers remain in Jesus' love (vss. 9-10), have joy (vs. 11), bear fruit (vs. 16), and have prayer answered.

We still have not answered our key question: What is the fruit that God is looking for in our lives? What is it that God wants to produce in our lives? What is it that will automatically come when a believer draws his life from Jesus Christ?

The answer is simple: love. Verse 17 says it all: "These things I command you, that ye love one another."

We enjoy Christ's love for ourselves more as we love one another. As we follow the guidance and protection of Jesus Christ, love will be produced in our lives.

CHILDREN'S CORNER

It is at an early age that most people develop a personal concept of love. Our lesson will help children understand the nature of true, Christlike love.

The simplest and best way to bring them to this understanding is by focusing on Jesus' call for obedience (John 15:10). Children understand what it is to obey their parents out of love. They understand the difference between obeying because they have to and obeying because they love them. It is the same with our relationship with Jesus.

—Martin R. Dahlquist.

LESSON 13   MAY 28, 2023

SCRIPTURE LESSON TEXT

JOHN 17:6 I have manifested thy name unto the men which thou gavest me out of the world: thine they were, and thou gavest them me; and they have kept thy word.

7 Now they have known that all things whatsoever thou hast given me are of thee.

8 For I have given unto them the words which thou gavest me; and they have received *them,* and have known surely that I came out from thee, and they have believed that thou didst send me.

9 I pray for them: I pray not for the world, but for them which thou hast given me; for they are thine.

10 And all mine are thine, and thine are mine; and I am glorified in them.

11 And now I am no more in the world, but these are in the world, and I come to thee. Holy Father, keep through thine own name those whom thou hast given me, that they may be one, as we *are.*

12 While I was with them in the world, I kept them in thy name: those that thou gavest me I have kept, and none of them is lost, but the son of perdition; that the scripture might be fulfilled.

13 And now come I to thee; and these things I speak in the world, that they might have my joy fulfilled in themselves.

14 I have given them thy word; and the world hath hated them, because they are not of the world, even as I am not of the world.

15 I pray not that thou shouldest take them out of the world, but that thou shouldest keep them from the evil.

16 They are not of the world, even as I am not of the world.

17 Sanctify them through thy truth: thy word is truth.

18 As thou hast sent me into the world, even so have I also sent them into the world.

19 And for their sakes I sanctify myself, that they also might be sanctified through the truth.

20 Neither pray I for these alone, but for them also which shall believe on me through their word;

21 That they all may be one; as thou, Father, *art* in me, and I in thee, that they also may be one in us: that the world may believe that thou hast sent me.

NOTES

Jesus Prays for Believers

Lesson Text: John 17:6-21

Related Scriptures: Luke 22:31-32; John 17:22-24; Hebrews 7:24-27

TIME: A.D. 30   PLACE: Jerusalem

GOLDEN TEXT—"[I pray] that they all may be one; as thou, Father, art in me, and I in thee, that they also may be one in us: that the world may believe that thou hast sent me" (John 17:21).

Introduction

Jesus' teaching on prayer is quite extensive. Especially in His Sermon on the Mount, He taught His disciples about prayer. He taught them to pray for their enemies (Matt. 5:44-45) and to pray in private and with simplicity (6:5-8).

Jesus also taught the need to be persistent in prayer (Matt. 7:7-11) and to pray with humility (Luke 18:9-14). He taught that prayer must be made in His name—that is, on the basis of His character and authority (John 14:13-14). And, of course, Jesus gave His disciples a model of prayer (Luke 11:1-4.)

As important as this teaching is, it is dramatically enhanced by Jesus' own example.

Jesus' prayer in John 17 is better described as the "Lord's Prayer" than is His model prayer in Luke 11. It is the most extensive prayer of Jesus recorded in the Gospels. It reminds us of the importance of prayer in Jesus' life, but it is more than a mere example. It reveals the heart of Jesus, and it focuses first on His disciples and then on future believers. It is a prayer for us!

LESSON OUTLINE

I. **PRAYER FOR GOD'S GLORY**—John 17:6-8

II. **PRAYER FOR THE DISCIPLES**—John 17:9-19

III. **PRAYER FOR FUTURE BELIEVERS**—John 17:20-21

Exposition: Verse by Verse

PRAYER FOR GOD'S GLORY

JOHN 17:6 I have manifested thy name unto the men which thou gavest me out of the world: thine they were, and thou gavest them me; and they have kept thy word.

7 Now they have known that all things whatsoever thou hast given me are of thee.

8 For I have given unto them the words which thou gavest me; and they have received them, and have

known surely that I came out from thee, and they have believed that thou didst send me.

Through keeping God's word (John 17:6). {The lengthy prayer of Jesus recorded in John 17 took place on the night of His betrayal and shortly before His arrest in Gethsemane. He apparently prayed these words after leaving the upper room in Jerusalem on His way to the Garden of Gethsemane, just outside the city.}Q1

First, Jesus prayed for Himself—that God would glorify Him so that through Him God would be glorified (vss. 1-6). His prayer then turned to His disciples.

God would receive glory through Jesus' imminent death on the cross. But He would also be glorified through Jesus' disciples. {Jesus had manifested God's name to these men; that is, He fully revealed God's nature and character to them through His words and His works.}Q2

These men, whom the Father had given to Jesus from out of the world, had kept God's word. They had their failings, but the course of their lives—with the exception of Judas, who had already left them (John 13:21-30)—was one of obedience to God's commands. Their continued obedience would be the means by which Jesus would be glorified (cf. 17:10).

Through knowing the truth (John 17:7-8). {Jesus affirmed that at this point the disciples had come to understand that everything Jesus had been given was indeed given by the Father.}Q3 This "appears to mean the knowledge that Jesus' mission is divine, that he has nothing except what the Father has given him. All is of God. . . . What is central is that all that we see in him is of God" (Morris, *The Gospel According to John,* Eerdmans).

Jesus went on to say that the disciples had received His words as coming from God (John 17:8). This confirmed that Jesus "came from the Father and was sent from the Father (see 16:28-30)" (Comfort and Hawley, *Opening the Gospel of John,* Tyndale).

While Jesus' words here are more a statement about His disciples' faith in Him than a prayer for them, their obedience and understanding of Him were means by which He would be glorified. Thus, these words establish the importance of the subsequent petitions of Jesus on the disciples' behalf.

PRAYER FOR THE DISCIPLES

9 I pray for them: I pray not for the world, but for them which thou hast given me; for they are thine.

10 And all mine are thine, and thine are mine; and I am glorified in them.

11 And now I am no more in the world, but these are in the world, and I come to thee. Holy Father, keep through thine own name those whom thou hast given me, that they may be one, as we are.

12 While I was with them in the world, I kept them in thy name: those that thou gavest me I have kept, and none of them is lost, but the son of perdition; that the scripture might be fulfilled.

13 And now come I to thee; and these things I speak in the world, that they might have my joy fulfilled in themselves.

14 I have given them thy word; and the world hath hated them, because they are not of the world, even as I am not of the world.

15 I pray not that thou shouldest take them out of the world, but that thou shouldest keep them from the evil.

16 They are not of the world, even as I am not of the world.

17 Sanctify them through thy truth: thy word is truth.

18 As thou hast sent me into the world, even so have I also sent them into the world.

19 And for their sakes I sanctify myself, that they also might be sanctified through the truth.

To confirm their position (John 17:9-10). While Jesus did not lack compassion for the world, His disciples were the particular objects of His prayer here. They were the ones the Father had given to Him, and thus they belonged to both the Father and the Son. And they were the ones through whom Jesus would be glorified after His return to heaven.

So certain was Jesus' glorification in them that He stated it as if it were already accomplished. It must have greatly encouraged the disciples as they heard this, for it assured them that even with all their failures, God would use them in a significant way. It should encourage us as well to know that the Lord uses people who are faithful, not perfect.

To give them unity (John 17:11-12). Jesus knew that He would soon leave this world, but He would leave His disciples behind. Therefore, {He asked the Father to "keep" them and to preserve their unity. When He asked the Father to keep His disciples and said, "I kept them in thy name," He was probably referring to keeping them from evil, or the evil one.}Q4 What Jesus had done up to this point, He now asked the Father to do.

Jesus had kept them from the evil one—except for Judas, whom He described as the "son of perdition" (vs. 12), meaning one who is doomed to perish (cf. II Thess. 2:3). By his own choice and in fulfillment of Scripture, Judas rejected Christ and sealed his own doom (John 13:18).

{Jesus prayed that the disciples would "be one" (John 17:11) just as He and the Father are one. This speaks not of some outward, organizational unity but of an inward, spiritual one.}Q5 "Believers experience this through the Holy Spirit as they are made sharers of God's life. Of course, spiritual unity will manifest itself in peaceable relations, but mere organizational unification is no substitute for spiritual oneness" (Kent, *Light in the Darkness,* BMH).

Jesus' prayer was not that His followers would become one but that they would continually be one. Unity is something we are given; it is up to us to maintain it, and this was what Jesus' prayer was about. As we individually draw closer to God, we also draw closer to one another, and the unity of the Spirit is maintained among us (cf. Eph. 4:3).

To give them joy (John 17:13). Jesus looked forward to the joy He would soon experience in the Heavenly Father's presence. His disciples would remain in the world, however, and His desire was that they might know that joy themselves. He prayed that they might experience the fullness of His joy (cf. 15:11).

To protect them (John 17:14-15). It must have been very comforting to the disciples to know that the Lord wanted them to have joy to the fullest, for as Jesus Himself acknowledged before the Father, the world—sinful mankind and the whole world system under Satan—hated them. They could expect no approval or acceptance from a world that also hated their Master (cf. 15:18-19).

{Because they had been given God's word, or message, and had accepted it, thereby identifying with God and God's Son, they were not a part of the world, just as Jesus was not of the world. It was therefore certain that the world would express hatred for them.}Q6

Yet Jesus knew that for all the hatred and opposition the disciples would face in the world, it was not the Father's will to take them out of the world at this time. {Jesus' prayer, therefore, was that God would protect them *in* the world, that He would "keep them from the evil" (17:15). "The evil" here refers to Satan, the evil one.}^Q7 Thus, Jesus "prayed that they would be preserved from the clutches of Satan" (Kent).

The disciples had God's message; what they needed now was His protection as they faced the temptations and attacks of Satan that would surely come as they proclaimed that message to others. We too have been entrusted with the gospel, and because of that, satanic attacks and opposition and temptation will come. We should pray for God's spiritual protection, knowing that this is the prayer of Christ Himself.

To sanctify them (John 17:16-17). Verse 16 repeats what Jesus had just said: that the disciples were not of the world just as He was not of the world. This reinforced the truth that they would be left in a hostile environment to carry on the Lord's work. Consequently, they would need God's protection from Satan (vs. 15), as well as the sanctifying work of God (vs. 17).

{Jesus' prayer was that God the Father would sanctify the disciples through His truth. He further identified the truth with God's Word. To sanctify means "to make holy" or "set apart." It is most often used of setting someone or something apart from sin and unto God for His use.}^Q8

There is a past aspect of the doctrine of sanctification in that God has set apart every believer for Himself, clothing him positionally with the holiness of Christ (cf. I Cor. 1:2; 6:11). There is also a future aspect in that believers will be conformed completely to Christ in holiness and completely separated from sin when He returns (I Thess. 5:23; I John 3:2-3).

Finally, there is a present aspect of sanctification. {This is the progressive setting apart of believers as they grow in holiness. This type of sanctification is accomplished by the Word of God (Eph. 5:25-26). This is the sanctification of which Jesus spoke in John 17:17.}^Q9

Jesus' prayer was for God to make the disciples "holy men, separated from the world to be of service to the world" (Morris). This He would accomplish through His Word. "As the disciples lived for God day by day, the application of God's truth to their lives would have a purifying effect as it would call sin to their attention, and cause confession and restoration to follow. By this means they would be set apart from sin and consecrated to the ministry to which Christ had called them" (Kent).

The "word" in John 17:17 here refers to the truths Jesus had given them. These truths are now contained in God's completed revelation, the Bible. God has called us all to holiness, or sanctification (I Thess. 4:7). This is God's will for us, and it will be accomplished only as we read, absorb, and submit to the teachings of Scripture.

To equip them (John 17:18-19). Jesus' words here again reinforce the need for the disciples' protection (vs. 15) and sanctification (vs. 17). Just as the Father had sent Jesus into the world, so He had sent His disciples into the world. Both Jesus and the disciples were sent to take God's message of salvation to a hostile world.

Jesus said that it was for His followers' sakes that He sanctified Himself. He did indeed set Himself apart to God's service. However, that service included His death on the cross. The primary idea here seems to be that Jesus sanctified or set Himself apart for death. He "sanctifies or consecrates himself as a priest would consecrate a sacrifice! He is priest and sacrificial victim at the same time" (Michaels, *John,* Hendrickson).

In relation to His disciples, Jesus set Himself apart for death and died in their place to give them life and so that they too could be sanctified through the truth. They could be set apart for God's service only because He had set Himself apart to complete God's mission by dying on the cross.

PRAYER FOR FUTURE BELIEVERS

20 Neither pray I for these alone, but for them also which shall believe on me through their word;

21 That they all may be one; as thou, Father, art in me, and I in thee, that they also may be one in us: that the world may believe that thou hast sent me.

The focus of the Lord's prayer now turned to a wider group. The importance of Jesus' disciples to His continuing work on earth is evidenced by the amount of space given to them in His prayer. But Jesus' prayer was not limited to the few disciples who had accompanied Him for three years. He also prayed for those who would believe in Him through their preaching.

It was through the apostles of Jesus—through their personal ministries and writings—that future believers would come to faith in Christ. It was for all these subsequent believers that He now prayed, and these believers include us!

How wonderful it is to know that even as Jesus faced the cross, He was thinking not only of His family and His disciples but also of you and me! {He prayed for us, and He prayed that we might be unified. His desire for us is that we be united as one in Him and in the Father, just as Jesus and the Father are in each other.}Q10 There is no closer unity imaginable than that which exists between God the Father and God the Son. This kind of unity is the pattern for our unity with God and with one another in the body of Christ.

Jesus desired this unity for us because it would mean that many people in this world would believe in Him as a result. The unity Jesus foresaw was not a man-made unity. We do not effect unity by setting aside truth in order to minimize our differences. Rather, unity comes naturally as we focus on the truth of God and grow in our knowledge of and relationship with Him.

As we grow closer to God, we grow closer to one another and present to the world a faith that is serious and committed to the truth. It is the testimony of a faith that is truly committed to the truth of the gospel that will draw people to Christ.

—*Jarl K. Waggoner.*

QUESTIONS

1. What was the setting of Jesus' prayer in John 17?
2. How had Jesus manifested God's name to His disciples (vs. 6)?
3. What did Jesus affirm about the disciples' spiritual understanding?
4. From what did Jesus ask the Father to keep His disciples?
5. What kind of unity did Jesus want for His disciples?
6. Why would the world hate the disciples after Jesus' departure?
7. What did Jesus pray in light of that?
8. What did Jesus mean when He asked the Father to sanctify the disciples (vs. 17)?
9. How is personal sanctification accomplished?
10. What did Jesus pray in regard to us?

—*Jarl K. Waggoner.*

Preparing to Teach the Lesson

Many people think of the prayer in Matthew 6:9-13 as the Lord's Prayer. In that passage, the Lord gave us a model for our praying, but it was not really *His* prayer. The text we will study in this lesson was His actual prayer for His disciples throughout the ages. In the fullest sense, John 17 is the *Lord's* prayer.

From this prayer we know what the Lord's desires are for His disciples throughout all time. As we live our lives, let us make His desires our desires.

TODAY'S AIM

Facts: to understand the Lord's desires for His disciples.

Principle: to make the Lord's desires our desires.

Application: to carry out the Lord's desires for us.

INTRODUCING THE LESSON

We who know and love the Lord want to fulfill His desires for our lives. We can discover His desires for us throughout Scripture. For example, in I John 2:15-17 we read that we are not to desire the things of the world; rather, we are to desire the things of God.

We also find God's desires for us in His prayer in John 17. We find His desires for His first disciples (vss. 6-19) and for those who would come after them (vss. 20-21). If the Lord prays for something He would like to see in the lives of His followers, that tells you what His desires are for you. His desires should then become your spiritual goals.

Let us endeavor as we live our lives to understand more clearly the Lord's desires for us and to adopt them as our own desires in the coming months and years.

DEVELOPING THE LESSON

1. Jesus' desire concerning His Word (John 17:6-10). In verses 6-19, Jesus prayed for His disciples—"the men which thou gavest me out of the world." Yet His prayer includes all believers, for we are His followers, or disciples, today (vs. 20).

In these verses, Jesus acknowledged several important truths about His disciples. He knew that they belonged to God the Father vss. 6, 8), that the Father had given them to Him (vss. 6, 9, 10), and that He was glorified in them (vs. 10).

Jesus' prayer also showed that His disciples recognized some important spiritual truths about Him. They understood that everything Jesus had was from the Father (vs. 7) and that Jesus had come from the Father (vs. 8).

In His prayer for His disciples, Jesus spoke several times about their relationship to God's Word. "They have kept thy word" (vs. 6). "For I have given unto them the words which thou gavest me; and they have received them" (vs. 8; cf. vs. 14).

These statements about His disciples show Jesus' desire for us concerning God's Word. We need to be people who gladly receive God's Word (Acts 2:41) and keep it (Jas. 1:22).

2. Jesus' desire concerning spiritual protection (John 17:11-16). Jesus acknowledged that His disciples would not be thought of or treated well in this world. "The world hath hated them, because they are not of the world, even as I am not of the world." Yet His plan was not to take them out of the world but rather to protect them from Satan in the world. "Keep through thine own name those whom thou hast given me."

Jesus' will for His disciples is to protect them from the spiritual attacks of Satan. The Lord is committed to protecting us, for He prayed for it specifically (vs. 15). We also are to act for our own spiritual protection by being alert to Satan's schemes (II Cor. 2:11; I Pet. 5:8-9).

3. Jesus' desire concerning sanctification (John 17:17-19). Jesus prayed that God, His Father, would sanctify His disciples. Sanctification is the divine process of purifying and dedicating someone for service to God. Jesus acknowledged that such sanctification could come only from the truth found in God's Word. "Sanctify them through thy truth: thy word is truth."

Christ's desire for the sanctification of His disciples is still active today. He wants us to purify ourselves and to set ourselves apart from the world so that we can serve Him effectively.

4. Jesus' desire concerning unity (John 17:20-21). Earlier, Jesus had prayed for unity for His disciples: "That they may be one, as we are" (vs. 11). Then He extended that desire to all His followers: "That they all may be one; as thou, Father, art in me, and I in thee, that they also may be one in us: that the world may believe that thou hast sent me" (vs. 21).

The unity Jesus desires among believers is a spiritual unity. All true believers, anywhere in the world, are united by being part of God's family. This unity is based on the unity of the Godhead and testifies to the world that we are from Christ, who is from God. We should therefore endeavor to "keep the unity of the Spirit in the bond of peace" (Eph. 4:3).

ILLUSTRATING THE LESSON

We should understand the desires of our Lord for His followers and make them our own desires.

CONCLUDING THE LESSON

Now that we know the desires of our Lord for His followers, we should make them our desires as well. As we look at the remainder of our lives and the call to live a life pleasing to the Lord, to which of the Lord's desires do we need to give greater attention?

• Do we need to commit to reading and receiving His Word more than we have in the past? If so, what steps can we take to do that?

• Do we need to commit to a greater effort of guarding ourselves from the attacks of Satan? If so, what steps can we take to guard ourselves better?

• Do we need to commit to pursuing a greater degree of sanctification in the days ahead? If so, what steps can we take to advance toward this crucial goal?

• Do we need to strive for greater spiritual unity with fellow believers? If so, what steps can we take to live in greater unity with other Christians?

ANTICIPATING THE NEXT LESSON

Next quarter we will look at the glorious kingdom Christ came to proclaim and what He taught about preparing for it and entering it.

—Don Anderson.

PRACTICAL POINTS

1. Jesus' gracious love for us displays God and His glory to the world (John 17:6-10).
2. We should seek unity with one another that will in some sense reflect the unity within the Trinity (vs. 11).
3. We do not have to worry about an evil power being stronger than Jesus (vs. 12).
4. Knowledge of God's truth will sanctify us as we live in the world (vss. 13-19).
5. Jesus prayed for all His followers in the future to be unified, including you and me (vss. 20-21).

—Stuart Olley.

RESEARCH AND DISCUSSION

1. Who are the people God has given to Jesus (John 17:6-10, 20)? Was Jesus praying for believers today?
2. What can the members of our local church do to reflect something of the unity within the Trinity (John 17:11; cf. Eph. 4:1-6)?
3. How certain can we be that God will save us if we have faith in Him (John 17:12; cf. 10:27-30)?
4. What are some of the practices that help us in sanctification (17:13-19)? How can our progress in sanctification be a witness in the world (Col. 4:5-6)?
5. How does Jesus' prayer for you encourage you (John 17:20-21)?
6. What gifts does God equip us with that are part of His nature (John 17:22-26; cf. II Pet. 1:3-11)?

—Stuart Olley.

ILLUSTRATED HIGH POINTS

My joy (John 17:13)

One summer I worked in a factory along with five other college students. One day, Clayton came in with a sad look. Upon inquiry, we learned that he and his girlfriend had just broken up. We tried to cheer him up, but he insisted on being sad. "After all," he said, "Jesus never laughed."

It is true that there is no verse that says Jesus laughed. But although He was "a man of sorrows" (Isa. 53:3), He was also a man of genuine joy. His joy did not depend on outward circumstances but was the abiding enjoyment of His Father and the Word of God.

The world hath hated them (vs. 14)

In America, atheists are stepping up their attacks on Christianity. Several years ago, they put up a billboard in Times Square. Under a picture of Santa Claus was the caption "Keep the Merry!" Above the picture of Jesus was "Dump the Myth!" This is ironic, since Santa is truly a myth and only Jesus can provide lasting joy and blessing!

That they also may be one

A father gave his young son a tied-up bundle of sticks and asked him to break them up.

He returned a short time later to find the bundle intact and the boy frustrated. He had tried to smash it against his knee, only to be bruised. He had stomped on it and slammed it against a tree—both to no avail.

Taking the bundle, the father untied the cord and simply began to break the sticks—one at a time.

It is so with the church of Christ. If we remain united, we are strong. When we are divided, we can be easily broken apart.

—David A. Hamburg.

Golden Text Illuminated

"[I pray] that they all may be one; as thou, Father, art in me, and I in thee, that they also may be one in us: that the world may believe that thou hast sent me" (John 17:21).

"By this shall all men know that ye are my disciples, if ye have love one to another" (John 13:35). Our relationships with fellow believers are an important priority to our Saviour. In His last recorded prayer with His disciples (nearly all of John 17), He prayed that His followers would be unified in love. The reason is listed twice: that the world would know that Jesus was sent from God.

Jesus prayed His final high priestly prayer for His disciples, both current and future. In John 17:9, Jesus said, "I pray not for the world, but for them which thou hast given me." Later, Jesus expanded His prayer to include not only current believers but future ones as well (vs. 20). Jesus prayed for us!

A song from 1968 declares, "And they'll know we are Christians by our love" (Scholtes). Many like to conclude that the world will know that Jesus was sent from God because of our love for the lost. But according to Jesus, it is our love for each other that proves to the world that He is who He said He is.

So, if our world does not believe that Jesus was sent from God, the fault may be partly ours. Many believe Christ was merely a good man or a good teacher. We know that is not enough. However, this passage shows us that what will convince people is not just ardent evangelism, careful argumentation, or even great compassion for the lost. It is our love for one another as Christians that will convince others.

Why is unity so hard? A church in our local area recently split—an unhappy divorce among God's people, providing the world with one more reason not to believe that Jesus is our Lord and Saviour. By having such conflict among us, we send the false and shameful message to the world that Jesus' claims are in doubt.

Psalm 133:1 exclaims, "Behold, how good and how pleasant it is for brethren to dwell together in unity!" Is your church a pleasant place? Do the believers love one another? Are they unified in purpose as Jesus was unified with God, testifying to the world that His Spirit of love is within us?

How can we become unified as Jesus intends?

Remember who we really are. When we recall that our hearts are desperately wicked (Jer. 17:9) and that even "our righteousnesses are as filthy rags" (Isa. 64:6), we also remember that God's grace is an undeserved gift. If God gave it to us, we should likewise extend it to others out of love for Him.

Recognize we are not in charge. It is not our job to judge. It is God's! "Who art thou that judgest another man's servant? to his own master he standeth or falleth" (Rom. 14:4).

We must forgive each other. Max Lucado once said, "Only hold a grudge when God does." Jesus expressed emphatically that if we are forgiven, we must likewise forgive others (Mark 11:26)—even seventy times seven times (Matt. 18:22)!

A church of believers who are unified by Jesus' love would change the world! Sometimes it is easier to love the lost than it is to love our brothers and sisters in Christ, but if we want to be like Jesus, we must make love a priority.

—Kimberly Rae.

Heart of the Lesson

John 17 could be called the Lord's Prayer, since it is the prayer of the Lord Jesus on our behalf. He offered this prayer in the presence of His disciples. Do not worry that John could not have remembered the entire prayer. It was common then for people to remember long passages of spoken words. In addition, the Holy Spirit was inspiring John to write these exact words; so there is no error or omission here. We believe and know that this is the prayer the Lord Jesus uttered.

1. Convictions (John 17:6-8). Many things people believe are conveniences, not convictions. When pushed to the limit, people may abandon their convenient beliefs. However, a true conviction is a truth for which one would die. The Lord Jesus stated repeatedly that He had received the truth from the Heavenly Father and had given it to His disciples. God's name equals who and what He is; it is the true nature of God. They had received Christ's message that He had come forth from the Father in heaven and had taught them the truth about the Father. Jesus said they had kept His word.

2. Safety (John 17:9-16). The Lord Jesus specifically stated in His prayer that He was praying for His disciples and for those who would later believe through their words. That includes us today. He asked that His joy might be made full in us. He also made it clear that believers are not of this world, just as the Lord Jesus is not of this world. The world hated Him, and it hates us; but the Lord will keep us from spiritual harm by anyone, including Satan himself.

3. Sanctification (John 17:17-19). The basic idea of sanctification is separation to God from anything that defiles us or makes us unfit for fellowship with Him. We are set apart for God as we believe and obey the truth He has given us.

The Lord Jesus prayed that the Father would sanctify us. He said that He sanctifies Himself, which He can do; but He prayed that the Father would sanctify us, which we cannot do.

4. Unity (John 17:20-21). This is by far the greatest theme of the prayer. It is also the hardest to get our minds around. It is hard enough for us to understand the Trinity—the Triune God, the Father, Son, and Holy Spirit.

The unity that the Lord Jesus enjoys with the Father He wants us to have with each other.

When we are divided, we make it harder—if not impossible—for people to believe the gospel. The Lord Jesus specifically prayed, "That they all may be one; as thou, Father, art in me, and I in thee, that they also may be one in us: that the world may believe that thou hast sent me" (John 17:21).

Jesus included in His prayer those who would believe in Him through His disciples' preaching. This certainly includes you and me and all those who have believed since the time of Christ.

The scope and breadth of this prayer is staggering. We should spend much time meditating upon it.

This prayer will be fulfilled perfectly and completely in God's perfect timing. We will not see it completely answered in this life, but God will most certainly answer this high priestly prayer of the Lord Jesus. It was prayed by the perfect and holy Son to the faithful Father, whose great, eternal plan it seeks to implement. You and I were in the heart of Jesus as He prayed. Eternal love and gratitude must be our constant response.

—*Brian D. Doud.*

World Missions

As Christians, we have the privilege and opportunity to walk into the very presence of God Himself. To use an analogy from the Old Testament, we can walk into the Holy of Holies and meet face-to-face with God. One of the distinctive factors of our faith is that we can talk with God and meet with Him at any time. This is wonderful in itself. He is always there, waiting to listen to our deepest needs. We also have the privilege of praying for others in need.

We all know someone who is very close to us who either is not living as Jesus would want him to or has never committed his life to Jesus. Even if we cannot penetrate his world with the good news of Jesus, we can always pray for that person. There are no walls that can keep prayer out! God knows our thoughts, and He knows the hurts within us. We all care for those who are close to us. When they hurt, we hurt. When they succeed, we celebrate with them. There is a heart-to-heart connection that comes with such relationships.

Jesus prayed for His disciples. They were those who were closest to Him in the ministry that He set out to do. We also should pray for those closest to us. We are specially called to pray for those who are closest to us in regard to their salvation. We must point them to Jesus Christ and help those who make the decision to follow Jesus as their Lord to fulfill their calling as Christians. It hurts us deeply when someone close to us rejects Jesus.

Christians therefore have an obligation to pray for those who are close to them. Parents are to pray for their children. Workers are to pray for their coworkers. Those who pray for others close to them often find greater witnessing opportunities. All need to know of the salvation that Jesus paid such a high price for. God may have put you in your job so that you might be an instrument in His hand to help others find salvation through our Lord Jesus, using what you say and do. God responds to the prayers of the faithful.

Jesus prayed for His disciples, knowing their faults. We too can pray effectively for those close to us because we know them intimately, warts and all. There is something about prayer that changes outcomes for the better. Many a person bound for hell has been converted through prayers. Augustine was converted after years of his mother's fervent prayers. She prayed relentlessly for her wayward son until God intervened on her behalf and Augustine turned to God. God responds to prayer.

There is a world out there that is dying and on its way to hell because the people have never heard of Jesus and His love. They are floundering in the darkness of sin without hope of salvation. Jesus calls each of us to pray, following His example. We lift people up before the Heavenly Father daily by name so that they may encounter God in response to our prayers. God expects us to invite people into His kingdom, especially those we can influence daily because they are close to us.

We often excuse ourselves from this responsibility because we are too embarrassed to bring up the matter of faith lest we offend others. But God has given us this responsibility. The gospel is to be shared person to person. God could use angels, but He chooses us!

—A. Koshy Muthalaly

The Jewish Aspect

Four times in John 17 Jesus referred to God's "name" (17:6, 11, 12, 26). Reading those verses, we may miss their impact on Jesus' Jewish disciples, who knew the importance of a "name" in their culture.

Americans typically give names primarily to identify or perhaps to memorialize. For example, we may name a child after a grandparent. Rarely do we think of a child's "name" as signifying the character of that child. In Jewish thinking, however, "the name conveys the nature and essence of the thing named. It represents the history and reputation of the being named" ("The Name of God," www.jewishvirtuallibrary.org). This applies especially to God's "name." Many names for God are used in Scripture. These include *Elohim, El, Elyon, El Shaddai,* and *Adonai.* The most important name, however, is YHWH, the tetragrammaton, a word that comes from a Greek term meaning "four letters."

Jews considered "YHWH" to be the only proper name of God. All the other names were viewed as titles that conveyed various elements of God's character. This name of God occurs over 6,500 times in the Old Testament, and every one refers to the true Lord of heaven and earth. Exactly how this name was pronounced in ancient times is not known. This is because "in Second Temple times [530 B.C.–A.D. 70], as an expression of reverence, Jews began to avoid uttering it, substituting 'adonai' and other surrogates" (Berlin and Brettler, eds., *The Jewish Study Bible,* Oxford).

By Jesus' time, even the priests in the temple did not pronounce this name. The Talmud even said that "'whoever pronounces the Name forfeits his portion in the future world' (Sanh. xi. 1)" ("Names of God," www.jewishencyclopedia.com). The Masoretes, Jewish scholars between the seventh and eleventh centuries A.D., inserted the vowels from the name "Adonai" into the consonants "YHWH," which led to it being pronounced as "Jehovah." Current scholars believe that "Yahweh" is probably more accurate, although modern Jews still do not pronounce the word.

The name "YHWH" was revealed to Moses at the burning bush (Ex. 3). Moses asked what he should tell Israel when they asked what God's name is. God responded, "I AM THAT I AM: and he said, Thus shalt thou say unto the children of Israel, I AM hath sent me unto you" (vs. 14). To show the importance of this, *The Jewish Study Bible* translates this verse emphasizing each Hebrew word: "And God said to Moses, "'Ehyeh-Asher-Ehyeh.'" He continued, "'Thus shall you say to the Israelites, 'Ehyeh' sent me to you.'" The verb from which the name comes has the idea of "to be, to live." "The meaning would, therefore, be 'He who is self-existing, self-sufficient,' or, more concretely, 'He who lives'" ("Names of God"). This divine name of God was and is considered by Jews to be equal to God Himself.

This stress on the importance of God's "name" helps us to see how Jesus' disciples understood it when Jesus referred to God's name in His prayer in John 17. Jesus said to His Father, "I have manifested thy name" (vs. 6). He had declared God's name to the disciples (vs. 26), thus revealing "the essential nature of God to men" (Morris, *The Gospel According to John,* Eerdmans). That essential nature of God is what protects His children (vss. 11-12).

—*R. Larry Overstreet.*

Guiding the Superintendent

Who has never eavesdropped on a conversation? It is very hard to resist doing this. Our lesson this week will allow us to listen in on one of the most fascinating conversations ever—the conversation that Jesus had with His Father on the eve of the Cross.

John 17 has been called the high priestly prayer of Jesus. What a comfort it is to realize that Jesus intercedes for His people!

This prayer contains Jesus Christ's priorities for His disciples and the church they would lead.

As we listen in on Jesus' prayer, we can get a sense of what is really important to Him and thus for us as His followers.

DEVOTIONAL OUTLINE

Jesus started His prayer with His concern that He bring glory to the Father, especially in light of the Cross, which was just hours away. His focus here was not directly on Himself but on God and God's glory. What a lesson for us! Even when facing deep pain and tragedy, we should always be focused on God's glory.

1. Christ described His disciples (John 17:6-8). Before His actual prayer for His disciples, Jesus described who they are. Jesus viewed the disciples as God's special gift to Him. A disciple is one who believes in Jesus Christ, knowing that He has been sent by the Father on a special mission.

2. Christ prayed for His disciples (John 17:9-19). Jesus' prayer for His disciples is very special. He prayed that their confidence in Him would continue in spite of the difficulties that were coming. He prayed for their protection in the midst of a hostile world. And He prayed that His followers would have true joy as they lived for Him.

3. Christ prayed for His future followers (John 17:20-21). The prayer now moves in a vital direction for us. Jesus went beyond His disciples to the followers He would have in the future. He was now praying for you and me!

As He faced the Cross, Christ was very confident that in spite of what would happen to Him shortly, there would always be those who believed in Him. He prayed for the unity of His followers so that the world would believe that God had sent Him (John 17:21). The fact that the unity of the believers was a main concern of Jesus' final prayer indicates that this continues to be a major issue in the church. How encouraging it is to realize that when believers are struggling to be united, Jesus is praying for us about this very thing!

The entire prayer closes with Jesus speaking of His and the Father's love for His people and expressing His desire to be with them forever (John 17:22-26).

CHILDREN'S CORNER

In this prayer, Jesus reminds His followers of His love for them. This lesson will help children understand Jesus' love for them.

Children can be told that Jesus not only prayed for them in this passage's prayer, but that He is still praying for them every day (Heb. 7:25). And they can be assured that His prayers will always be answered without fail and without delay!

—Martin R. Dahlquist.

EDITORIALS
(Continued from page 3)

and foremost to save His people from their sin, and that necessitated confronting them about it, often in stark terms.

In this, Christ was following in the footsteps of the prophets who had ministered long before—and with much the same results. He warned His opponents, "Behold, I send unto you prophets, . . . and some of them ye shall kill and crucify; and some of them shall ye scourge in your synagogues, and persecute them from city to city" (Matt. 23:34). And He stood at the apex of their fury, as He made clear in the parable of the vineyard owner and caretakers (21:33-41, 45).

The brute fact is that when Jesus came to earth as a man, He was entering enemy territory. Ever since Adam's Fall in Eden, mankind has been under the thrall of evil (I John 5:19) and living in enmity toward God (Rom. 8:7; Jas. 4:4).

In all this darkness, however, a bright ray of hope shines brightly. Jesus broke the stranglehold of sin through His sacrifice on the cross and His defeat of death in His resurrection. Those of us who trust Him He has rescued from the power of darkness and brought into His eternal kingdom (Col. 1:13; II Pet. 1:11). And one day that glorious kingdom will be the only reality in heaven and on earth (Rev. 11:15; 21:1-5). How we long for that day!

In the meantime, however, we face an unavoidable choice. If we are to follow Jesus faithfully and carry out His mission to make disciples of all nations, we must accept that we will not always please the world.

This does not mean that every unbeliever we encounter will despise us, but if we are faithful in shining Christ's light into our world, we must be prepared for opposition, even fierce persecution. Many brethren around the world right now are suffering greatly for their faith in Christ. But if we set our hearts on pleasing the Father as Jesus did, we will know His peace and joy even now, and it will never be taken from us throughout all eternity.

Pleasing the Father— Our Privilege and Imperative

KENNETH SPONSLER

When we consider how Jesus pleased the Father, we stand amazed. He did what no one has ever done or could ever hope to do—live a life pleasing to God in perfect and unbroken fruition. Yet now, because of Him, the way has been opened for ordinary sinners like us to actually live lives that are genuinely pleasing to the Father. We will never do so perfectly on this earth, but what was once an impossible prospect now beckons us with compelling potential.

We rejoice that we have been given this unimaginably great privilege, but Scripture makes it repeatedly clear that pleasing the Father is also our main obligation, our mission in life. Jesus reminds us that the greatest command in the law directs us to love God with all our heart, soul, mind, and strength (Mark 12:30). We cannot love someone without wanting to please him.

Jesus very pointedly told those who came to hear Him, "Not every one that saith unto me, Lord, Lord, shall enter into the kingdom of heaven; but he that doeth the will of my Father which is in heaven" (Matt. 7:21). He was not talking about perfect performance but about having a heart to please God by doing His will as He makes it known to us.

The Lord expanded on this idea in the parable of the two sons and the vineyard. The father asked both sons to do some work in the family vineyard. One son brazenly refused the request but later changed his mind and went and did the work. The other son promised heartily to fulfill the request but then somehow never made it into the vineyard. Jesus asked His listeners (the religious authorities) which one did the will of his father. They had to answer, the first (Matt. 21:28-31).

That we are called to please our Father in heaven and should earnestly desire to do so is clear and indisputable; most believers would never question it. But we may ask, *How* do we please Him? Most of us may well wonder, How is it possible for a sinner like me to be pleasing to One who is infinitely holy?

On one level, that question cannot be fully answered in a short article like this. The whole of Scripture was written to show us how we are to please God. In II Timothy 3:16-17 we read that all Scripture is given "for reproof, for correction, for instruction in righteousness: that the man of God may be perfect, throughly furnished unto all good works." Learning to please our Heavenly Father is a lifelong endeavor, in which the Bible is our number-one guide.

What are some of the main specifics that the Bible gives us about how we please the Father? Several could be enumerated, but for the remainder of this article, we will focus on three.

First, we please the Father *by faith*. Hebrews 11:6 tells us plainly, "Without faith it is impossible to please him." When Jesus was asked by the crowds that were following Him around, "What shall we do, that we might work the works of God?" (John 6:28), He replied, "This is the work of God, that ye believe on him whom he hath sent" (vs. 29). We cannot ever hope to please God in anything apart from faith in Jesus Christ; trusting Him is the foundation and driving force of living for His glory and pleasure.

The necessity of faith for pleasing God was true even for Old Testament saints. They of course did not possess the full revelation of Christ, but they pleased God by believing what He told them. The pattern is established early on. Abraham "believed in the Lord; and he counted it to him for righteousness" (Gen. 15:6). The whole of Hebrews 11 is a testament to the faith of Old Testament believers. They were not saved by fulfilling the law; rather, they followed God by faith and thereby pleased Him.

Second, we please the Father by *abiding in Christ*. This, of course, is a close corollary of faith; we cannot abide in Christ without exercising faith in Him. But the passage in John 15 in which Jesus speaks on this theme draws us into a more specific emphasis and promise: as we abide in Christ, we bear much fruit (vs. 5) and the Father is glorified (vs. 8). Conversely, if we do not remain in Christ, we can do nothing of value to the Father (vss. 4, 6).

It is in the context of pleasing the Father by abiding in Christ and bearing fruit to His glory that we are given the promise, "Ye shall ask what ye will, and it shall be done unto you" (vs. 7). Scripture never countenances making selfish requests directed toward worldly pleasure (cf. Jas. 4:3), but God is delighted and pleased when we pray to Him in faith, seeking His glory and the accomplishment of His will.

Third, we please the Father *by the power of the Holy Spirit*. This is, in fact, the foundation for (and perhaps really another side of) abiding in Christ. Romans 8 is the watershed passage on living by the Spirit, something possible to us because of what Jesus did for us (vss. 2-4). Paul states categorically, "They that are in the flesh cannot please God" (vs. 8), but then he declares, "But ye are not in the flesh, but in the Spirit, if so be that the Spirit of God dwell in you" (vs. 9). If we are in Christ, we have been given the Spirit, and through His power we live as children of God.

It is intimated in Scripture that Jesus Himself accomplished His mighty works by the power of the Spirit (Luke 4:1, 14, 18). This begins to touch on the mystery of the Trinity, which we cannot fully comprehend. But if even Jesus, who was sinless and perfect, depended on the Spirit, how much more do we need to do the same?

TOPICS FOR NEXT QUARTER

June 4

Upside-Down Kingdom

Matthew 5:1-16

June 11

A Perfect Kingdom

Matthew 5:17-18, 21-22, 27-28, 38-39, 43-44

June 18

A Victorious Kingdom

Mark 3:13-29; 6:6*b*-13

June 25

Growing God's Kingdom

Matthew 13:24-33

July 2

Praying to God

Luke 11:1-13

July 9

Accept God's Invitation!

Luke 14:7-11, 15-24

July 16

A Warning for the Hard-Hearted

Luke 16:19-31

July 23

Separating the Sheep and the Goats

Matthew 25:31-46

July 30

Ears to Hear

Matthew 13:9-17

August 6

Forgiving One Another

Matthew 18:21-35

August 13

A Story of Forgiveness

Luke 15:11-24

August 20

God's Gracious Rewards

Matthew 20:1-16

August 27

God's Great Mercy

Luke 18:9-14

PARAGRAPHS ON PLACES AND PEOPLE

TREASURY (OF THE TEMPLE)

As the book of Joshua makes clear, Israel needed a place where they could store their treasures dedicated to God (cf. 6:19, 24). David's instructions to Solomon for the temple included a treasury (I Chr. 28:12). Solomon's temple contained a place for storing the gold and silver that was dedicated to the Lord (I Kgs. 5:17). In the time of Jesus, the priests served as administrators of the treasures in the temple.

The exact location of the temple treasury has been disputed, but because women had access to giving offerings, it is thought to have been located by the Court of the Women, which was located in the outer court, past the Beautiful Gate. There were boxes, with openings shaped like inverted megaphones, that were positioned to receive the donations of the worshippers. Jesus saw the widow give her two mites there (Mark 12:41).

JESUS' TOMB

For centuries, emperors, kings, historians, archaeologists, and filmmakers have searched for the location of Jesus' temporary tomb. Most Bible scholars will caution that there is not enough proof of its exact location.

Two locations are the main contenders. The first contender is the Garden Tomb, also known as Gordon's Tomb, named after Charles Gordon, who discovered a tomb two-hundred-and-seventy-five yards outside Jerusalem, in a garden, near a rock formation that looked like a skull (supposedly Golgotha).

The second, and strongest, contender is the tomb in the Church of the Holy Sepulchre. In A.D. 325, Emperor Constantine sent a group to find the tomb. They followed local tradition that it was under a temple built by Emperor Hadrian in the second century. When they leveled the temple, they found a tomb underneath. They then built a shrine around it. Scholars verify that the tomb existed in the first century, but no one can say with certainty that Jesus rested there. Located in the Christian Quarter of the Old City, the site draws many visitors yearly.

ALL THAT ARE IN THE GRAVES

Jesus referred to the resurrection of the righteous and the unrighteous that would take place in the last day. Both will physically rise from their graves to stand before God, who will determine their eternal destinies. Christ's perfect work on the cross gives Him the authority to raise the dead to life. Those who have put their trust in Him will live for eternity in heaven.

ALL THOSE WHO CAME BEFORE ME

Jesus' statement in John 10:8 that all who came before Him were thieves and robbers must be taken within the context of His being the door of the sheepfold. He was not referring to Old Testament prophets, because none of them claimed to be the Messiah, and they all pointed to Him.

Jesus was talking about those who pretended to be the means by which all others could come to God. They claimed to be the mediators between man and God.

—*Don Ruff*

Daily Bible Readings for Home Study and Worship

(Readings are for the week previous to the lesson topics.)

1. March 5. Jesus' Baptism
M — The Saviour and His Forerunner. Luke 1:67-80.
T — The Lamb of God. John 1:29-34.
W — Make Way for the Lord. Matt. 3:1-12.
T — Listen to My Son. Mark 9:2-8.
F — A Voice from Heaven. John 12:27-32.
S — Eyewitnesses to Christ's Majesty. II Pet. 1:16-21.
S — The Beloved Son. Mark 1:4-13.

2. March 12. Overcoming Temptation with the Word
M — God's Care in the Wilderness. Deut. 8:1-10.
T — Worship and Trust God. Ps. 95:1-11.
W — Resist the Devil. Jas. 4:7-12.
T — The Whole Armor of God. Eph. 6:10-20.
F — Stand Against Temptation. I Cor. 10:9-13.
S — Cast Your Cares upon Him. I Pet. 5:6-11.
S — Temptation in the Wilderness. Matt. 4:1-14*a*.

3. March 19. Doing the Father's Work
M — Made Whole by the Son. John 5:1-17.
T — In the Father's House. Luke 2:41-52.
W — Jesus Praises His Father. Luke 10:17-24.
T — Jesus Does What His Father Does. John 10:31-39.
F — Doing the Father's Will. John 8:25-30.
S — Obeying the Father. John 14:28-31.
S — The Son Honors the Father. John 5:19-29.

4. March 26. Submitting to the Father's Will
M — Placing Hope in God. Ps. 42:1-11.
T — Jesus' Hour Has Come. John 12:20-26.
W — Peace from Trusting Jesus. John 16:29-33.
T — Jesus' Work Complete. John 17:1-5.
F — The Will of Him Who Sent Me. John 6:37-40.
S — Cry Out to the Lord. Ps. 88:1-13.
S — Agony in the Garden. Matt. 26:36-50.

5. April 2. Crucified for Sinners
M — Jesus Sentenced to Die. Luke 23:13-31.
T — Christ's Death Foretold. Ps. 22:1-18.
W — Golgotha. John 19:16-24.
T — The Suffering Saviour. Isa. 53:3-12.
F — The Faith of the Thief. Luke 23:32-43.
S — It Is Finished. John 19:28-30.
S — Forsaken by God? Matt. 27:38-54.

6. April 9. Risen from the Dead! (Easter)
M — The Stone Rolled Away. Mark 16:1-11.
T — No Hope Without Resurrection. I Cor. 15:12-19.
W — God's Mighty Power. Eph. 1:15-23.
T — He Is Risen! Luke 24:1-12.
F — The Sign of Jonah. Matt. 12:38-42.
S — Not Abandoned to the Grave. Ps. 16:1-11.
S — An Empty Tomb. John 20:1-10, 19-20.

7. April 16. Proofs of the Resurrection
M — Many Infallible Proofs. Acts 1:1-4.
T — Christ Arose. I Cor. 15:3-8.
W — The Word of Life. I John 1:1-4.
T — Jesus with the Disciples. Mark 16:12-14.
F — The Road to Emmaus. Luke 24:13-35.
S — The Third Appearance. John 21:1-14.
S — Scripture Now Fulfilled. Luke 24:36-53.

8. April 23. The Bread of Life
M — The Feeding of the Five Thousand. John 6:1-13.
T — God Sends Manna. Ex. 16:4-18.
W — Complaints About Manna. Num. 11:4-10.
T — Judgment for Ungrateful Hearts. Ps. 78:17-31.
F — God's Mercy on Mankind. Isa. 55:1-7.
S — One with Christ. John 6:47-58.
S — The True Bread from Heaven. John 6:22-35.

9. April 30. The Light of the World
M — A Light to the Nations. Isa. 9:2-4.
T — The True Light. John 1:1-10.
W — Believers Shine Forth in the World. Phil. 2:12-16.
T — Life Through the Son. I John 5:5-13.
F — Out of the Darkness into the Light. John 3:16-21.
S — The Path of the Just. Prov. 4:14-22.
S — The Light of Life. John 8:12-20; 12:44-46.

10. May 7. The Good Shepherd
M — The Lord Is My Shepherd. Ps. 23:1-6.
T — The Lord's Flock. Ezek. 34:10-25.
W — Peter Commissioned to Shepherd. John 21:15-17.
T — Shepherd the Flock. I Pet. 5:1-4.
F — He Will Feed His Flock. Isa. 40:9-14.
S — Perfect in Every Good Work. Heb. 13:20-21.
S — The Door to Eternal Life. John 10:7-18.

11. May 14. The Resurrection and the Life
M — The Death of Lazarus. John 11:1-16.
T — Lazarus Raised to Life. John 11:28-45.
W — Awakening to Life or to Shame. Dan. 12:1-3.
T — The Resurrection of the Dead. I Cor. 15:20-26.
F — The Power of His Resurrection. Phil. 3:7-14.
S — The Resurrection of the Just and Unjust. Acts 24:10-21.
S — Those in Christ Will Never Die. John 11:17-27.

12. May 21. The True Vine
M — The Parable of the Vineyard. Isa. 5:1-7.
T — The Lord's Vineyard. Isa. 27:2-6.
W — Rooted in Christ. Col. 2:6-10.
T — A Fruitless Vine. Ezek. 15:1-8.
F — A Vine out of Egypt. Ps. 80:8-19.
S — My Servant the Branch. Zech. 3:6-10.
S — Abide in Me. John 15:1-17.

13. May 28. Jesus Prays for Believers
M — Our High Priest and Intercessor. Heb. 7:24-27.
T — Jesus Prays for our Oneness with God. John 17:22-26.
W — The Lord Prays for Peter's Faith. Luke 22:24-34.
T — Believe and Confess Jesus Is Lord. Rom. 10:5-17.
F — The Lord's Favor. Isa. 61:1-11.
S — Ask in Confidence. I John 3:19-24.
S — Prayer for Protection. John 17:6-21.

REVIEW

What have you learned this quarter?

Can you answer these questions?

Jesus Pleases His Father

UNIT I: By His Works

March 5
Jesus' Baptism

1. What were people indicating when they were being baptized by John?
2. What is repentance, and what results when a person repents?
3. How did John convey his recognition of the Messiah's greatness?
4. What made Jesus' baptism different from all other baptisms?
5. What occurred that confirmed to Jesus that He was pleasing to God?

March 12
Overcoming Temptation with the Word

1. Why did the devil encourage Jesus to use His power to turn stones into bread?
2. How did the devil misuse Scripture in tempting Jesus?
3. What shortcut did the devil propose to Jesus for getting what rightfully belonged to Him?
4. Why was Jesus successful in overcoming Satan's attacks?
5. Why was Galilee a strategic center for Jesus' early ministry?

March 19
Doing the Father's Work

1. Why did the Jews become upset when Jesus said He was working in the same way as His Father?
2. What did Jesus claim regarding His authority to judge?
3. Why did He say that it is important to recognize His equality with God?
4. What certain truth did Jesus state about believing in Him?
5. What takes place when people believe in Jesus Christ?

UNIT II: By His Sacrifice

March 26
Submitting to the Father's Will

1. What did Jesus tell His disciples to do in the Garden of Gethsemane?
2. How did Jesus receive strength after His first prayer?
3. Why did Jesus tell His sleepy disciples to watch and pray?
4. What does Jesus' example in repeating His prayer teach us?
5. In what way did all the disciples let Jesus down?

April 2
Crucified for Sinners

1. For how long did Jesus suffer in darkness?
2. Why was Jesus forsaken by God the Father?
3. How did the spectators ridicule Jesus' cry to the Father?
4. How did the rending of the temple veil symbolize the significance of Jesus' death?
5. What happened when the earthquake opened many graves?

April 9
Risen from the Dead (Easter)

1. Why was Mary so loyal to Jesus?
2. What was the disciples' initial response to what the women told them?
3. Who decided to check out their story, and what did they do when they arrived at the tomb?
4. What was it that led to John's belief in the resurrection?
5. When after His resurrection did Jesus appear to His disciples?

April 16
Proofs of the Resurrection
1. What do we know about Christ's body after His resurrection?
2. Why did the disciples think they had seen a spirit?
3. What is meant by the Law, Prophets, and Psalms?
4. What is repentance? Why is it necessary for us to repent?
5. What were the disciples to wait for in Jerusalem?

UNIT III: By His Teachings

April 23
The Bread of Life
1. What misguided ideas of the people did Jesus continually encounter?
2. What enabled the people to go to Capernaum to seek Jesus?
3. What kind of food did Jesus tell them they should be looking for?
4. How did Jesus describe the work they should do?
5. Why did they ask for a sign?

April 30
The Light of the World
1. Why is there so much darkness in the world, and what is our hope?
2. How did Jesus say His judgment would differ from that of the Pharisees?
3. What did Jesus mean when He said that the Pharisees knew neither Him nor His Father?
4. Why was no one able to apprehend Jesus?
5. What must happen before people can understand true spirituality?

May 7
The Good Shepherd
1. What did Jesus mean when He referred to Himself as the Door (John 10:7)?
2. How does the sheepfold picture our salvation?
3. What was the difference between a shepherd and a hireling?
4. Who are the "other sheep" (vs. 16)?
5. What important truth did Jesus communicate about His death?

May 14
The Resurrection and the Life
1. Why did Jesus delay His return to Bethany?
2. What did Jesus promise Martha?
3. What kinds of death are referred to in Scripture?
4. What "I am" statement did Jesus make at this time, and what was He claiming by it?
5. What did Jesus mean by saying that believers will never die?

May 21
The True Vine
1. Who was Jesus referring to when He spoke of the vine, the husbandman, and the branches?
2. What is necessary if a Christian is going to produce spiritual fruit for the Lord?
3. What is one rewarding result that comes from abiding in Christ?
4. What is the highest standard of love that can be shown to anyone?
5. How can we be both a slave and a friend of our Lord?

May 28
Jesus Prays for Believers
1. What was the setting of Jesus' prayer in John 17?
2. How had Jesus manifested God's name to His disciples (vs. 6)?
3. What kind of unity did Jesus want for His disciples?
4. Why would the world hate the disciples after Jesus' departure?
5. How is personal sanctification accomplished?